The Gen X Seri

ENGLISH OLYMPIAD 9

Useful for English Olympiads Conducted at School, National & International Levels

Author
Suparna Sengupta
Peer Reviewer
P. Shyamla

Strictly According to the Latest Syllabus of English Olympiad

Published by:

F-2/16, Ansari road, Daryaganj, New Delhi-110002
☎ 23240026, 23240027 • *Fax:* 011-23240028
Email: info@vspublishers.com • *Website:* www.vspublishers.com
Online Brandstore: *amazon.in/vspublishers*

Regional Office : Hyderabad
5-1-707/1, Brij Bhawan (Beside Central Bank of India
Lane) Bank Street, Koti, Hyderabad - 500 095
☎ 040-24737290
E-mail: vspublishershyd@gmail.com

Branch Office : Mumbai
Jaywant Industrial Estate, 1st Floor–108, Tardeo Road
Opposite Sobo Central Mall, Mumbai – 400 034
☎ 022-23510736
E-mail: vspublishersmum@gmail.com

BUY OUR BOOKS FROM: AMAZON FLIPKART

ISBN 978-93-579407-7-1
New Edition

DISCLAIMER

While every attempt has been made to provide accurate and timely information in this book, neither the author nor the publisher assumes any responsibility for errors, unintended omissions or commissions detected therein. The author and publisher makes no representation or warranty with respect to the comprehensiveness or completeness of the contents provided.
All matters included have been simplified under professional guidance for general information only, without any warranty for applicability on an individual. Any mention of an organization or a website in the book, by way of citation or as a source of additional information, doesn't imply the endorsement of the content either by the author or the publisher. It is possible that websites cited may have changed or removed between the time of editing and publishing the book.
Results from using the expert opinion in this book will be totally dependent on individual circumstances and factors beyond the control of the author and the publisher.
It makes sense to elicit advice from well informed sources before implementing the ideas given in the book. The reader assumes full responsibility for the consequences arising out from reading this book.
For proper guidance, it is advisable to read the book under the watchful eyes of parents/guardian. The buyer of this book assumes all responsibility for the use of given materials and information.

Printed at : TechShresta Solutions Private Limited, India

Publisher's Note

The current decade has firmly established V&S Publishers as one of the Leading Publishers of General Trade Mass Appeal Books across popular genres along with Academic Books for school children. Having been in publishing trade for over 40 years we understand the need of the hour when it comes to Books. After successfully publishing over 600 titles in a rather short time span of 5 years and establishing a pan India network of booksellers & distributors including ecommerce platforms viz – Amazon, Flipkart etc; an extensive market research lead us to publishing our Bestselling Series ever – OLYMPIAD BOOKS.

The Olympiad Series launched 4 years back under our GEN X SERIES Imprint gained widespread popularity amongst students and teachers immediately owing to its rich, high quality content and unique presentation. Published for Classes 1–10 across subjects English, Maths, Science & Computers, these books are holistic in nature and unlike run of the mill workbooks in the market, which are mere replicas of one another, these books deal with the content in a much comprehensive manner. Recourse to the 'Principles of Applied Psychology of Student Learning' has been utilised to upgrade levels of conceptual understanding in all designated subjects among class 1 to 10 students.

Encouraged by this huge acceptability of our Olympiad Series among parents and students and after revolutionising the way Olympiad books were written and published, we at V&S Publishers decided to take this to the next level.

We present to you Brand New Edition of our book – **ENGLISH OLYMPIAD CLASS 9.**

Each book originally written by Subject Matter Expert, is now further Peer Reviewed by top School Teachers and HODs to eliminate the slightest of errors that were present earlier. Furthermore to ensure authenticity and accuracy of content the book is now completely revised and reformatted as per the guidelines of the examining body. The New and Revised Olympiad Book is now suited to Olympiad examinations conducted at School Level, National Level or International Level by any and all organisations/companies.

The New Edition of this English Olympiad Class 9 is written in a Guide like pattern with images and illustrations at every step & is divided into different sections. Each chapter comes with Basic Theory and Solved Examples. Multiple Choice Questions with their Answer Keys and Solutions are liberally included. In order to help students become aware of and to simulate the actual exam conditions, a bunch of OMR Sheets have been enclosed with the book as well.

Amalgamation of Technology with Content has always been at the forefront for V&S Publishers and our new Student Portal for Olympiad Practice–**www.vsexamprep.com** is further testimony to that. We recommend students logging in and using it to their benefit.

P.S. While every care has been taken to ensure correctness of content, if you come across any error, howsoever minor, anywhere in the book, do not hesitate to discuss with your teachers while pointing that out to us in no uncertain terms.

We wish you All The Best!

Contents

SECTION 1: WORD AND STRUCTURE KNOWLEDGE

SECTION 2: READING COMPREHENSION

SECTION 3: SPOKEN AND WRITTEN EXPRESSIONS

SECTION 4: ACHIEVERS' SECTION

SECTION 1

WORD AND STRUCTURE KNOWLEDGE

Noun

1

Noun is a part of Speech in English language. It's basically a 'naming' word.

Example: Raman, Delhi, cow, pen, beauty, etc.

Kinds of Noun

Nouns are divided into five major classes.

(i) Common noun → Concrete / Material

(ii) Proper noun

(iii) Collective noun

(iv) Concrete noun

(v) Abstract noun

Common Noun

Common noun is a name given in common to every person or thing of the same class or kind.

Example: Boy, woman, girl, officer.

Countable noun

Countable noun is the noun that can be counted and it is further classified into singular or plural.

Example: People, animal, pens, planets.

Uncountable noun

Uncountable noun is the noun that can't be counted. It is the opposite of a countable noun.

Example: Sand, salt, hair, wool.

Proper Noun

Proper noun is the name of a particular person or place.

Example: Bangkok, Rohit, Kolkata, Rahul.

Collective Noun

Collective noun is the name given to a collection of people, animals or things.

Example: Class, herd, army, family.

Concrete Noun

Concrete noun refers to the name of something that we experience through our senses.

Example: A room, a person, an animal.

Abstract Noun

Abstract noun is the name of a quality, action or state. It is the opposite of a concrete noun and it can't be touched or felt.

Example: Anger, love, beauty, liberty.

Material Noun

Material noun is the name of a substance or material from which things can be/are made. Material nouns are a subset of common nouns because they are not proper nouns. They don't have individual names but something can be made out of them. Material nouns are not countable.

Example: Iron, copper, silk, glass.

Functions of a Noun

Noun as a subject: A noun functions as a subject of the sentence. The subject is usually placed at the beginning of the sentence. The subject is shown in italics in the beginning of the following sentences.

Example: *Tanmay* buys the house.

The cat chases the mouse.

Noun as an object: A noun functions as an object in the sentence. The object is usually placed at the end of the sentence. The object is shown in italics in the following sentences.

Example: Tanmay buys *the house.*

The cat chases *the mouse.*

Noun as a possessive phrase: A noun shows ownership in the sentence. We usually use an's to show ownership. The possessive is shown in italics in the following sentences:

Example: That is *Tanmay's* house.

The *cat's* eyes are yellow.

Noun as an objective complement: Nouns and noun phrases can function as objective complement. An objective complement is a word, phrase, or clause that directly follows and describes the direct object. The italicized noun phrases are example of objective complements in the following sentences.

Example: Indira named her son *Rajeev.*

We elected you as a *team leader.*

Noun as a prepositional complement: A prepositional complement is a word, phrase, or clause that directly follows the preposition in a prepositional phrase. Prepositional complements are also called complements of prepositions and objects of prepositions. Nouns and noun phrases function as prepositional complements. The italicized noun phrases are example of prepositional complements in the following sentences.

Example: Rohit gave his toy to *his brother.*

The mother warned her children not to go in *the jungle.*

Noun as an appositive phrase: An appositive is a word, phrase, or clause that modifies or explains another noun or noun phrase. Nouns and noun phrases also function as appositives. The following italicized noun phrases are the Example of appositives in the following sentences.

Example: A. R. Rahman, *the musician,* is a famous person worldwide.

Mr. Bishan Singh, *the captain*, is a good internal player.

Usage of Nouns

☞ Collective nouns are followed by singular verbs when we are talking of the group as a whole. They take a plural verb when we are talking about the individual members of the group.

Example: The jury is in the court room. (Here we use a singular verb because we are talking of the group as a whole.)

The jury are still debating the case. (Here we use a plural verb because it is the individual members of the group who are debating the case.)

☞ Some nouns are always followed by plural verbs. Example are: binoculars, scissors, spectacles, glasses, knickers, pyjamas, tongs, shears, trousers etc. Note that it is wrong to say 'a binocular' or 'a spectacle'. If the singular aspect is to be expressed use the expression 'a pair of'. Example are: a pair of trousers, a pair of tongs etc.

Example: The binoculars are very useful at the races.

His new glasses were on the table.

The garden shears are used to clip the hedges.

Note: We use a singular verb when the phrase 'a pair of' comes before the noun.

Bring me the knickers that are on the line.

Bring me a pair of knickers that is on the line.

Pyjamas are in the drawer.

A pair of pyjamas is in the drawer.

☞ When a singular noun and a plural noun are connected by or, the verb agrees with the nearest noun.

Example: Grapes or a melon is suitable. (Here we use a singular verb because the nearest noun (melon) is singular in number.)

A melon or grapes are necessary. (Here we use a plural verb because the nearest noun (grapes) is plural in number.)

☞ When two singular nouns are joined by 'or', a singular verb is used.

Example: Jam or butter was not available in the store.

(Note that it would be better to use the plural noun second; then a plural verb is necessary.)

☞ A singular noun is used after 'one of', 'none of', 'each of' and similar expressions.

Example: One of the calves is sick. (NOT One of the calves are sick.)

One of our students has won a prize.

Noun: Person

Pronouns can be of different grammatical persons whereas all nouns are in the third person.

Form	Function	Example	Pronoun
First person	represents the person speaking	---	I, we
Second person	represents the person spoken to	---	you
Third person	represents the person spoken about	poet	he, she, it, they

Noun: Number

Form	Function	Example	Pronoun
Singular	represents the name of one of someone or something	poet	he
Plural	represents the name of two or more of someone or something	poets	they

Noun: Gender

Gender is a grammatical classification of sexes. There are four kinds of gender as follows:

(i) Masculine
(ii) Feminine
(iii) Common
(iv) Neuter

Masculine Gender

Masculine gender is a noun that denotes a male animal or person.

Example: Lion, king, nephew, father

Feminine Gender

Feminine gender is a noun that denotes a female animal or person.

Example: Lioness, queen, niece, mother

Common Gender

Common gender is a noun that includes both a male and a female and does not discriminate according to gender.

Example: Parents, crowd, doctor, artist, children

Neuter Gender

Neuter gender is a noun that denotes neither male or female or animal, it's commonly used in reference to things.

Example: Radio, tree, college, book.

Noun: Case

Form	Function	Example	Pronoun
Nominative	subject of a verb subject complement	poet	I, we, you, he, she, they
Accusative	object of a finite verb object of a non-finite verb object of a preposition object complement	poet	me, us, you, him, her, them
Genitive	shows possession, ownership or relationship	poet's	mine
Dative	indirect object	poet	him
Vocative	used as an address	poet	---

Practice Exercise

I. Choose the correct option.

1. Which of the following is a collective noun?
   (a) Apple (b) Writer
   (c) Choir (d) Lily
2. Which of the following is a proper noun?
   (a) Sinjini (b) Freedom
   (c) Love (d) Capital
3. Which of the following is a common noun?
   (a) Iron (b) London
   (c) Swarm (d) Officer
4. Which of the following is an abstract noun?
   (a) Birds (b) Greed
   (c) Clown (d) Elephant
5. Which of the following is an uncountable noun?
   (a) Cattle (b) Boy
   (c) Star (d) Milk
6. Which of the following is a concrete noun?
   (a) Lies (b) Forest
   (c) Bottle (d) Sweet
7. Which of the following is a material noun?
   (a) Feathers (b) Light
   (c) Air (d) Deer
8. Which of the following is a countable noun?
   (a) Shadow (b) Studio
   (c) Tea (d) Red
9. Which of the following is a collective noun?
   (a) Team (b) Rugby
   (c) Sugar (d) Happiness
10. Which of the following is a proper noun?
    (a) Whale
    (b) Velvet
    (c) Taiwan
    (d) Perfume

II. Choose the correct option according to the instruction given in brackets.

11. Do you ever need to give request? (Which word is a count noun?)
    (a) Ever (b) Give
    (c) Request (d) You
12. Teacher asked students to use colour pencils during art period. (Which word is a compound noun?)
    (a) Colour pencil (b) Students
    (c) Period (d) Teacher
13. Australian government will bring tougher anti-terror laws. (Which word is a nominative noun?)
    (a) Bring
    (b) Australian
    (c) Anti-terror
    (d) Government
14. They like swimming. Whenever they have a leisure time. (Which word is a verbal noun?)
    (a) Leisure (b) Free
    (c) Like (d) Swimming
15. Solar energy can be an alternative source of power. (Which word is a predicative noun?)
    (a) Solar
    (b) Can be
    (c) Alternative source of power
    (d) Energy
16. Mice's can nibble the food. (Which word is a plural possessive noun?)
    (a) Can (b) Mice's
    (c) Nibble (d) The
17. Be careful, there is a hive of bees on tree. (Which word is a collective noun?)
    (a) Tree (b) There
    (c) Hive of bees (d) Careful
18. "O, you pass me my ball, buddy." (Which word is a naming noun?)
    (a) My (b) Pass
    (c) Buddy (d) You
19. Good friends are beauty of life. (Which word is a countable noun?)
    (a) Friends (b) Good
    (c) Beauty (d) Are
20. My grandmother is good at telling funny stories. (Which word is a plural noun?)
    (a) Telling (b) Stories
    (c) Funny (d) Goad

III. Directions (21-30): Determine the type of noun the italicized word and choose the correct option. Be careful, some of them are not nouns.

21. What type of noun is the word *Moon* as it is used in the following sentence?

    Scientists believe that the Moon formed from an ancient planet called Theia that collided with the Earth billions of years ago.

    (a) Singular noun (b) Plural noun
    (c) Possessive noun (d) Not a noun

22. What type of noun is the word *Neil* as it is used in the following sentence?

    Neil Armstrong is remembered for being the first person to walk on the Moon and for he memorable words that he spoke: "That's one small step for a man, one giant leap for mankind."

    (a) Proper noun (b) Plural noun
    (c) Possessive noun (d) Not a noun

23. What type of noun is the word *Halley's* as it is used in the following sentence?

    At every 76th year or so, Earthlings have a chance to view Halley's Comet with the naked eye, and (assuming that you are an Earthling) your next chance will be in middle of the year 2061.

    (a) Proper noun (b) Plural noun
    (c) Possessive noun (d) Not a noun

24. What type of noun is the word *Pluto's* as it is used in the following sentence?

    Pluto's status as a planet was called into question after numerous icy objects similar to Pluto were found orbiting the Sun.

    (a) Singular noun (b) Plural noun
    (c) Possessive noun (d) Not a noun

25. What type of noun is the word *galaxies* as it is used in the following sentence?

    The Milky Way is the galaxy in which we live, but there are billions of galaxies in the known Universe.

    (a) Singular noun
    (b) Plural noun
    (c) Possessive noun
    (d) Not a noun

26. What type of noun is the word *crashes* as it is used in the following sentence?

    A meteoroid becomes a meteorite when it crashes into the Earth.

    (a) Singular noun (b) Plural noun
    (c) Possessive noun (d) Not a noun

27. What type of noun is the word *Saturn's* as it is used in the following sentence?

    Saturn's rings are made almost entirely of ice, though they have traces of rocky material.

    (a) Singular noun (b) Plural noun
    (c) Possessive noun (d) Not a noun

28. What type of noun is the word *expanding* as it is used in the following sentence?

    Edwin Hubble is best remembered for proving that the Universe is expanding.

    (a) Singular noun (b) Plural noun
    (c) Possessive noun (d) Not a noun

29. What type of noun is the word *night* as it is used in the following sentence?

    The North Star is closely aligned with Earth's axis of rotation, so its position in the sky changes very little throughout the night.

    (a) Singular noun (b) Plural noun
    (c) Possessive noun (d) Not a noun

30. What type of noun is the word *effects* as it is used in the following sentence?

    No one has ever seen a black hole with their own eyes, but scientists believe that they have witnessed their effects.

    (a) Singular noun (b) Plural noun
    (c) Possessive noun (d) Not a noun

IV. Fill in the blanks with the correct word given in the box.

[orange, class, hatred, herd, cloud, habits, voice, Nile, hive, wise]

1. I just saw a ________ of elephants passing by.
2. The _______ is a long river.
3. Old ________ die hard.
4. He gave me an ________.
5. I recognized his _________ at once.
6. Don't disturb the bee ______.
7. Solomon was a ________ king.

8. Every ________ has a silver lining.
9. Our ________ is preparing for a test.
10. ________ is an ugly thing.

V. Identify the type of the following nouns.

1. Japan : ____________
2. Oxygen : ____________
3. Childhood : ____________
4. Traveller : ____________
5. Mob : ____________
6. Table : ____________
7. Clay : ____________
8. Earphones : ____________
9. Ice : ____________
10. Galaxy : ____________

VI. Find out the gender of the following nouns.

1. Sir
2. Doe
3. Czar
4. Gander
5. Mare

Pronoun

2

Pronoun is a word that is used in place of a noun, e.g. he, she, it, they, his, her, him, its, etc.

Example: Robert is an intelligent student. He always goes to school. He studies seriously. He is making a preparation for examination. He will get high marks in examination.

In the above paragraph, pronoun 'he' is used instead of noun 'Robert'. If we do not use pronoun in above paragraph, we will have to use the noun 'Robert' again and again in each sentence. So, the purpose of pronoun is to avoid the repetition of a noun.

Example: He, she, it, they, you, I, we, who, him, her, them, me, us, whom, his, its, their, your, mine, our and whose, myself, himself, herself , yourself, which, this, that, these, those etc. are pronouns.

Types of Pronoun

There are five types of pronoun

(i) Personal Pronoun

(ii) Possessive Pronoun

(iii) Reflexive Pronoun

(iv) Relative Pronoun

(v) Demonstrative Pronoun

Personal Pronoun

Personal pronoun describes a particular person or thing or group. Personal pronoun describes the person speaking (I, me, we, us), the person spoken to (you), or the person or thing spoken about (he, she, it, they, him, her, them).

Example: He helps the poor.

The pronoun 'he' in above sentence describes a person who helps the poor.

Personal pronouns: Number and person

		Personal Pronoun	
Number	**Person**	**Subject**	**Object**
Singular	1st Person	I	Me
	2nd Person	You	You
	3rd Person	He, She, It	Him, Her, It
Plural	1st Person	We	Us
	2nd Person	You	You
	3rd Person	They	Them

Personal pronouns change their form in the predicts of the sentence. For example 'I' changes to me as below.

a) I asked the boy to sit down.

The boy was asked to sit down by me.

Example: She is intelligent

They are playing chess.

It is raining.

We love our country.

I met him yesterday.

Possessive Pronoun

Possessive pronoun indicates close possession or ownership or relationship of a thing/person to another thing/person. e.g. yours, mine, his, hers, ours, theirs, hers.

Example: This book is mine.

The pronoun 'mine' describes the relationship between book and a person (me) who possesses this book or who is the owner of this book.

Possessive pronoun: Number and person

Number	Person	Possessive Pronoun
Singular	1st Person	Mine
	2nd Person	Yours
	3rd Person	Hers, his, its
Plural	1st Person	Ours
	2nd Person	Yours
	3rd Person	Theirs

Example:

a) Your book is old. Mine is new.
b) The pen on the table is mine.
c) The smallest cup is yours.
d) The voice is hers.
e) I have lost my camera. May I use yours?

Note: Possessive adjectives (my, her, your) cannot be used in place of possessive pronouns because possessive adjective modifies noun in terms of possession. Both possessive adjective and possessive pronoun show possession pronoun or ownership, but possessive adjective is used (with noun) to modify the noun while possessive pronoun is used in place of a noun.

Example: This is my book. (Possessive adjective: 'my' modifies the noun 'book')

This book is mine. (Possessive pronoun: 'mine' is used instead of noun 'to whom the book belongs')

Reflexive Pronoun

Reflexive pronoun describes noun when the action affects the subject itself; e.g, himself, yourself, herself, ourselves, themselves, itself are reflexive pronouns.

Reflexive pronouns always act as objects not subjects, and they require an interaction between the subject and an object.

Number	Person	Subject	Reflexive Pronoun
Singular	1st Person	I	Myself
	2nd Person	You	Yourself
	3rd Person	He, She, It	Himself, Herself, Itself
Plural	1st Person	We	Ourselves
	2nd Person	You	Yourselves
	3rd Person	They	Themselves

Example:

a) I looked at myself in the mirror.
b) You should think about yourself.
c) They prepared themselves for completion.
d) She pleases herself by thinking that she will win the prize.

Note: Reflexive noun can also be used to give more emphasis on subject or object. When a reflexive pronoun is used to give more emphasis on a subject or an object, it is called "Intensive Pronoun".

Example: She herself started to think about herself.

In the above sentence, the first "herself" is used as intensive pronoun while the second "herself" is used as a reflexive pronoun.

See the following Example of intensive pronouns.

Example: I did it myself. OR I myself did it.

She herself washed the clothes.

He himself decided to go to New York.

Reciprocal Pronoun

Reciprocal pronouns are used when two subjects act in same way towards each other, or, more subjects act in same way to one another.

Example: A loves B and B loves A. We can say that A and B love each other.

There are two reciprocal pronouns.

- Each other
- One another.

Example:

a) John and Marry are talking to each other.
b) The students gave cards to one another.
c) The people helped one another in hospital.
d) The car and the bus collided with each other.

Relative Pronoun

Relative Pronoun describes a noun which is mentioned before and more information is to be given about it.

OR

Relative pronoun is a pronoun which joins relative clauses and relative sentences.

Example: It is the person who helped her.

In this sentence the word 'who' is a relative pronoun which refers to the noun (the person) which is already mentioned in beginning of sentence (It is the person) and more information (he helped her) is given after using a relative pronoun (who) for the noun (the person).

Similarly, in the above sentence the pronoun 'who' joins two clauses which are 'it is the person' and 'who helped her'.

Example: The most commonly used five relative pronouns are, who, whom, whose, which, that.

'Who' is used for subject and 'whom' is used for object. 'who' and 'whom' are used for people. 'Whose' is used to show possession and can be used for both people and things. 'Which' is used for things. 'That' is used for people and things.

Example:

a) It is the girl who got first position in the class.
b) The man whom I met yesterday is a nice person.
c) The boy who is laughing is my friend.

Demonstrative Pronoun

Demonstrative pronoun is a pronoun that points to a thing or things; e.g, this, that, these, those, none, neither. These pronouns point to thing or things in short distance/time or long distance/time.

- **Pronouns that show short distance or time:** This, these.
- **Pronouns that show long distance or time:** That, those.

Demonstrative pronouns 'this or that' are used for singular thing while 'these or those' are used for plural things.

Example:

a) This is black.
b) That is heavy.
c) Can you see these?
d) Those look attractive.

Usage of Pronoun

- Subject pronouns are used when the pronoun is the subject of the sentence. You can remember subject pronouns easily by filling in the blank subject space for a simple sentence.

Example: ___ did the job.

I, he, she, we, they, who, whoever, etc., all can be filled in the blank and are, therefore, subject pronouns.

- Subject pronouns are also used if they rename the subject. They will follow to be verbs, such as is, are, was, were, am, will be, had been, etc.

Example: It is he.

This is she speaking.

It is we who are responsible for the decision to downsize.

> **Note:** In informal English, most people tend to follow 'to be' verbs with object pronouns like me, her, them.
>
> ***Example:*** It could have been them.
>
> It could have been they. (Technically correct)
>
> It is just me at the door.
>
> It is just I at the door. (Technically correct)

- When 'who' refers to a personal pronoun (I, you, he, she, we, they), it takes the verb that agrees with that pronoun.

Example:

a) It is I who am sorry. (Correct)
b) It is I who is sorry. (Incorrect)
c) It is you who are mistaken. (Correct)
d) It is you who's mistaken. (Incorrect)

☞ Object pronouns are known more specifically as direct object, indirect object, and object of a preposition. Object pronouns include me, him, herself, us, them, themselves.

Example:

a) Jean saw him. (Him is the direct object of the verb 'saw'.)
b) Give her the book.

(The direct object of 'give' is book, and her is the indirect object. Indirect objects always have an implied 'to' 'or' for in front of them: Give [to] her the book. Do [for] me a favour.)

c) Are you talking to me? (Me is the object of the preposition to.)

☞ The pronouns who, that, and which become singular or plural depending on the subject. If the subject is singular, use a singular verb. If it is plural, use a plural verb.

Example: He is the only one of those men, who is always on time.

The word who refers to one. Therefore, use the singular verb is.

Sometimes we must look more closely to find a verb's true subject:

Example: He is one of those men who are always on time.

The word who refers to men. Therefore, use the plural verb are.

In this last example, many would mistakenly use singular verb. But look at it this way: Of those men who are always on time, he is one.

☞ Pronouns that are singular (I, he, she, everyone, everybody, anyone, anybody, no one, nobody, someone, somebody, each, either, neither, etc.) require singular verbs. The pronouns each, either, and neither, followed by of always take singular verbs. Do not be misled by what follows of.

Example:

a) Each of the girls sings well.
b) Either of us is capable of doing the job.
c) Neither of them is available to speak right now.

Exception: When 'each' follows a noun or pronoun in certain sentences, even experienced writers sometimes get tripped up:

Example: The women each gave her approval. (Incorrect)

The women each gave their approval. (Correct)

These examples do not contradict the above usage because each is not the subject, but rather an adjunct, describing the true subject.

☞ To decide whether to use the subject or object pronoun after the words 'than' or 'as', mentally complete the sentence.

Example: Raman is taller than I/me.

It means: Raman is taller than I am.

Danny would rather talk to her than I/me.

We can interpret this sentence in two ways: Danny would rather talk to her than to me. OR Danny would rather talk to her than I would. A sentence's meaning can change considerably, depending on the pronoun you choose.

☞ The possessive pronouns yours, his, hers, its, ours, theirs, and whose never need apostrophes. Avoid mistakes like her's and your's.

Example: This pen is your's. (Incorrect)

This pen is yours. (Correct)

☞ The only time it's has an apostrophe is when it is used for contraction for 'it is' or 'it has'. The only time who's has an apostrophe is when it means 'who is' or 'who has'. There is no apostrophe in oneself. Avoid "one's self," a common error.

Example:

a) It's been a cold morning.
b) The thermometer reached its highest reading.
c) He's the one who's always on time.
d) He's the one whose wife is always on time.
e) Keeping oneself ready is important.

☞ Reflexive pronouns are used when both the subject and the object of a verb are the same person or thing. There are nine reflexive pronouns: myself, yourself, himself, herself, itself, oneself, ourselves, yourselves, and themselves.

Example: Ashok helped himself.

If the object of a preposition refers to a previous noun or pronoun, use a reflexive pronoun:

Example: Ashok bought it for himself.

Reflexive pronouns help avoid confusion. Without them, we might be stuck with sentences like Ashok helped Ashok.

Example:

a) I worked myself to the bone. (Correct)

The object myself is the same person as the subject I, performing the act of working.

b) My brother and myself did it. (Incorrect)

c) My brother and I did it. (Correct)

Don't use myself unless the pronoun I or me precedes it in the sentence.

Example: Please give it to John or myself. (Incorrect)

Please give it to John or me. (Correct)

Myself refers back to me in the act of being.

A sentence like Help yourself looks like an exception to the rule until we realize it's shorthand for You may help yourself.

In certain cases, a reflexive pronoun may come first.

Example: Doubting himself, the man proceeded cautiously.

Reflexive pronouns are also used for emphasis.

Example: He himself finished the whole job.

☞ The use of they and their with singular pronouns is frowned upon by many scholars. To be consistent, it is a good practice to try to avoid they and its variants (e.g., them, their, themselves) with previously singular nouns or pronouns.

Example:

❒ Someone has to do it, and they have to do it well. (Not consistent)

The problem is that someone is singular, but they is plural. If we change they to he or she, we get a rather clumsy sentence, even if it is technically correct.

❒ Someone has to do it, and he or she has to do it well. (Technically correct)

Replacing an inconsistent sentence with a poorly written one is a bad bargain. The better option is to rewrite.

❒ Someone has to do it, and has to do it well. (Rewritten)

Many writers do not like the idea of using he or she solution. Following are more example of why rewriting is a better idea than using he or she or him or her to keep sentences consistent.

Example: No one realizes when their time is up. (Inconsistent)

No one realizes when his or her time is up. (Awkward)

None realize when their time is up. (Rewritten)

Note: Please see our note regarding the word none under Rule 6 of Subject-Verb Agreement.

☞ If two people possess the same item, and one of the joint owners is written as a pronoun, use the possessive form for both.

Example: Raghu and my home (Incorrect)

Mine and Raghu home (Incorrect)

Raghu and my home (Correct)

He and Raghu home (Incorrect)

Him and Raghu home (Incorrect)

His and Raghu home (Correct)

You and Raghu home (Incorrect)

Yours and Raghu home (Incorrect)

Raghu and your home (Correct)

Note: When one of the co-owners is written as a pronoun, use possessive adjectives (my, your, her, our, their). Avoid possessive pronouns (mine, yours, hers, ours, theirs) in such constructions.

Do not combine a subject pronoun and an object pronoun in phrases like her and I or he and me. Whenever "and" or "or" links an object pronoun (her, me) and a subject pronoun (he, I), one of those pronouns will always be wrong.

Example: Her and I went home. (Incorrect)

She and I went home. (She went and I went.) (Correct)

Practice Exercise

I. Choose the correct option to fill in the blanks.

1. ____________ did you invite to preside over the meeting?
   (a) Who (b) Whom
   (c) What (d) Whose

2. She asked ____________ I preferred, tea or coffee?
   (a) Who (b) That
   (c) Which (d) Whom

3. Of ____________ are you speaking?
   (a) Who (b) Whom
   (c) Whose (d) None of these

4. ____________ do you want to do?
   (a) What (b) Which
   (c) That (d) Whom

5. ____________ shall I give this to?
   (a) Whom (b) What
   (c) Whose (d) Which

6. ____________ of these books will you take?
   (a) Which (b) Whom
   (c) That (d) Whose

7. I don't know __________ of them will actually get it?
   (a) Whom (b) What
   (c) Which (d) Whose

8. ____________ said these words?
   (a) Who (b) Whom
   (c) What (d) Which

9. To __________ boy are you speaking?
   (a) Whom (b) Who
   (c) Which (d) That

10. __________ do you want to see?
    (a) Who
    (b) Whom
    (c) Which
    (d) Whose

11. ________did he come here for?
    (a) Why (b) What
    (c) Whom (d) Who

12. _________ do you think is the correct answer to this question?
    (a) What (b) Which
    (c) Who (d) Whom

13. To ____________ did she give her necklace?
    (a) Whom (b) Whose
    (c) What (d) Which

14. _______ do you think he is?
    (a) What (b) That which
    (c) Who (d) Which

15. With __________ were you exchanging pleasantries?
    (a) Whom (b) What
    (c) Which (d) Who

16. __________ is better, honour or riches?
    (a) Which (b) Who
    (c) That (d) Whom

17. ________ of them wants to see me?
    (a) Which (b) What
    (c) That (d) Whom

18. To ____________ do you pass on the notes?
    (a) Who (b) Whom
    (c) What (d) Which

19. _______ animal is your favourite?
    (a) How (b) What
    (c) Which (d) Who

20. ______ was it that hurt you?
    (a) What (b) Whom
    (c) How (d) Who

II. Fill in the blanks with personal pronoun.

Once upon a time there was a girl called Little Red Riding Hood. Together with ___1___ mum, ___2___ lived in a big forest. One fine day, Little Red Riding Hood's mother said, "___3___ grandma is ill. Please go and take this cake and a bottle of wine to ___4___. Grandma's house is not too far from ___5___ house, but always keep to the path and don't stop!". So, Little Red Riding Hood made ___6___ way to Grandma's house. In the forest ___7___ met the big bad wolf. Little Red Riding Hood greeted ___8___ and the wolf asked: "Where are ___9___ going, Little Red Riding Hood?" "To ___10___ grandma's house." answered Little Red Riding Hood. "Can you tell ___11___ where grandma lives?"

"___12___ lives in a little cottage at the edge of the forest." "Why don't ___13___ pick some nice flowers for ___14___?" asked the wolf.

III. Fill the blanks with demonstrative pronouns.

1. ______ is a gift from my brother.
2. Both watches are good; but __________ is better than that.
3. My views are in accordance with _______ of the Chairman.
4. ______ are mere excuses.
5. ______ is the Red Fort.
6. Kolkata mangoes are better than _______ of Bangalore.
7. _________ flowers are very beautiful.
8. _______ days were the best.
9. ______ horse is faster than ______ horse.
10. The streets of Mumbai are busier than _______ of Lucknow.

IV. Choose the correct option according the hint given in brackets.

1. We cannot go to movie, until my mom gives permission to go. Subjective pronoun in sentences.
   (a) my (b) we
   (c) until (d) can
2. Success is only for those who believe in hard working. Relative pronoun in sentence.
   (a) is (b) for
   (c) who (d) in
3. Someone called fire fighters when a house was on fire. Indefinite pronoun in sentence.
   (a) someone (b) when
   (c) was (d) on
4. What are others thinking about me? I do not care it. Interrogative pronoun in sentence.
   (a) other (b) me
   (c) I (d) What
5. That was the boy whom I saw in party last night. Relative pronoun in sentence.
   (a) that (b) I
   (c) whom (d) them
6. Ali and Imran are helping each other in completing their projects. Reciprocal pronoun in sentence.
   (a) in
   (b) each other
   (c) their
   (d) to
7. What have you decided to do? Will you resign the job? Interrogative pronoun in sentence.
   (a) what (b) you
   (c) will (d) have
8. Each of boy in my class knows how to keep discipline. Distributive pronoun in sentence
   (a) my (b) how
   (c) each (d) the

◆◆◆

Adjective

3

Types of Adjectives

Adjectives are the words that are used to describe nouns and pronouns and to quantify and identify them.

Example: He was wearing a blue shirt. (Here 'blue' is an adjective as it is describing the noun 'shirt' by answering the question 'what kind of shirt?')

There are seven rooms in the house. (Here 'seven' is also an adjective as it's telling the quantity/ the number of the noun 'rooms', answering the question 'how many rooms?'.)

There are different types of adjectives based upon their effect on a noun and what do they tell about the noun. There are five types of adjective.

I. Adjectives of Quality

These adjectives are used to describe the nature of a noun. They give an idea about the characteristics of the noun by answering the question 'what kind'; e.g. Honest, Kind, Large, Bulky, Beautiful, Ugly, etc.

Example: New Delhi is a large city with many historical monuments.

Sheila is a beautiful woman.

II. Adjectives of Quantity

These adjectives help to show the amount or the approximate amount of the noun or pronoun. These adjectives do not provide exact numbers; rather they tell us the amount of the noun in relative or whole terms; e.g. All, Half, Many, Few, Little, No, Enough, Great, etc.

Example: They have finished most of the rice.

Many people came to visit the fair.

III. Adjectives of Number

These adjectives are used to show the number of nouns and their place in an order. There are three sub-categories of adjectives of number; they are:

(a) Definite numeral adjective

Those adjectives which clearly denote an exact number of nouns or the order of the noun.

Example: One, Two, Twenty, Thirty-Three, etc. also known as Cardinals.

First, Second, Third, Seventh, etc. also known as Ordinals.

(b) Indefinite numeral adjective

Those adjectives that do not give an exact numerical amount but just give a general idea of the amount; e.g. Some, Many, Few, Any, Several, All, etc.

Example: There were many people present at the meeting.

(c) Distributive numeral adjective

Those adjectives that are used to refer to individual nouns within the whole amount; e.g. Either, Neither, Each, Another, Other, etc.

Example: Taxes have to be paid by every employed citizen.

IV. Possessive Adjective

A possessive adjective modifies a noun by telling whom it belongs to. It answers the question 'Whose?'; e.g. His, her, its, my, our, their, and your.

Example:

a) You can share my rice.
b) Have you seen their house?
c) This is his room.
d) They are our friends.

V. Demonstrative Adjective

These adjectives are used to point out or indicate a particular noun or pronoun:

☞ This, That, These and Those.

Example:

a) That bag belongs to Neil.
b) Try using this paintbrush in art class.
c) I really like those shoes.
d) These flowers are lovely.

VI. Distributive Adjective

There are four distributive adjectives in English: each, every, either and neither. Distributive adjectives are used with singular nouns.

Example:

a) *Each* boy must attend the class.

b) *Every* person should contribute to the growth of the country.

VII. Interrogative Adjective

These adjectives are used to ask questions about nouns or in relation to nouns, they are: Where, What, Which and Whose.

Example:

a) What assignment did I miss out on?

b) Whose pen is this?

Coordinate and Non-coordinate Adjective

Sometimes we find that we need to use more than one adjective to describe a noun in a satisfactory manner. In these cases, commas are used to separate the adjectives but some series of adjectives do not require a comma. Therefore, we need to know the difference between Coordinate and Non-coordinate Adjectives.

Coordinate Adjective

These adjectives can be re-arranged in the series easily and are still grammatically sound. This kind of series makes use of commas. This series can also insert 'and' between them and still be correct.

Example:

a) She was a kind, generous, loving human being.

b) She was a generous, loving, kind human being.

c) She was a loving, kind and generous human being.

Here we can see that all three sentences are grammatically correct. In this case, the adjectives only need to be separated by commas.

Non-coordinate Adjective

These adjectives cannot be rearranged in the series. These do not use commas to separate the adjectives. Also, this kind of series do not make sense if we insert 'and' between them.

Example: She has two energetic playful dogs. (Correct)

She has playful two energetic dogs. (Incorrect)

She has energetic and playful and two dogs. (Incorrect)

Here we see that only the first sentence makes sense and is grammatically correct. The second and third ones are incorrect. Hence, the sentence uses non-coordinate adjectives and does not need commas.

Placement of Adjectives

There are certain rules regarding the placement of different kinds of adjectives in a sentence. The general order followed is: Determiner + Quality/ Quantity + Noun

Determiners

Determiner is a word or phrase that preceeds a noun or noun phrase to show how the noun is being used various articles (the, a, an), demonstratives (this, that, these, those), possessives (my, mine, your, yours, -'s), quantifiers (all, many, etc.), numerals (one, twenty, thirty-seven, etc.) and distributives (each, every, neither, either)

Quality/Quantity and Opinion

The adjectives that give a quantity (also known as post-determiners) and subjective opinion to the noun, telling 'how much' and 'how' was the noun; e.g. Few, Most, One, Three/ Beautiful, Ugly, Difficult, etc.

Example: The beautiful house

Size

The third position after observations is for the adjectives that tell about the size of the noun, they can be used for an object as well as living thing; e.g. Huge, Little, Bulky, Thin, Vast, Tiny, Lean, etc.

Example: The beautiful little house

Age

The adjectives that tell about the age of a noun either by itself or in relation to another noun show the age at the fourth place; e.g. Young, Old, Teenage, Mature, Recent, Bygone, etc.

Example: The beautiful little old house

Shape

The adjectives that tell about the shape or appearance of the noun come at fifth place; e.g. Circular, Crooked, Triangular, Oval, Wavy, Straights, etc.

Example: The beautiful little old square house

Colour
The adjectives that tell the shade and hue of a noun come at fourth position; e.g. Pastel, Red, Blue, Metallic, Colourless, Translucent, etc.

Example: The beautiful square blue coloured house

Origin
The adjectives that show the different geographical locations associated with a noun come at fifth place; e.g. Southern, Northern, Lunar, Mexican, French, etc.

Example: The beautiful blue coloured Mexican house

Material
The adjectives that talk about raw material or texture of the objects or the behaviour of the living nouns indicate material quality; e.g. Wooden, Plastic, Steely, Metallic, Cottony, etc.

Example: The beautiful Mexican limestone house

Qualifier
At last the qualifier or the grammatical modifier comes, which is an additional word or phrase provided to change the meaning of the noun in a sentence.

☞ Pink + eye, Royal + treatment, etc.

Example: The beautiful Mexican limestone doll house

Identifying Adjectives
We know the adjectives usually by what they do (their function) in a sentence. However, some word endings (suffixes) are typical of adjectives.

Suffix	Example
-able, -ible	Comfortable, readable, incredible, invisible
-al, -ial	Comical, normal, musical, industrial, presidential
-ful	Beautiful, harmful, peaceful, wonderful
-ic	Classic, economic, heroic, romantic
-ical	Aeronautical, alphabetical, political
-ish	British, childish, Irish, foolish
-ive, -ative	Active, alternative, creative, talkative
-less	Endless, motionless, priceless, timeless
-eous, -ious, -ous	Spontaneous, hideous, ambitious, anxious, dangerous, famous
-y	Angry, busy, wealthy, windy

Comparison of Adjectives
When we want to compare two or more nouns using adjectives, we use the comparative and superlative forms of the adjective to show the comparison between the nouns.

Example: Honey is sweet, sugar is sweeter but victory is the sweetest.

In this sentence, we are comparing the three nouns using the positive, comparative and superlative forms of the word 'sweet'.

Positive Form
These are the simple adjectives that simply describe the noun without comparing it to another.

☞ Big, sweet, clean, etc.

Example:

a) She has a big black dog.
b) The cupboard is clean.

Comparative Form
These are used when we compare two nouns and need to show which noun possesses the adjective or character in a greater or lesser amount, when compared with the other.

☞ Bigger, sweeter, cleaner, etc.

Example:

a) I have a big dog but hers is bigger.
b) The cupboard is cleaner than before.

Superlative Form
This form is used when three or more nouns are being compared and we need to show that one or more of the nouns possess the adjective or characteristic to the highest amount possible. We usually add 'the' before the superlative form.

☞ Biggest, sweetest, cleanest, etc.

Example:

a) She has the biggest dog in the colony.
b) He is the sweetest boy in his class.
c) The cupboard is the cleanest thing in the house.

Irregular Comparisons

These adjectives do not make their comparative and superlative forms using the rules above. Their comparative and superlative forms are different words altogether.

Positive	Comparative	Superlative
Bad	Worse	Worst
Good	Better	Best
Far (time)	Further	Furthest
Far (place)	Farther	Farthest
Old (people)	Elder	Eldest
Little (amount)	Less	Least
Late (order)	Latter	Last

Forming Adjectives

Prefix

Prefixes such as un-, in-, im-, il- and ir- change the meaning of adjectives. Adding these prefixes makes the meaning negative:

Prefix	Example		
un-	fair – unfair	sure – unsure	happy – unhappy
in-	active – inactive	appropriate – inappropriate	complete – incomplete
ir-	responsible – irresponsible	regular – irregular	reducible – irreducible
im-	balance – imbalance	polite – impolite	possible – impossible
il-	legal – illegal	legible – illegible	logical – illogical

Suffix

Some adjectives are made from nouns and verbs by adding suffixes.

Noun	Adjective	Verb	Adjective
Hero	heroic	Read	readable
Wind	windy	Talk	talkative
Child	childish	Use	useful
Beauty	beautiful	Like	likeable

Example:

a) I hate windy days.

b) San Francisco is a very hilly place.

Some words ending in -ly can be both adjectives and adverbs. These include: daily, early, monthly, weekly, nightly, yearly.

Example: She gets a *weekly* payment from her parents. (Adjective)

I pay my rent *weekly*. (Adverb)

Some words ending in -ly are only adjectives and not adverbs. These include: costly, cowardly, deadly, friendly, likely, lonely, lovely, oily, orderly, scholarly, silly, smelly, timely, ugly, woolly.

Example: We enjoyed the trip to America but it was a costly holiday.

Some certain rules must be followed in the making of comparatives and superlatives of the adjectives. Not all adjectives form their comparatives and superlatives in the same way and there are also some irregular adjectives that form completely different comparative and superlative forms.

Word with Single or Double Syllable

Single syllable words and double syllable words ending with -y, -er, -ow, -le.

☞ We use '-er' to make the comparative and '-est' to make the superlative.

Positive	Comparative	Superlative
Black	Blacker	Blackest
Fair	Fairer	Fairest
Clever	Cleverer	Cleverest

☞ When there is a silent 'e' at the end of the positive form, we remove that and add '-er' and '-est'.

Positive	Comparative	Superlative
Nice	Nicer	Nicest
Late	Later	Latest

☞ When the adjective ends with a 'y', we convert the 'y' into 'i' before adding '-er' and '-est'.

Positive	Comparative	Superlative
Pretty	Prettier	Prettiest
Lazy	Lazier	Laziest

☞ If the adjective is a small one with little stress on the vowel, we double the last consonant.

Positive	Comparative	Superlative
Hot	Hotter	Hottest
Wet	Wetter	Wettest

Other Words with Two or More Syllables

For other double syllable words that do not end with -y, -er, -ow, -le, and for adjectives with more than two syllables we use more and most to form the comparatives and superlatives.

Positive	Comparative	Superlative
Difficult	More Difficult	Most Difficult
Careful	More Careful	Most Careful
Handsome	More Handsome	Most Handsome
Interesting	More Interesting	Most Interesting

Special Adjectives

There are a few adjectives that can use both '-er and -est' and 'more' and 'most' to form their comparative and superlative forms. The distinction between these is that '-er and -est' are used when we are comparing the noun to another noun and 'more' and 'most' is used when we are comparing characteristics within the noun.

Positive	Comparative	Superlative
Clever	Cleverer/More Clever	Cleverest/Most Clever
Quiet	Quieter/More Quiet	Quietest/Most Quiet
Brave	Braver/More Brave	Bravest/Most Brave
Sure	Surer/More Sure	Surest/Most Sure

Usage of Adjectives

☞ In comparing two things, the comparative degree should be used ; for more than two, superlative degree should be used.

Example:

a) He is the best of the two brothers. (Incorrect)

b) He is better of the two brothers. (Correct)

c) Among the three friends, Rahim is better. (Incorrect)

d) Among the three friends, Rahim is the best. (Correct)

☞ The use of double comparatives and superlatives should be avoided.

Example:

a) Ram is more smarter than Shyam. (Incorrect)

b) Ram is smarter than Shyam. (Correct)

c) Julius Caesar was stabbed by Brutus, which was the most unkindest cut of all. (Incorrect)

d) Julius Caesar was stabbed by Brutus, which was the unkindest cut of all. (Correct)

☞ When a comparative is followed by than, just any or all should not be used, other should be added to these.

Example:

a) He is cruder than any man living. (Incorrect)

b) He is cruder than any other man living. (Correct)

c) Birbal was wiser than any man living. (Incorrect)

d) Birbal was wiser than any other man living. (Correct)

☞ When the superlative degree is used, then other is avoided.

Example:

a) Birbal was the wisest of all other courtiers. (Incorrect)

b) Birbal was the wisest of all courtiers. (Correct)

☞ After the use of comparative like superior, inferior, prefer, preferable, junior, senior, posterior, anterior, prior, to should be used instead of than.

Example:

a) As a batsman, Jayasurya is superior than Tendulkar. (Incorrect)

b) As a batsman, Jayasurya is superior to Tendulkar. (Correct)

c) Orange is preferable than mausami. (Incorrect)

d) Orange is preferable to mausami. (Correct)

Note: Greater than or smaller than are often used incorrectly. Study the following Example carefully:

Example: The area of Bihar is greater than Jharkhand. (Incorrect)

The area of Bihar is greater than that of Jharkhand. (Correct)

The population of India is smaller than China. (Incorrect)

The population of India is smaller than that of China. (Correct)

☞ Some adjectives like perfect, universal, unique, chief, complete, entire, full, etc. are considered to be superlative, so they do not take any comparatives.

Example:

a) This is the most unique feature of the car. (Incorrect)

b) This is the unique feature of the car. (Correct)

c) This belief is most universally accepted. (Incorrect)

d) This belief is universally accepted. (Correct)

☞ Few and a few, little and a little have different meanings.

Few and little are negative, meaning : not many or hardly any.

A Few and a little are positive, meaning : some (though not much).

Example:

a) I have lost little money in the stock exchange. (hardly any)

b) I have lost a little money in the stock exchange (some).

Both the sentences have different meanings.

Similarly,

a) Few people believed what you said.

b) A few people believed what you said.

Both the sentences have different meanings.

But "Little knowledge is a dangerous thing" is incorrect. It should be "A little knowledge is a dangerous thing".

☞ Less is used for quantity, and fewer for numbers.

Example:

a) No less than twenty politicians have corruption cases registered against them. (Incorrect)

b) No fewer than twenty politicians have corruption cases registered against them. (Correct)

c) We buy no fewer than three crates of cold drinks. (Incorrect)

d) We buy no less than three crates of cold drinks. (Correct)

☞ Older and oldest may be used for persons and things, but elder and eldest are used only for persons, and that too usually of the same family.

Example:

a) My oldest sister is still unmarried. (Incorrect)

My eldest sister is still unmarried. (Correct)

b) Ram is elder than Shyam. (Incorrect)

Ram is older than Shyam. (Correct)

☞ Any is used in negative sentences and some is used in affirmative sentences ; both any and some can be used in interrogative sentences.

Example:

a) He did not give me something on my birthday. (Incorrect)

He did not give me anything on my birthday. (Correct)

b) I told him to give any money to the beggar. (Incorrect)

I told him to give some money to the beggar. (Correct)

☞ Latest and last are often incorrectly used.

Latest is the superlative form of late meaning most recent.

Last means final, or contrasted with first.

Example:

a) Do you know the last score ? (Incorrect)

b) Do you know the latest score ? (Correct)

c) He missed the latest train. (Incorrect)

d) He missed the last train. (Correct)

Practice Exercise

Fill in the blanks with the correct option.

1. Generally, girls are _______ than boys.
   (a) talkative (b) more talkative
   (c) most talkative (d) none of these
2. Cricket is an _______ game.
   (a) exciting (b) more exciting
   (c) most exciting (d) none of these
3. Arpita is looking _______ in this dress.
   (a) gorgeous (b) gorgeouser
   (c) gorgeousest (d) none of these
4. She has a very _______ voice.
   (a) sour (b) bitter
   (c) sweet (d) none of these
5. Diamond is the ______ natural material.
   (a) hard (b) harder
   (c) hardest (d) none of these
6. This exercise is quite _______.
   (a) simple (b) more simple
   (c) most simple (d) none of these
7. Rohan is a _______ boy.
   (a) trustworthy (b) trustworthier
   (c) trustworthiest (d) none of these
8. The entire staff of the hotel we stayed at was very _______.
   (a) friendly (b) friendlier
   (c) friendliest (d) none of these
9. You are getting _______ all the time!
   (a) good
   (b) better
   (c) best
   (d) none of these
10. Your efforts to accomplish this project are _______!
    (a) outstanding
    (b) more outstanding
    (c) most outstanding
    (d) none of these
11. An elephant's brain is _______ a whale's brain.
    (a) big than (b) bigger than
    (c) biggest (d) more big than
12. Monkeys are _______ learners than elephants.
    (a) faster (b) very fast
    (c) more fast (d) more faster
13. I am _______ my brother.
    (a) taller than (b) more taller than
    (c) tallest (d) more taller than
14. Tom thinks that his car is _______ than my car.
    (a) expensiver (b) more expensiver
    (c) most expensive (d) more expensive
15. This examination is _______ than the other examination.
    (a) more easy (b) more difficult
    (c) more easier (d) most easy
16. David is _______ than Emily. Emily is arrogant.
    (a) more modest (b) modest
    (c) most modest (d) arrogant
17. My town is _______ this city.
    (a) more peaceful
    (b) peacefuller
    (c) more peaceful than
    (d) most peaceful
18. The test says that Mark is more _______ Becky.
    (a) taller (b) creative than
    (c) faster than (d) happier than
19. Some students are more _______ than others.
    (a) cleverer (b) braver
    (c) slower (d) successful
20. I was ill yesterday but I am _______ today.
    (a) bitter (b) weller
    (c) better (d) gooder
21. I don't have _______ much time for reading _______ I would like to.
    (a) as/as (b) more/than
    (c) too/than (d) so/than
22. English is today the third _______ native language worldwide after Chinese and Hindi, with some 380 million speakers.
    (a) the most spoken (b) the more spoken
    (c) much spoken (d) most spoken

23. My students' sleepless nights became ______ as the finals approached.
   (a) so frequently
   (b) more frequent
   (c) as frequent
   (d) much more frequently

24. It is often said that the hyena is an aggressive animal, but in fact it is not ______ many people believe.
   (a) more vicious
   (b) so vicious that
   (c) as viciously as
   (d) so vicious as

25. The roots of the old tree spread out ______ thirty metres in all directions and damaged nearby buildings.
   (a) as much as
   (b) so much
   (c) as many as
   (d) so many as

Articles

4

Articles are the words which always give information about nouns and are always used with nouns. There are three articles – A, An, and The. They are also known as demonstrative adjectives.

Kinds of Articles

There are two kinds of articles: Definite Article (The) and Indefinite Article (A, An)

Definite Article (The)

It is an article used to refer to a particular person or thing.

Example: *The* cow is white.

The persons are professors.

Here the definite article '*the*' has been used to refer, to particular person or animal.

Indefinite Articles (A, An)

An article which is used in general and not in particular to anything.

Example: *A* boy of ten years.

An umbrella of black colour.

In these sentences '*A*' and '*An*' are indefinite articles.

☞ When we refer to any member of a group, we use a/an. It is not important which one we are talking about.

Example: I want to buy a new car. I want to buy the car, I looked at yesterday. [Here the use of article, 'the' is correct because we are talking about a specific car (the one I looked at already)].

☞ The usage of 'A' and 'An' depends on sound. 'An' is used with the words having vowel sounds like honest, upper, heir, etc. 'A' is used before the words that begin with consonant sound like yard, man, horse.

Uses of Articles

☞ The article A is used before singular, countable nouns which begin with consonant sounds.

Example: He is a teacher.

I saw a bear at the zoo.

☞ The article AN is used before singular, countable nouns which begin with vowel sounds.

Example: He is an actor.

She didn't get an invitation.

☞ Remember that A(AN) means 'one' or 'a single'. You cannot use A(AN) with plural nouns.

Example: I saw a bears in Yellowstone National Park. (Incorrect)

I saw bears in Yellowstone National Park. Correct

☞ If there is an adjective or an adverb-adjective combination before the noun, A(AN) should agree with the first sound in the adjective or the adverb-adjective combination.

Example: He is an excellent teacher.

I saw a really beautiful eagle at the zoo.

☞ Use A before words such as 'European' or 'university' which sound like they start with a consonant even if the first letter is a vowel. Also use A before letters and numbers which sound like they begin with a consonant, such as 'U', 'J', '1' or '9'. Remember, it is the sound not the spelling which is important. For example, '1' is spelled O-N-E; however, it is pronounced 'won' like it starts with a 'W'.

Example: She has a euro. Sounds like 'yu-ro'.

That number is a '1'. (Sounds like 'won'.)

☞ Use AN before words such as 'hour' which sound like they start with a vowel even if the first letter is a consonant. Also use AN before letters and numbers which sound like they begin with a vowel, such as 'F' or '8'. Remember, it is the sound not the spelling which is important. For example, 'F' is pronounced 'eff' like it starts with an 'E'.

Example: I only have an hour for lunch. (Sounds like 'au-er'.)

Does his name begin with an 'F'? (Sounds like 'eff'.)

☞ Some words such as 'herb' or 'hospital' are more complicated because they are pronounced differently in different English accents. In most American accents, the "h" in 'herb' is silent, so Americans usually say 'an herb'. In many British accents, the 'h' in 'herb' is pronounced, so many British say "a herb". In some British accents, the "h" in hospital is silent, so some British will say "an hospital" instead of "a hospital".

☞ In English, some nouns are considered uncountable such as: information, air, advice, salt and fun. We do not use A(AN) with these uncountable nouns. (Learn more about countable and uncountable nouns.)

Example: She gives a good advice. (Incorrect)

She gives good advice. (Correct)

Uses of Article (The)

The word 'the' is one of the most common word in English. It is the only definite article.

☞ Use 'the' to refer to something which has already been mentioned.

Example: I was walking past Sharma's Bakery when I decided to go into the bakery to get some bread.

There's a position/job available in my team. The job will involve some international travel.

☞ Use 'the' when you assume there is just one of something in that place, even if it has not been mentioned before.

Example: We went on a walk in the forest yesterday.

Where is the bathroom?

My father enjoyed the book you gave him.

☞ Use 'the' in sentences or clauses where you define or identify a particular person or object.

Example: The man who wrote this book is famous.

I live in the small house with a blue door.

He is the doctor I came to see.

☞ Use 'the' to refer to people or objects that are unique.

Example: The sun rose at 6:17 this morning.

You can go anywhere in the world.

Clouds drifted across the sky.

The president will be speaking on TV tonight.

☞ Use 'the' before superlatives and ordinal numbers.

Example: This is the highest building in New York.

She read the last chapter of her new book.

This is the third time I have called you today.

☞ Use 'the' with adjectives, to refer to a whole group of people.

Example: The French enjoy cheese.

The elderly require special attention.

☞ Use 'the' with decades.

Example: He was born in the seventies.

This is a painting from the 1820's.

☞ Use 'the' with clauses introduced by only.

Example: You are the only person he will listen to.

The only tea I like is black tea.

☞ Use 'the' with names of geographical areas, rivers, mountain ranges, groups of islands, canals, and oceans.

Example: They are travelling in the Arctic.

Our ship crossed the Atlantic in 7 days.

I will go on a cruise down the Nile.

☞ Use 'the' with countries that have plural names

Example: I have never been to the Netherlands.

Do you know anyone who lives in the Philippines?

☞ Use 'the' with countries that include the words "republic", "kingdom", or "states" in their names.

Example: She is visiting the United States.

James is from the Republic of Ireland.

☞ Use 'the' with newspaper names.

Example: I read it in the Times of India.

She works for the New York Times.

☞ Use 'the' with the names of famous buildings, works of art, museums, or monuments.

Example: Have you been to the Vietnam Memorial?

We went there and saw the Mona Lisa.

I would like to visit the Eiffel Tower.

☞ Use 'the' with the names of hotels and restaurants, unless these are named after a person.

Example: They are staying at the Hilton on 6th street.

We ate at the Golden Lion.

☞ Use 'the' with the names of families, but not with the names of individuals.

Example: We're having dinner with the Smiths tonight.

The Browns are going to the play with us.

When Not to Use 'The'

☞ Do not use 'the' with names of countries with singular names.

Example: Germany is an important economic power.

He's just returned from Zimbabwe.

☞ Do not use 'the' with the names of languages.

Example: French is spoken in Tahiti.

English uses many words of Latin origin.

☞ Do not use 'the' with the names of meals.

Example: Lunch is my favourite meal.

I like to eat breakfast early.

☞ Do not use 'the' with people's names.

Example: John is coming over later.

Mary Carpenter is my boss.

☞ Do not use 'the' with titles when combined with names.

Example: Prince Charles is Queen Elizabeth's son.

President Kennedy was assassinated in Dallas.

☞ Do not use 'the' after the 's possessive case.

Example: His brother's car was stolen.

Peter's house is over there.

☞ Do not use "the" with professions.

Example: Engineering is a well-paid career.

He'll probably study medicine.

☞ Do not use 'the' with names of shops.

Example: I'll get the card at Smith's.

☞ Do not use "the" with years.

Example: 1948 was a wonderful year.

He was born in 1995.

☞ Do not use 'the' with uncountable nouns.

Example: Rice is an important food in Asia.

War is destructive.

☞ Do not use 'the' with the names of individual mountains, lakes and islands.

Example: She lives near Lake Windermere.

Have you visited Long Island?

☞ Do not use 'the' with most names of towns, streets, stations and airports.

Example: Can you direct me to Bond Street?

She lives in Florence.

They're flying into Heathrow.

Omission of Articles "A" & "The"

'A' and 'the' are not used with

☞ Plural nouns

Example: "Boys like soccer." (Correct, as we are talking about boys in general (all boys).

The boys in my school like soccer.

But, when a noun refers to any specific or definite noun, one should use 'the' before that noun).

(Correct, as we are talking about specific boys (the ones in my school).

☞ Uncountable Nouns

Example: Pollution is a problem. (Pollution is an uncountable noun (a mass noun). But when the noun refers to a certain situation, one should use 'the' before that noun.)

Example: The pollution in my town is a problem. (Correct, as we are talking about a specific location).

"There is some pollution in my town."

(Correct, as the word 'some' tells us about the amount of pollution).

"There is a pollution in my town."

(Incorrect, as 'a' is only used with countable nouns (a car, a boy) but pollution is uncountable. Water, traffic and snow are Example of uncountable nouns.

☞ Proper Nouns

We do not use any article before the names of a person, or a place as these are proper nouns. i.e. the names of people or places, e.g. Mahatma Gandhi, New Delhi, etc.

Example: "I want to visit the Spain." (Incorrect)

Practice Exercise

I. Choose the correct option (article) to fill in the blanks.

1. Where's ______ knife I was just using?
   (a) no article needed (b) the
   (c) a (d) an
2. How much ______ snow do you get in winter?
   (a) a (b) no article needed
   (c) the (d) an
3. I had ______ fruit for lunch.
   (a) no article needed (b) the
   (c) a (d) an
4. I'm thinking about taking ___ holiday.
   (a) a (b) the
   (c) no article needed (d) an
5. Can you lend me ______ pen?
   (a) an (b) a
   (c) no article needed (d) the
6. ___ roses in your garden are beautiful.
   (a) the (b) an
   (c) no article needed (d) a
7. Make sure you drink plenty of ______ water.
   (a) no article needed (b) the
   (c) a (d) an
8. Let's eat out at ______ restaurant tonight. What type shall we go to?
   (a) no article needed (b) the
   (c) a (d) an
9. I should buy ______ new pair of shoes soon.
   (a) a (b) the
   (c) no article needed (d) an

II. Fill in the blanks with the correct article.

1. My father is _____ doctor and my mother is _____ artist.
2. I recommended ______ musician to Priya but she didn't like _____ artist at all.
3. There is _____ English and Hindi The-saurus.
4. I met _____ editor and ______ cartoonist of _____ magazine.
5. I am _____ Indian by birth.
6. Eric is ___ star football player as well as ___ impressive captain.
7. My father is ________ honorable person.
8. I saw _____ monkey and _____ elephant at ___ zoo.
9. Varanasi is ________ holy place.
10. There's _____ peacock on ______ fence.

III. Fill in the blanks with A, AN or (X) for 'no article'.

1. I have ______ two sisters and ______ brother. My brother has ______ son. That makes me ______ uncle.
2. Would you like ______ orange? Or would you prefer ______ banana? We also have ______ strawberries.
3. Does anyone have ______ cell phone? I need to make ______ emergency phone call.
4. John doesn't own ______ car. He rides ______ motorcycle to work.
5. Today, you ate ______ ice cream cone, ______ piece of pizza, ______ burrito and ______ doughnuts. That's not exactly ______ healthy diet.
6. Let's go see ______ movie. There's ______ adventure film that I have really been wanting to see.
7. Is there ______ Internet cafe around here? I need to send ______ important email.
8. Instead of making ______ traditional turkey for Thanksgiving dinner, she baked ______ enormous chicken.
9. It looks like it is going to be ______ rainy day. You should take ______ umbrella.
10. Phil and Debbie took ______ amazing vacation to Switzerland last year. They even climbed ______ mountain near Lucerne.
11. Because there was ______ huge rainstorm, the flight was delayed for more than ______ hour. The airport was full of ______ angry passengers.
12. You said that he was ______ well known player in ______ European football team, his name started with ______ "E", and his jersey had ______ "18" on it. I don't know who you are talking about.

13. That company makes _______ app to let you instantly translate _______ things with _______ iPhone. That's _______ useful tool for _______ frequent traveller.

14. Is this _______ phone number? It's really hard to read. Is that _______ "1" or _______ "7"?

15. With gas prices at _______ all-time high, I wish I didn't drive _______ SUV. I think _______ small compact car would be _______ much more cost-effective way to get around.

16. 'Photo' doesn't start with _______ "F"; it starts with _______ 'P'. And 'write' starts with _______ "W", not _______ 'R'.

17. He's quite _______ unique salesman. He has _______ unusual gift for keeping customers happy, and he has honest face which convinces _______ people to buy things.

18. I buy my music from _______ online music store. They charge Americans _______ dollar for _______ song and Europeans _______ euro. You can choose to download the song as _______ MP3 or in several other formats. If you purchase ten songs, they will even send you CD.

19. No, no, Margaret isn't _______ secretary; her husband is. In fact, he is quite _______ efficient secretary. He works for _______ well known law firm downtown.

20. Dr. Joshi is professor at Stanford University. She has _______ Ph.D. in biology from Yale and _______ MBA from Harvard. She is quite _______ educated lady.

IV. Fill in the blanks with the correct article.

Akansha Verma's freshman year at St. Cornelius School hadn't been ___1___ easy one. She was relieved that ___2___ summer break had finally arrived. Valerie and her two new friends, Deepika and Aradhana, had plans-BIG plans. This was going to be ___3___ best summer ever! Just one year had passed since ___4___ Vermas moved from ___5___ small suburb on ___6___ outskirts of Bengaluru to ___7___ huge megapolis of Mumbai. When Akanksha's parents had first announced ___8___ news about moving, her feelings were so convoluted, she could hardly speak! She hated ___9___ thought of moving away from her friends and relatives, but at ___10___ same time, Valerie was intrigued by ___11___ idea of life in ___12___ big city. Now that she was settled into ___13___ new neighbourhood and had survived that awkward first year in ___14___ new school, Valerie's memory of her ordinary life in her old town began to fade away. Mumbai was her home now. This is where her summer dreams would come true.

Verb

5

A verb is a part of speech which expresses an action, an occurrence, a state of being. It's the action word that denotes an action.

Verb

Verbs are the most important component of any sentence. These words talk about the action or the state of any noun or subject. This means that verbs show what the subject is doing or what is the state or situation of the subject.

Example: He ran to the store. (Here the verb 'ran' describes the action of the subject 'he')

She is a creative person. (Here there is no action being done. Instead the auxiliary verb 'is' shows the state of the subject 'she' as being 'creative'.)

Types of Verb

There are different types and classifications of verbs; some of the most important ones are following:

Action Verbs

These verbs talk about what the subject is doing in the sentence. Action verbs are one of the most easily identifiable types of verbs. To recognize them, you simply have to look for the word in the sentence that answers the question 'What is the subject doing?'

Example:

a) Tom is painting the kitchen walls. (The subject here is Tom, and what is Tom doing? Tom is painting. Hence, painting is action verb.)

b) My dog is sleeping on the sofa. (The subject here is dog, and what is the dog doing? The dog is sleeping. So sleeping is action verb.

There are two types of action verbs which describe the verb and the subject doing the action and the object on which the action is done, they are:

(i) Transitive Verbs

(ii) Intransitive Verbs

Transitive verbs

These action verbs have a definite object on which, or for which the action is being performed. That means that the action has a definite recipient or object. To identify them you can ask the question what did the subject do?

Example:

a) Tom is painting the kitchen walls.

Here the verb is painting and the subject is Tom.

If we form the question - what is Tom painting?

The answer is: The kitchen walls.

Thus, we see that there is a specific object on which the action of painting was being done.

b) Sudha gave him a big hug.

Here, we see that the action 'gave' is being performed by the subject Sudha. So the question is what did Sudha give? And the answer is - A big hug.

Here, we also have a indirect object as 'him'. This indirect object would be the answer to the question:

Who did the subject (Sudha) - verb - (give) the object (hug) to?

Intransitive verbs

These verbs also show an action but there is no specific object on which the action is being done. To recognize these verbs, we ask the question what did the subject do? If there is no answer present, then the verb in the sentence is an intransitive verb.

Example:

a) Tom is painting right now.

Here, if we ask the question what is Tom painting? There is no answer which means that in this sentence painting is an intransitive verb.

It is telling us about the action of the subject but there is no specific object for the action.

b) Sudha sneezed repeatedly.

Here, the verb is sneezed. If we ask the question what did Sudha sneeze? There is no answer present; so sneezed is an intransitive verb.

Linking Verbs

These verbs are unlike other verbs as they do not tell anything about a subject themselves, instead linking verbs connect the subject to a noun or adjective that helps in describing or providing additional information about the subject. Those nouns or adjectives are called the subject complements.

Example:

a) Sarita is greedy about food.

(Here we see the subject is Sarita and the linking verb is 'is' which is connecting Sarita to the subject complement 'greedy about food' which is giving additional information about Sarita preferences.)

b) The students felt relieved. The students are relieved. (Linking Verb)

(Hence 'felt' is a linking verb and not an action verb as 'felt' is simply connecting the subject to the adjective.)

Every student felt the relief. Every student is/am/are the relief. (Action Verb)

(Hence 'felt' is action verb as it is the action of 'feeling an emotion.')

Helping and Modal Auxiliary Verbs

Helping verbs or auxiliary verbs such as will, shall, may, might, can, could, must, ought to, should, would, used to, need are used in conjunction with main verbs to express shades of time and mood. The combination of helping verbs with main verbs creates what are called verb phrases or verb strings.

Example: As of next August, I *will have been* studying chemistry for ten years.

Students should remember that adverbs and contracted forms are not, technically, part of the verb.

Shall, will and forms of have, do and be combine with main verbs to indicate time and voice. As auxiliaries, the verbs be, have and do can change form to indicate changes in subject and time.

Example:

a) I *shall* go now.

b) He *had* won the election.

c) They *did* write that novel together.

d) I *am* going now.

e) He *was* winning the election.

f) They *have been* writing that novel for a long time.

☞ Uses of Shall, Will and Should

Shall is used to express the simple future for first person I and we, as in "Shall we meet by the river?" Will would be used in the simple future for all other persons. Using will in the first person would express determination on the part of the speaker, as in "We will finish this project by tonight, by golly!" Using shall in second and third persons would indicate some kind of promise about the subject.

Example:

a) "This shall be revealed to you in good time.

b) "Shall we go now?"

c) "Shall I call a doctor for you?"

(In the second sentence, many writers would use should instead, although should is somewhat more tentative than shall.)

☞ Shall is often used in formal situations (legal or legalistic documents, minutes to meetings, etc.) to express obligation, even with third-person and second-person constructions:

Example:

a) The board of directors *shall* be responsible for payment to stockholders.

b) The college president *shall* report financial shortfalls to the executive director each semester."

☞ Should is usually replaced, nowadays, by would. It is still used, however, to mean "ought to" as in

Example:

a) You really shouldn't do that.

b) If you think that was amazing, you should have seen it last night.

☞ In British English and very formal American English, one is apt to hear or read should with the first-person pronouns in expressions of liking such as "I should prefer iced tea" and in tentative expressions of opinion such as

Example:

a) I should imagine they'll vote Conservative.

b) I should have thought so.

Uses of Do, Does and Did

☞ In the simple present tense, do will function as an auxiliary to express the negative and to ask questions. (Does, however, is substituted for third-person, singular subjects in the present tense. The past tense did works with all persons, singular and plural.)

Example:

a) I don't study at night.

b) She doesn't work here anymore.

c) Do you attend this school?

d) Does he work here?

☞ These verbs also work as "short answers," with the main verb omitted.

Example: Does she work here? No, she doesn't work here.

☞ With "yes-no" questions, the form of do goes in front of the subject and the main verb comes after the subject:

Example:

a) Did your grandmother know Truman?

b) Do wildflowers grow in your back yard?

☞ Forms of do are useful in expressing similarity and differences in conjunction with so and neither.

Example:

a) My wife hates spinach and so does my son.

b) My wife doesn't like spinach; neither do I.

☞ Do is also helpful because it means you don't have to repeat the verb:

Example:

a) Larry excelled in language studies; so did his brother.

b) Rohit studies as hard as his sister does.

☞ The so-called emphatic do has many uses in English.

❒ To add emphasis to an entire sentence: "He does like spinach. He really does!"

❒ To add emphasis to an imperative: "Do come in." (actually softens the command)

❒ To add emphasis to a frequency adverb: "He never did understand his father." "She always does manage to hurt her mother's feelings."

❒ To contradict a negative statement: "You didn't do your homework, did you?" "Oh, but I did finish it."

❒ To ask a clarifying question about a previous negative statement: "Ridwell didn't take the tools." "Then who did take the tools?"

❒ To indicate a strong concession: "Although the Clintons denied any wrong-doing, they did return some of the gifts."

❒ In the absence of other modal auxiliaries, a form of do is used in question and negative constructions known as the get passive:

Example:

a) Did Rinaldo get selected by the committee?

b) The audience didn't get riled up by the politician.

Uses of Have, Has and Had

Forms of the verb to have are used to create tenses known as the present perfect and past perfect. The perfect tenses indicate that something has happened in the past; the present perfect indicating that something happened and might be continuing to happen, the past perfect indicating that something happened prior to something else happening. (That sounds worse than it really is!)

To have is also in combination with other modal verbs to express probability and possibility in the past.

❒ As an affirmative statement, to have can express how certain you are that something happened (when combined with an appropriate modal + have + a past participle): "Georgia must have left already." "Clinton might have known about the gifts." "They may have voted already."

❒ As a negative statement, a modal is combined with not + have + a past participle to express how certain you are that something did not happen: "Clinton might not have known about the gifts." "I may not have been there at the time of the crime."

❒ To ask about possibility or probability in the past, a modal is combined with the subject + have + past participle: "Could Clinton have known about the gifts?"

❒ For short answers, a modal is combined with have: "Did Clinton know about this?" "I don't know. He may have." "The evidence is pretty positive. He must have."

❒ To have (sometimes combined with to get) is used to express a logical inference:

Example: It's been raining all week; the basement has to be flooded by now.

He hit his head on the doorway. He has got to be over seven feet tall!

☞ Have is often combined with an infinitive to form an auxiliary whose meaning is similar to "must."

Example: I have to have a car like that!

She has to pay her own tuition at college.

He has to have been the first student to try that.

Modal Auxiliaries

Other helping verbs, called modal auxiliaries or modals, such as can, could, may, might, must, ought to, shall, should, will, and would, do not change form for different subjects. For instance, try substituting any of these modal auxiliaries for can with any of the subjects listed below.

I

you (singular)

he

we

you (plural)

they can write well.

Uses of Can and Could

The modal auxiliary can is used to express ability (in the sense of being able to do something or knowing how to do something):

Example: He can speak Spanish but he can't write it very well.

☞ To expression permission (in the sense of being allowed or permitted to do something):

Example: Can I talk to my friends in the library waiting room? (Note that can is less formal than may. Also, some writers will object to the use of can in this context.)

☞ To express theoretical possibility:

Example: American automobile makers can make better cars if they think there's a profit in it.

☞ The modal auxiliary could is used to express an ability in the past:

Example: I could always beat you at tennis when we were kids.

☞ To express past or future permission:

Example: Could I bury my cat in your back yard?

☞ To express present possibility:

Example: We could always spend the afternoon just sitting around talking.

☞ To express possibility or ability in contingent circumstances:

Example: If he studied harder, he could pass this course.

☞ In expressing ability, can and could frequently also imply willingness:

Example: Can you help me with my homework?

Can Versus May

Uses of May and Might

☞ Two of the more troublesome modal auxiliaries are may and might. When used in the context of granting or seeking permission, might is the past tense of may. Might is considerably more tentative than may.

Example: May I leave class early?

If I've finished all my work and I'm really quiet, might I leave early?

☞ In the context of expressing possibility, may and might are interchangeable present and future forms and might + have + past participle is the past form:

Example:

a) She might be my advisor next semester.

b) She may be my advisor next semester.

c) She might have advised me not to take biology.

☞ Avoid confusing the sense of possibility in may with the implication of might, that a hypothetical situation has not in fact occurred.

Example: Let's say there's been a helicopter crash at the airport. In his initial report, before all the facts are gathered, a newscaster could say that the pilot "may have been injured." After we discover that the pilot is in fact all right, the newscaster can now say that the pilot "might have been injured" because it is a hypothetical situation that has not occurred.

A body had been identified after much work by a detective. It was reported that "without this painstaking work, the body may have remained unidentified." Since the body was, in fact, identified, might is clearly called for.

Uses of Will and Would

- In certain contexts, will and would are virtually interchangeable, but there are differences. Notice that the contracted form 'll is very frequently used for will.
- Will can be used to express willingness:

Example: I'll wash the dishes if you dry.

We're going to the movies. Will you join us?

- It can also express intention (especially in the first person) or prediction:

Example: I'll do my exercises later on.

Specific: The meeting will be over soon.

Timeless: Humidity will ruin my hairdo.

Habitual: The river will overflow its banks every spring.

- Would can also be used to express willingness:

Example: Would you please take off your hat?

- It can also express insistence (rather rare, and with a strong stress on the word "would"):

Example: Now you've ruined everything. You would act that way.

- Customary: After work, he would walk to his home in West Hartford.
- Typical (casual): She would cause the whole family to be late, every time.
- In a main clause, would can express a hypothetical meaning:

Example: My cocker spaniel would weigh a ton if I let her eat what she wants.

- Finally, would can express a sense of probability:

Example: I hear a whistle. That would be the five o'clock train.

Uses of Used to

- The auxiliary verb construction used is used to express an action that took place in the past, perhaps customarily, but now that action no longer customarily takes place:

Example: We used to take long vacation trips with the whole family.

- The spelling of this verb is a problem for some people because the "-ed" ending quite naturally disappears in speaking: "We yoostoo take long trips." But it ought not to disappear in writing. There are exceptions, though. When the auxiliary is combined with another auxiliary, did, the past tense is carried by the new auxiliary and the "-ed" ending is dropped. This will often happen in the interrogative:

Example: Didn't you use to go jogging every morning before breakfast?

It didn't use to be that way.

- Used to can also be used to convey the sense of being accustomed to or familiar with something:

Example: The tyre factory down the road really stinks, but we're used to it by now.

I like these old sneakers; I'm used to them.

- Used to is best reserved for colloquial usage; it has no place in formal or academic text.

Moods of a Verb

The modes which are used to explain a certain action are called moods. There are three types of moods:

Indicative Mood

They are used to indicate a question, a fact or supposition.

Example: You must *read* the newspaper daily. (statement)

Are we going out? (Question)

If you've *studied*, you should be able to answer the questions. (Supposition)

Imperative Mood

These verbs are used to express a command or some form of advice or request.

Example: *Shut* the door. (Command)

Be *kind* to the poor. (Advice)

Subjunctive Mood

The verbs in subjuntive mood are used to express a desire or hope, uncertainty, possibility, etc.

Example: Long *live* the queen! (wish)

Usage of Verbs

- A verb must agree with its subject in number, person and gender.

Example:

a) Sudha *learns* her lesson well. (Subject: singular, third person, feminine gender)

b) One of the boys *was selected*. (Here the singular verb *'was'* agrees with the singular subject one.)

☞ The subject of a sentence should be followed by a verb. Note that a sentence must have at least one verb.

Example:

a) He who has won the prize, let him *speak*. (incorrect)

b) Let him who has won the prize *speak*. (correct)

☞ An infinitive should be in the present tense unless it represents an action prior to that mentioned by the principal verb.

Example:

a) I should have liked *to win*. (correct)

b) I should have liked *to have won*. (incorrect)

c) He seems *to have enjoyed* his stay at the hill station. (Here, the stay at the hill station took place earlier than the action mentioned by the main verb).

☞ The participle should not be left without proper agreement.

Example: *Having bitten* the postman, the farmer killed the dog. (incorrect) In the above sentence, it was the farmer who bit the postman.

Having bitten the postman, the dog was killed by the farmer. (correct)

OR

The dog *having bitten* the postman, the farmer killed it. (correct)

☞ The verbs of perception; e.g., see, hear, smell and make are followed by noun/pronoun + plain infinitive.

Example: They *made* the child *drink* the whole milk. (NOT They made the child to drink ...)

I *heard* her *sing* a happy song. (NOT I heard her to sing ...)

☞ The verbs enjoy, avoid, miss, postpone and suggest should be followed by gerunds, and not by to-infinitives.

Example: He *enjoys* singing. (NOT He enjoys to sing.)

Mother *suggested* consulting a doctor. (NOT Mother suggested to consult.)

Practice Exercise

I. Underline the verbs in the following sentences.

1. There was a raging fire that ran through the neighborhood.
2. We felt disappointed with her failure.
3. The film is directed by one of the new directors of the academy.
4. They are living in abject poverty.
5. The dog is chained.
6. Rajiv Gandhi was assassinated.
7. She is feeling a pain in her hip.
8. The train is delayed.
9. The rain has stopped.
10. We played chess for an hour.

II. Fill in the blanks with the correct form of verb given in the bracket.

1. I ______ for Medicine last year. (study)
2. My father ______ from service last year. (retire)
3. My uncle ______ the paper daily. (read)
4. Rachel _____ to church every Sunday. (go)
5. It ______ heavily last night. (rain)
6. All roads ______ to Rome. (lead)
7. The earth _____ around the sun. (revolve)
8. Edison ______ the photograph. (take)
9. Nature ______ our best physician. (be)
10. Megha ______ a good memory. (has)
11. The Sun ______ in the east. (rise)
12. Slow and steady ______ the race. (win)
13. Time and tide ______ for none. (wait)
14. I ______ for the Congress. (vote)
15. Gandhi ______ freedom for India. (want)

III. Fill in the blanks with the correct form of verbs given in brackets.

1. If you ______ (are, were) a fool, you would accept that offer.
2. If she ______ (was, were) a teacher, she would be able to explain it well.
3. If I ______ (have, had) money, I would lend it to you.
4. If Padma has asked me, I ______ (would have given it, could have given it) to her.
5. It is the time we ______ (realize, realized) the value of time.
6. It is time she ______ (returns, returned) home.
7. If I ______ (know, knew) her address, I would have written a letter to her.
8. She walks as if she ______ (is, were) a qualified teacher.
9. She talks as though she _____ _ (is, were) a qualified teacher.
10. I would rather ______ you (stop, stopped) smoking.
11. I wish I ______ (can, could) kill a tiger.
12. I wish I ______ (see, saw) her again.
13. If you ______ (give, will give) respect, you will receive respect from others.
14. She wishes she _____ (belongs, belonged) to a rich family.
15. If you _____ (are, were) my wife, I would be happy.

IV. Choose the correct option to fill in the blanks with the correct form of verb.

1. I ______ tennis every Sunday morning.
   (a) playing (b) play
   (c) am playing (d) am play
2. Don't make so much noise. Sarika ____ to study for her ESL test!
   (a) try (b) tries
   (c) tried (d) is trying
3. Manav ______ his teeth before breakfast every morning.
   (a) will cleaned (b) is cleaning
   (c) cleans (d) clean
4. Sorry, she can't come to the phone. She ______ a bath!
   (a) is having (b) having
   (c) have (d) has
5. ______ many times every winter in Frankfurt.
   (a) It snows (b) It snowed
   (c) It is snowing (d) It is snow

6. How many students in your class _______ from Korea?
   (a) comes (b) come
   (c) came (d) are coming
7. Weather report: "It's seven o'clock in Frankfurt and _______ ."
   (a) there is snow (b) it`s snowing
   (c) it snows (d) it snowed
8. Babies _______ when they are hungry.
   (a) cry (b) cries
   (c) cried (d) are crying
9. Jane: "What _______ in the evenings?"
   Mary: "Usually I watch TV or read a book."
   (a) you doing (b) you do
   (c) do you do (d) are you doing
10. Jane: "What _______ ?"
    Mary: "I'm trying to fix my calculator."
    (a) you doing (b) you do
    (c) do you do (d) are you doing
11. Jane _______ her blue jeans today, but usually she wears a skirt or a dress.
    (a) wears (b) wearing
    (c) wear (d) is wearing
12. I think I _______ a new calculator. This one does not work properly any more.
    (a) needs (b) needed
    (c) need (d) am needing
13. Sorry, you can't borrow my pencil. I _______ it myself.
    (a) was using (b) using
    (c) use (d) am using
14. At a school dance:
    Jane: " _______ yourself?"
    Mary: "Yes, I'm having a great time!"
    (a) You enjoying
    (b) Enjoy you
    (c) Do you enjoy
    (d) Are you enjoying
15. I've just finished reading a story called Dangerous Game. It's about a man who _______ his wife because he doesn't want to lose her.
    (a) kills (b) killed
    (c) kill (d) is killing
16. What time _______
    (a) the train leaves?
    (b) leaves the train?
    (c) is the train leaving?
    (d) does the train leave?
17. Jane: "Are you going to the dance on Friday?"
    Mary: "No, I'm not. I _______ school dances; they're loud, hot and crowded!"
    (a) not enjoy
    (b) don`t enjoy
    (c) doesn`t enjoy
    (d) am not enjoying
18. I _______ for my pen. Have you seen it?
    (a) will look (b) looking
    (c) look (d) am looking
19. You can keep my iPod if you like. I _______ it any more.
    (a) don`t use (b) doesn`t use
    (c) didn`t use (d) am not using
20. The phone _______ Can you answer it, please?
    (a) rings (b) ring
    (c) rang (d) is ringing
21. Have you ever _______ abroad?
    (a) went (b) been
    (c) to (d) go
22. She's _______ a show at the moment.
    (a) taken (b) takes
    (c) take (d) taking
23. I always _______ before bed.
    (a) read (b) to read
    (c) reading (d) is read
24. He will _______ you later.
    (a) to call (b) calls
    (c) calling (d) call
25. I don't know who _______ the chair.
    (a) breaking (b) broke
    (c) breaks (d) break
26. We've all been _______ about you.
    (a) thinking (b) thought
    (c) thinks (d) to think
27. Someone _______ moved my bag.
    (a) have (b) having
    (c) has (d) haves

28. We ______ playing cards all afternoon.
(a) were (b) was
(c) is (d) be

29. Those______ the type I like.
(a) isn't (b) aren't
(c) don't (d) won't

30. James asked me ______ him.
(a) emailed (b) to email
(c) emailing (d) email

31. Ted's flight from Amsterdam took more than 11 hours. He ______ be exhausted after such a long flight.
(a) must (b) had better
(c) can (d) none of these

32. The book is optional. My professor said we could read it if we needed extra credit. But we _____ read it if we don't want to.
(a) cannot (b) don't have to
(c) must not (d) none of these

33. Susan ______ hear the speaker because the crowd was cheering so loudly.
(a) couldn't (b) can't
(c) might not (d) none of these

34. The television isn't working. It ______ damaged during the move.
(a) must have been (b) must
(c) must be (d) none of these

35. Kate: ______ hold your breath for more than a minute?
Jack: No, I can't.
(a) are you able to (b) might you
(c) can you (d) none of these

36. You ______ be rich to be a success. Some of the most successful people I know haven't got a penny to their name.
(a) can't (b) shouldn't
(c) don't have to (d) none of these

37. I've redone this math problem at least twenty times, but my answer is wrong according to the answer key. The answer in the book ______ be wrong!
(a) have to (b) should
(c) must (d) none of these

38. You ______ do the job if you don't speak Japanese fluently.
(a) won't be able to (b) can't
(c) couldn't (d) none of these

39. You ______ worry so much. It doesn't do you any good. Either you get the job, or you don't. If you don't, just apply for another one. Eventually, you will find work.
(a) can't (b) should't
(c) don't have to (d) none of these

40. You ______ be kidding! That can't be true.
(a) ought to (b) have to
(c) should (d) none of these

41. You ______ leave the table once you have finished your meal and politely excused yourself.
(a) would (b) may
(c) might (d) none of these

42. Jenny's engagement ring is enormous! It ______ a fortune.
(a) must cost (b) must have cost
(c) must be costing (d) none of these

43. ______ we move into the living room? It's more comfortable there and there's a beautiful view of the lake.
(a) must (b) will
(c) shall (d) none of these

44. If I had gone white water rafting with my friends, I ______ down the Colorado River right now.
(a) would float
(b) would be floating
(c) would have float
(d) none of these

45. At first, my boss didn't want to hire Sam. But, because I had previously worked with Sam, I told my boss that he ______ take another look at his resume and reconsider him for the position.
(a) has to (b) ought to
(c) must (d) none of these

46. You ______ take along some cash. The restaurant may not accept credit cards.
(a) have to (b) can
(c) had better (d) none of these

47. The machine _______ on by flipping this switch.
(a) could be turning (b) may turn
(c) can be turned (d) none of these

48. I can't stand these people. I _______ get out of here. I'm going to take off for awhile while you get rid of them.
(a) have got to (b) might
(c) had better (d) none of these

49. You _______ forget to pay the rent tomorrow. The landlord is very strict about paying on time.
(a) couldn't (b) don't have to
(c) must not (d) none of these

50. Do you always have to say the first thing that pops into your head. _______ you think once in a while before you speak?
(a) can't (b) don't
(c) shouldn't (d) none of these

51. Terry and Frank said they would come over right after work, so they _______ be here by 6:00.
(a) should (b) can
(c) have to (d) none of these

52. Yesterday, I _______ cram all day for my French final. I didn't get to sleep until after midnight.
(a) should
(b) must
(c) had to
(d) none of these

53. We _______ no longer suffer the injustice of oppression! Freedom shall be ours!
(a) would
(b) shall
(c) might
(d) none of these

54. If I had gone to the University of Miami, I _______ participate in their Spanish immersion program.
(a) could be
(b) could have
(c) could
(d) none of these

55. The lamp _______ be broken. Maybe the light bulb just burned out.
(a) must not (b) might not
(c) could not (d) none of these

◆◆◆

Adverbs

6

Adverbs are the words which add another dimension or layer in the meaning of the verb they accompany. They express how to the verbs are being used or have been used to clarify the meaning of the verb.

Example: *She* sings *beautifully*. (the adverbial word '*beautifully*' tells how she '*sings*')

He explained the problem thoroughly. (The word 'thoroughly' has been used to indicate each and every point of the problem.)

Kinds of Adverb

Following are different kinds of adverbs:

(i) **Adverb of manner:** It is used to show how an action is done, e.g. *happily, gracefully, fast, etc.*

(ii) **Adverb of time:** It is used to show when an action takes place or is going to take place, e.g. *early, soon, yesterday, etc.*

(iii) **Adverb of place:** It is used to show where an action is performed or has taken place, e.g. *below, away, up, etc.*

(iv) **Adverb of degree:** It is used to show how much or in what degree or the extent of an action has been performed, e.g. *almost, hardly, enough, etc.*

(v) **Adverb of frequency:** It is used to show how often an action is done or how often it takes place, e.g. *twice, occasionally, seldom, etc.*

(vi) **Relative adverb:** It is used to relate two clauses or statements, e.g. *when, where, why, etc.*

(vii) **Interrogative adverb:** It is used to ask a question, e.g. *how, why, when, etc.*

Characteristics of Adverb

- A **simple adverb** is used to modify the meaning of a verb, an adjective, or an adverb
- An **interrogative adverb** is used to ask questions.
- A **relative adverb** is used to join two clauses or statements.
- **Adverb of manner** answers the question 'how'.
- **Adverb of place** answers the question of 'where'.
- **Adverb of time** answers the question of 'time'.
- **Adverb of frequency** answers the question of 'how often'.
- **Adverb of degree** answers questions like 'how much'.

Some words can be used as adverbs and *adjectives.*

Example: *Kapil* is a *fast* bowler. (the word 'fast' is used as an adjective in this sentence)

I cannot walk *fast*. (the word 'fast' is used as an adverb in this sentence)

Degrees of Comparison of Adverbs

The evolved forms of adverbs are known as comparative and superlative degrees. These forms are a comparison of adverbs.

Positive	Comparative	Superlative
Hard	Harder	Hardest
Swiftly	More swiftly	Most swiftly
Good	Better	Best

In the above box degrees of comparion of adverbs have been shown. The last example is known as an irregular comparison. The comparative adverbs can be formed using 'er' or 'more and 'ly' or the word changes entirely. The superlative adverbs can be formed using 'est' and 'most' and the same rule for the comparative adverbs applies here for an irregular comparison.

Position of Adverbs

Adverbs should come as near as possible to the verbs they qualify. This is because the meaning of a sentence can change with the change in the position of the adverb.

Example: *Only* he lent me five cents. (= He and nobody else lent me five cents.)

He *only* lent me five cents. (= He only lent me the money, he didn't do anything else.)

He lent me *only* five cents. (= He didn't lend me more than five cents.)

He lent *only* me five cents. (i.e. to nobody else)

You will have noticed that the meaning of the sentence changes considerably with the change in the position of the adverb *only*.

Most adverbs, however, can be placed in different positions with no significant change in meaning. The following are a few rules regarding the position of adverbs.

Rule 1: When the verb is *intransitive* (verbs that do not have objects), place the adverb immediately after it.

Example:

a) He walked *slowly*.

b) She smiled *beautifully*.

c) He spoke *fluently*.

d) They worked *hard*.

Rule 2: When the verb is *transitive* with an object following, place the adverb immediately after the object.

Example:

a) She endured the pain *bravely*.

b) He offered his help *willingly*.

c) She sang the song *beautifully*.

d) He drove the car *fast*.

e) He did the job *well*.

f) He gave his consent *immediately*.

g) He took the matter *lightly*.

Rule 3: Adverbs of Time and Frequency normally come before the verb.

Example:

a) They *seldom* visit us.

b) She *never* admitted her fault.

c) You *always* speak the truth.

d) It is *never* too late to mend.

Rule 4: When the verb consists of an auxiliary, the adverb goes after it.

Example:

a) I *have always* wanted to be a writer.

b) He *was greatly* praised for his novel idea.

c) I *have not* had the time to look into the matter.

d) We *must always* obey our parents.

Rule 5: An adverb which modifies an adjective or another adverb comes before it.

Example: She is *very* beautiful. (Here, the adverb 'very' modifies the adjective beautiful.)

They are *highly* competitive. (Here, the adverb 'highly' modifies the adjective competitive.)

Note: adverb enough comes after the adjective it modifies.

He was *foolish enough* to trust her.

Our army is *strong enough* to defend our country.

Rule 6: The words *only, merely, even, not* and *never* are usually placed before the words they modify.

Example:

a) I *merely* wanted to know his name.

b) She was *not* clever enough to see through his scheme.

c) He *never* keeps his word.

Forming Adverbs from Adjectives

☞ In a large number of the cases, the adverb can be formed by simply adding '-ly' to the adjective.

Adjective	Adverb
Cheap	Cheaply
Quick	Quickly
Strong	Strong

☞ If the adjective ends in with 'y', replace the 'y' with an 'i' and add '-ly'.

Adjective	Adverb
Ready	Readily
Merry	Merrily
Easy	Easily

☞ If the adjective ends with '-le', replace the 'e' at the end with 'y'.

Adjective	Adverb
Understandable	Understandably
Forcible	Forcibly
Possible	Possibly

☞ If the adjective ends with '-ic', add '-ally'.

Adjective	Adverb
Idiotic	Idiotically
Tragic	Tragically
Basic	Basically

An exception to this rule is 'public', whose adverbial form is 'publicly'.

☞ Some adjectives do not change form at all.

Adjective	Adverb
Fast	Fast
Straight	Straight
Hard	Hard

☞ In the case of the adjective 'good', the corresponding adverb is 'well'.

Uses of Adverb

☞ Adverbs are used to give us more information and are used to modify verbs, clauses and other adverbs.

☞ The difficulty with identifying adverbs is that they can appear in different places in a sentence.

☞ The simplest way to recognise an adverb is through the common ending –ly. Example of –ly adverbs are: quickly, quietly, fortunately.

☞ Most adverbs are made by adding –ly to adjectives:

Careful → Carefully

Loud → Loudly

Slow → Slowly

Adverbs with Verbs

Adverbs give us more information about the verb. Here, the adverbs are in bold and the verbs are in italics.

Example: She **slowly** *entered* the room.

He **carefully** *drove* through the city.

Adverbs with Adjectives

Adverbs give us more information about the adjective. Here, the adverbs are in bold and the adjectives are in italics.

Example: The test was **extremely** *difficult*.

I'm **incredibly** *sorry* about what I did.

Adverbs with Adverbs

The first adverb gives us more information about the second. Here, both adverbs are in bold.

Example: The cheetah runs **incredibly quickly**.

He talks **exceptionally loudly**.

Adverb: Independent Use

Adverbs can be used to change the entire meaning of a sentence. The adverbs are in bold.

Example: **Unfortunately**, I will be out of the office for the next 3 days.

Surprisingly, the team was beaten in the final.

Confusing Adverbs

We have seen how many adverbs are made by adding –ly to the adjective: strong → strongly

Some adverbs are very different from the adjective:

good → adjective But well → adverb

Example: He's a good golfer.

He plays golf well.

Look at the following sentences; both have adverbs and are shown in bold.

Example:

a) I work **hard**.

b) I **hardly** work.

(Hard, which is also an adjective, here means 'with a lot of effort.'

Hardly here means 'very little.')

a) He's a fast runner. (Here fast is an adjective.)

b) He runs fast. (Here fast is an adverb.)

Combining Two Clauses

We can join two independent clauses (sentences) together using conjuctive adverbs. Conjunctive adverbs show cause and effect, sequence, contrast, comparison, or other relationships.

The most common of these are:

Accordingly, Afterwards, Also, Consequently, However, Indeed, Likewise, Moreover, Nevertheless,

Nonetheless, Otherwise, Similarly, Still, Therefore

When writing, we must use a semi-colon (;) before the conjunctive adverb. Use a comma (,) after the conjunctive adverb.

Example: I wanted to eat pizza; however, my wife wanted curry.

It had snowed all day; therefore, he decided not to drive in the dangerous conditions.

Note: In the following sentence no semi colon is needed because it does not separate two clauses. Instead it shows a thought:

Example: In my opinion, however, it makes no difference.

Practice Exercise

I. Choose the correct option/adverb to fill in the blanks.

1. You need to work harder; ____________, you'll get fired.
   (a) otherwise (b) moreover (c) instead (d) None of these
2. We wanted to go to Goa; ____________, we went to Pune.
   (a) instead (b) accordingly
   (c) otherwise (d) None of these
3. He is a very weak president; __________, most people support him.
   (a) otherwise (b) instead
   (c) nevertheless (d) none of these
4. We wanted to go to the beach;___________, it started to rain and we stayed at home.
   (a) otherwise (b) however
   (c) namely (d) none of these
5. She is a very smart woman; ____________, it is not at all surprising that she got the job.
   (a) nevertheless (b) similarly
   (c) therefore (d) none of these
6. He has a terrible voice; ______________, he will go down in history as the worst singer ever.
   (a) undoubtedly (b) otherwise
   (c) still (d) none of these
7. John has very little money; ______________, his brother Jojo is a millionaire.
   (a) in contrast (b) nonetheless
   (c) similarly (d) none of these
8. Sheela didn't have all the ingredients to bake a cake; ______________, she decided to prepare something else.
   (a) finally (b) indeed
   (c) therefore (d) none of these
9. He couldn't tell her the truth; ______________, he lied.
   (a) finally (b) similarly
   (c) instead (d) none of these
10. I really don't know why he came; ______________, I would tell you.
    (a) otherwise (b) instead
    (c) in contrast (d) none of these

II. Choose the correct adverb/option to fill in the blanks.

1. I found his home very _______.
   (a) easily (b) difficultly
   (c) frequently (d) none of these
2. Rohan behaves very _____ with his elders.
   (a) goodly (b) badly
   (c) easily (d) none of these
3. My father will be ______ of town this weekend.
   (a) inside (b) outside
   (c) out (d) none of these
4. Rohan plays football _________.
   (a) aggressively (b) sympathetically
   (c) hardly (d) none of these
5. He doesn't care for anything and _______ looks happy every time.
   (a) since (b) ago
   (c) hence (d) none of these
6. They called the police ________ after the accident.
   (a) immediately (b) slowly
   (c) peacefully (d) none of these
7. Kiran is a ______ paid employee of this company
   (a) lowly (b) highly
   (c) hardly (d) none of these
8. I was stuck in a jam for _______ two hours.
   (a) nearly (b) simply
   (c) correctly (d) none of these
9. How _______do you go there?
   (a) never (b) seldom
   (c) often (d) none of these
10. Thomas was ______ happy when he got his first job.
    (a) extremely (b) fully
    (c) halfly (d) none of these

11. ________ I met my childhood friend Meeta.
(a) Yesterday (b) Tomorrow
(c) This Sunday (d) none of these

12. You need to run ______ to win this race.
(a) slow (b) steadily
(c) fast (d) none of these

13. I won't say it ________.
(a) progressively (b) repeatedly
(c) necessarily (d) none of these

14. Speak ________, I cannot hear you.
(a) loudly (b) slowly
(c) hardly (d) none of these

15. You should ________ smoke as it is dangerous for your health.
(a) always (b) usually
(c) never (d) none of these

16. We searched ________ but were unable to find her lost jewellery.
(a) nowhere (b) anywhere
(c) everywhere (d) none of these

17. I hope to see you ________!
(a) soon (b) never
(c) randomn (d) none of these

18. Deepak never dresses _______ for work
(a) formally (b) coolly
(c) dirtily (d) none of these

19. The manager looked at me with an _______ expression when I reached late!
(a) sad (b) regret
(c) angry (d) none of these

20. Carlos is an excellent student. He ________ goes to class.
(a) always (b) usually
(c) sometimes (d) seldom
(e) never

21. I hate vegetables. I ________ eat carrots.
(a) always (b) usually
(c) sometimes (d) seldom
(e) never

22. Robert goes to the gym only two or three times a year. He ________ goes to the gym.
(a) always (b) never
(c) usually (d) seldom

23. Harold never leaves the college on Friday. He ________ eats at the cafeteria on Fridays.
(a) always (b) never
(c) seldom (d) none of these

24. Ms. Biethan is always in a good mood. She is ________ sad.
(a) always (b) usually
(c) never (d) none of these

25. Teresa is not a pleasant person. She is ________ in a bad mood.
(a) never (b) seldom
(c) always (d) none of these

26. My sister usually drives to work with a friend. She ________ drives alone.
(a) never (b) always
(c) usually (d) seldom

27. I never lend money to Curtis. He _______ pays me back.
(a) sometimes (b) always
(c) never (d) usually

28. Susan goes to the beach whenever she can. She _______ misses a chance to go to the ocean.
(a) never (b) always
(c) usually (d) none of these

29. It almost always rains in Seattle. The sun ________ shines there.
(a) always (b) usually
(c) seldom (d) none of these

30. When my teacher talks too ___, it's difficult to understand him.
(a) slowly (b) quickly
(c) clumsily (d) none of these

31. I always study ___ for a big test.
(a) hardly (b) goodly
(c) hard (d) none of these

32. My dad used to shout ___ when he was angry.
(a) loudly (b) loud
(c) noise (d) none of these

33. Please try to behave ___ when you meet my family.
(a) softly (b) quickly
(c) normally (d) none of these

34. She did ___ in her tennis match last week. She won.
(a) well (b) goodly
(c) bad (d) none of these

35. Please close the door ___ when you enter my room.
(a) gently (b) stupidly
(c) successfully (d) none of these

36. I'm sitting ___ so I don't want to move.
(a) normally (b) quickly
(c) comfortably (d) none of these

37. My husband sings ___ when he's in the shower. Even the neighbours can hear him.
(a) enthusiastically (b) bigly
(c) quietly (d) none of these

38. She laughs ___ at my jokes.
(a) happily (b) well
(c) angrily (d) none of these

39. Sometimes I need my teacher to talk more ___ so that I can hear her better.
(a) slowly (b) successfully
(c) hardly (d) none of these

Preposition

7

Prepositions are those words which are used to connect nouns, pronouns and phrases in any sentence. Usually preposition indicates the relationship between nouns that how they are connected to each other. It shows the manner in which the words are connected through time, space and place.

Example: I found the pen on the table. (Here the preposition is 'on' because it is showing a relationship between pen and the table.)

I am watching cricket match in the bedroom. (Here the preposition is 'in' because it shows my place where I am sitting.)

Types of Preposition

There are five types of Prepositions given below.

(i) Simple Preposition
(ii) Compound Preposition
(iii) Phrase Preposition
(iv) Participle Preposition
(v) Double Preposition

Simple Preposition

Simple preposition is used in simple sentences. A few simple prepositions are given below.

In, on, at, to, from, with, by etc.

Example:

a) I am not coming with you.
b) She is in the IT park.
c) We are going to the market.

Compound Preposition

When we connect two nouns, pronouns and phrases, we use compound preposition. A few compound prepositions are given below.

About, across, among, between, beside, before etc.

Example:

a) The book is inside the cupboard.
b) The fan is about the table.

Phrase Preposition

According to, in spite of, an account of, in front of, in order to, for the sake of, by means of, with reference to, in addition to, due to etc. are some phrase preposition.

Example:

a) According to me, there are three members in this company.
b) She is now in front of me.

Participle Preposition

A few participle prepositions are concerning, pending, and considering etc.

Example: I think I can do it easily considering my knowledge.

Double Preposition

A few double prepositions are outside of, out of, from behind and because of etc.

Example:

a) We have to solve two questions out of five.
b) It was just because of you that we won the game.

Uses of Prepositions

Prepositions of Place

These prepositions are used to show the place where something is located. Basically three prepositions of places are there.

AT

☞ At is used for a point

Example: At the end of the line

At the exit/entrance

At the corner

Note: We have some exceptions which do not follow this rule.

Example: At work

At home

At office/college/school

At the side

IN

☞ In is used for spaces

Example: In Haryana/India

In the bedroom

In the shop

In my bag

In the building

Note: We have some exceptions which do not follow this rule.

Example: In the book/newspaper/magazine

In the sky

ON

☞ On is used for surfaces

Example: On the roof

On the sofa

On the bike

On the cover

On the page

Note: We have some exceptions which do not follow this rule.

Example: On the bus/train/car

On the radio/laptop

On the right/left

On the way

Prepositions of Time

These prepositions are used to show time relationship between nouns. We have basically three prepositions of time. AT, IN, ON

AT

☞ At is used for precise time

Example: At nine o'clock

At 2:30pm

At the moment/same time/ present time

At sunrise/sunset/noon

Note: At night is an exception to this rule.

IN

☞ In is used for months, year, decades, and for a long time.

Example: In March

In 2000

In the 80's

In this century

Note: In the morning/afternoon/evening are the exceptions to this rule.

ON

On is used for week days.

Example: On sunday on the weekend.

Prepositions of Movement

We have nine prepositions of movements.

TO

☞ To is used when we want to indicate a specific destination. The destination can be a number of things like

Example: A place

I am going to the post-office

An event

Are you going to the fresher party?

A person

I am going to your mother to complain about you.

A position

The kitchen is to your left.

TOWARDS

☞ Towards is basically used to show the direction rather than a destination.

Example: John was running towards me.

THROUGH

☞ Through is basically used to show the movement across something.

Example: I cut through knife.

INTO

☞ Into shows the movement from outside to inside.

Example: I got into the room.

ACROSS

☞ Across is used to show the movement from one end to other end.

Example: Mark walked across the road.

OVER

☞ Over is used to show the position of something when it is above something else.

Example: The box is over the desk in the kitchen.

ALONG

☞ Along is used to show the movement with the line on object.

Example: We were walking along the river.

IN

☞ In is used to show the position of something relation to the place surrounding it.

Example: I am going to have a picnic in the park.

ON

☞ On is used to show the position of something in relation to a surface.

Example: There was a box of pens on the table.

Uses of Some other Prepositions

OF

☞ It is used to show the relation.

Example:

a) Mr. Vinod Kapoor is the principle of my school.

b) Rahul is the monitor of my class.

c) It is used to show quality of reason.

d) He died of jaundice. (Reason)

e) He is a man of high character. (Quality)

FROM

☞ It is used to tell about a place.

Example:

a) He comes back from Punjab.

b) With point of time.

c) She plays from morning till evening.

d) From is used to show the source.

e) Light comes from the sun.

SINCE

☞ It is used in perfect tense with certain time.

Example: I have known him since 1970.

FOR

☞ With perfect tense

Example: She has been living here for three years.

☞ It is used to exchange one thing for another.

Example: She bought a shirt for five hundred rupees.

☞ It is used for any goal.

Example: I did it for your good.

BY

☞ It is used to denote the latest time for completion of the task.

Example: The work should be finished by next Monday.

☞ It is used with watch.

Example: It is three by my watch.

☞ It is used to show the source.

Example: Ram caught me by the neck.

(Similarly by train, by car, by bus, by land, by caste etc.)

WITH

☞ It is used to accompany the other.

Example: He went to Gujarat with his brother.

☞ It is used to tell about the manner.

Example: The teacher punished the boy with a stick.

AFTER

☞ It is used in past indefinite tense.

Example: He came after 10 a.m.

☞ To show the order.

Example: We ran after the thief.

BEHIND

☞ A man stood behind the curtain.

DURING

☞ It is used to express idea:

(a) That an occurrence continues, or a situation persists throughout the whole of a specified period.

Example: During the war food was rationed.

(b) That an event took place within a specified period of time.

Example: I will call to see you during the weekend.

Rules of Preposition

Rule 1: A preposition generally, but not always, goes before its noun or pronoun. Just do not use extra prepositions when the meaning is clear without them.

Example: Where did you get this? (Correct)

Where did you get this at? (Incorrect)

Where did he go? (Correct)

Where did he go to? (Incorrect)

Rule 2a: The preposition like "similar to" or "similarly to should be followed by an object of the preposition (noun, pronoun, noun phrase), not by a subject and verb.

Example: You look like your mother. (Correct)

Meaning you look similar to her. (Mother is the object of the preposition like.)

You look like your mother does. (Incorrect)

Rule 2b: Instead of like, use as, as if, as though, or the way while making a comparison with a subject and verb.

Example:

a) You look the way your mother does. (Correct)

Do like I ask. (No one would say Do similarly to I ask.) (Incorrect)

b) Do as I ask. (Correct)

You look like you're angry. (Incorrect)

b) You look as if you're angry. (Correct)

Some speakers and writers, to avoid embarrassment, use 'as' when they mean like.

Example: They are considered as any other English words. (Incorrect)

They are considered as any other English words would be. (Correct)

They are considered to be like any other English words. (Correct)

Remember: Like means 'similar to' or 'similarly to'; as means 'in the same manner that.' Rule of thumb: Do not use 'as' unless there is a verb involved.

Example: I, as most people, try to use good grammar. (Incorrect)

I, like most people, try to use good grammar. (Correct)

I, as most people do, try to use good grammar. (Correct)

Rule 3: The preposition 'of ' should never be used in place of the helping verb 'have'.

Example: I should of done it. (Incorrect)

I should have done it. (Correct)

Rule 4: It is a good practice to use 'different' with the preposition 'from'. Most traditionalists avoid the use of 'different' with than. If you can replace 'different than' with 'different from' without having to rewrite the rest of the sentence, why not do so?

Example: You're different than I am. (Polarizing)

You're different from me. (Correct)

Rule 5: Use 'into' rather than 'in' to express motion toward something. Use 'in' to tell the location.

Example:

a) I swam in the pool. (Correct)

b) I walked into the house. (Correct)

c) I looked into the matter. (Correct)

d) I dived in the water. (Incorrect)

e) I dived into the water. (Correct)

f) Throw it in the trash. (Incorrect)

g) Throw it into the trash. (Correct)

Practice Exercise

I. Choose the correct option to fill in the blanks.

1. My best friend lives ________ M.G. Road.
   (a) in (b) at
   (c) on (d) none of these
2. I'll be ready to leave ______ ten minutes.
   (a) on (b) within
   (c) by (d) none of these
3. Since his new job, Jai never seems to be ________ home.
   (a) at (b) below
   (c) in (d) none of these
4. Seema's children responded to her parenting _______ throwing a tantrum.
   (a) with (b) from
   (c) by (d) none of these
5. He spent the entire afternoon ________ the laptop.
   (a) at (b) on
   (c) beside (d) none of these
6. You have to go ________ the field to reach your destination.
   (a) across (b) in
   (c) under (d) none of these
7. What are the main ingredients ________ tonight's chicken pizza?
   (a) with (b) from
   (c) of (d) none of these
8. The police caught the thief hiding _______ the bridge
   (a) at (b) under
   (c) in (d) none of these
9. I will wait _______ 8 p.m. for the delivery to arrive.
   (a) until (b) for
   (c) since (d) none of these
10. Rima's not interested in sports _______ she prefers science.
    (a) against
    (b) since
    (c) for
    (d) none of these

II. Fill in the blanks with the correct preposition.

1. Compare your answers ________ your partner.
2. The book holds a special meaning ________ me.
3. Write ______ me soon.
4. Have you got a piece ___ gum.
5. We have a house _______ a swing set.
6. I come _______ a small family.
7. Is your house _______ the city?
8. Match the animal ________ the sound.
9. This pen is _______ my exam.
10. I'm moving __________ my dream.

III. Fill in the blanks with correct preposition. Write cross (X) if no prepositions is required.

1. There was a loud noise which woke us up _______ midnight.
2. Do you usually eat chocolate eggs _______ Easter?
3. What are you doing _______ the weekend?
4. Last week I worked until 9 pm _______ every night.
5. My father always reads the paper _______ breakfast time.
6. She plays tennis _______ Fridays.
7. The trees here are really beautiful _______ the spring.
8. I'll see you _______ Tuesday afternoon then.
9. Shakespeare died _______ 1616.
10. She studies _______ every day.
11. John is going to buy the presents _______ today.
12. In my hometown, the shops open early _______ the morning.
13. She met her husband _______ 1998.
14. The party is _______ next Saturday.
15. We are meeting _______ Friday morning.
16. I often get sleepy _______ the afternoon.

17. His daughter was born ______ the 24th of August.
18. Mobile phones became popular ______ the nineties.
19. Luckily the weather was perfect ______ her wedding day.
20. Pass me the dictionary, it's ______ the bookshelf.
21. Jennifer is ______ work.
22. Berlin is ______ Germany.
23. You have something ______ your face.
24. Turn left ______ the traffic lights.
25. She was listening to classical music ______ the radio.
26. He has a house ________ the river.
27. The answer is ________ the bottom of the page.
28. Julie will be ________ the plane now.
29. There are a lot of magnets ________ the fridge.
30. She lives ______ London.
31. John is ______ a taxi. He's coming.
32. I'll meet you ______ the airport.
33. She stood ______ the window and looked out.
34. The cat is ______ the house somewhere.
35. Why are you calling so late? I'm already ______ bed.
36. I waited for Lucy ______ the station.
37. There was a picture of a flower ______ her T-shirt.
38. She has a house ______ Japan.

IV. Fill in the blanks with the correct preposition.

1. It's so noisy that I can't concentrate ______ my homework.
2. Don't worry. I'll pay ______ the tickets.
3. The car belongs ______ my father.
4. I borrowed a pen ______ my classmate.
5. I've been waiting ______ the bus for more than twenty minutes!.
6. Julie: "What time shall we eat dinner?" Gill: "It depends ______ John. We'll eat when he gets home".
7. When we arrived ______ the cinema, the film had already started.
8. Please explain this problem ______ us.
9. She was listening ______ the radio when the doorbell rang.
10. John worries ______ his exam results all the time.
11. My flatmate listens ______ a lot of jazz.
12. David paid ______ the drinks.
13. Who does that house belong ______ ?
14. Don't worry ______ Gemma, she'll be fine.
15. She borrowed a jumper ______ Julie.
16. Please be quiet. I need to concentrate ______ this book.
17. I want to go to the beach tomorrow but it depends ______ the weather.
18. Who are you waiting ______ ?
19. When will we arrive ______ Beijing?
20. A policeman explained ______ the children why they should never run across the road.

◆◆◆

Conjunction

8

Conjunction is a word that connects words, phrases, clauses or sentences; e.g., and, but, or, nor, for, yet, so, although, because, since, unless, when, while, where etc. are conjunctions.

Types of Conjunction

There are three types of conjunctions:

(i) Coordinating Conjunction

(ii) Subordinate Conjunction

(iii) Correlative Conjunction

Coordinating Conjunction

Coordinating conjunctions join words, phrases (which are similar in importance and grammatical structure) or independent clauses. A few coordinating conjunctions are and, but, or, nor, for, so, yet.

Coordinating conjunction joins two equal parts of a sentence,

(i) Word + word

(ii) Phrase + phrase

(iii) Clause + clause

(iv) Independent clause + independent clause

Example:

a) She likes tea and coffee. (word + word)

b) He may be in the room or on the roof. (phrase + phrase)

c) What you eat and what you drink affect your health. (clauses + clause)

d) The cat jumped over the mouse and the mouse ran away. (independent clause + independent clause)

Note: ❐ Independent clause is a clause which can stand alone as a sentence and have complete thought of its own.

Example: I called him but he didn't pick up the phone.

He shouted for help, but no body helped him.

❐ Coordinating conjunctions always come between the words or clauses that they join. A comma is used with conjunction if the clauses are long.

❐ If both clauses have same subjects, the subject of 2nd clause may not be written again.

Example: She worked hard and succeeded.

The player stopped and kicked the ball.

Subordinating Conjunction

Subordinating conjunctions join subordinate clause (dependent clause) to main clause; e.g. although, because, if, before, how, once, since, till, until, when, where, whether, while, after, no matter how, provided that, as soon as, even if,

(i) Main Clause + Subordinate Clause

(ii) Subordinate Clause + Main Clause

Subordinate clause is combination of words (subject and verb) which cannot stand alone as a complete sentence. Subordinate clause is also called dependent clause because it is dependent on main clause. Subordinate clause usually starts with relative pronoun (which, who, that, whom etc). Subordinate clause gives more information in relation to main clause to complete the thought.

Subordinating conjunction joins subordinate clause to main clause. Subordinating conjunction always come before the subordinate clause, no matter the subordinate clause is before main clause or after the main clause.

Example:

a) He does not go to school because he is ill.
b) I will call you after I reach my home.
c) I bought some cookies while I was coming from my office.
d) As far as I know, this exam is very difficult.
e) You can get high grades in exam provided you work hard for it.

Correlative Conjunction

These are paired conjunctions which join words, phrases or clauses that have reciprocal or complementary relationship.

The most commonly used correlative conjunctions are as follows:

Either … or, Neither … nor, Whether … or, Both … and, Not only … but also

Example:

a) Neither John nor Marry passed the exam.
b) Both red and yellow are attractive colours.
c) I like neither tea nor coffee.
d) He will be either in the room or in the hall.

Practice Exercise

I. Fill in the blanks with the correct conjunction.

1. You can come to the meeting ______ you don't say anything.
   (a) so that (b) as long as
   (c) while (d) as if
2. I'm not leaving ______ I get an apology from you.
   (a) so that (b) as long as
   (c) until (d) as if
3. I came here ______ you could give me an explanation.
   (a) so that (b) as long as
   (c) while (d) until
4. Rima is very tall ______ Mira is very short.
   (a) as if (b) as long as
   (c) while (d) so that
5. You look ______ you've seen a ghost.
   (a) so that (b) as long as
   (c) as if (d) until
6. I refuse to pay anything ______ you do the work properly.
   (a) while (b) as long as
   (c) so that (d) until
7. I'm going shopping for food this evening ______ I don't have to go at the weekend.
   (a) so that (b) as long as
   (c) while (d) until
8. You look ______ you haven't eaten for a week.
   (a) consequently (b) for
   (c) as though (d) until
9. I came early ______ I could talk to you privately.
   (a) so that (b) as long as
   (c) until (d) as if
10. ______ I don't think she's perfect for the job, she's certainly better qualified than Raj.
   (a) But
   (b) as long as
   (c) while
   (d) for
11. I don't mind if you go out for lunch ______ you would be back for the meeting at 2 pm.
   (a) as if (b) till
   (c) while (d) provided that
12. Are you OK? You look ______ you have a problem.
   (a) but (b) as though
   (c) as well as (d) until
13. ______ the job is very interesting, it's also very badly paid.
   (a) Although (b) till
   (c) since (d) until
14. We'll go to the mountains on Saturday ______ it doesn't rain.
   (a) before (b) as long as
   (c) if (d) that
15. Here the winters are very cold ______ the summers are very hot.
   (a) since (b) but
   (c) while (d) until
16. You can write the report when you want ______ it's ready by the end of the month
   (a) on the condition that
   (b) in order that
   (c) consequently
   (d) as long as
17. It looks ______ the government has got a lot of problems.
   (a) as if (b) as long as
   (c) only (d) that
18. I want Savitri to be in charge ______ I get back from holiday.
   (a) because (b) only
   (c) while (d) until
19. ______ I don't approve of what you do, I'm not going to punish you for it.
   (a) so that (b) as long as
   (c) as well as (d) until
20. I'm learning English ______ I can get a better job.
   (a) so that (b) else
   (c) since (d) therefore

II. Fill in the blanks with correct conjunction.

1. Receptionists must be able to relay information _______ pass messages accurately.
   (a) or (b) and
   (c) but (d) because
2. I did not go to the show _______ I had already seen it.
   (a) until (b) because
   (c) so (d) but
3. Manasvi is a member of the Historical Society _______ the Literary Society
   (a) as (b) or
   (c) and (d) but
4. Read over your answers _______ correct all mistakes before you pass them up.
   (a) or (b) and
   (c) because (d) while
5. Keep the food covered _______ the flies will contaminate it.
   (a) or (b) and
   (c) until (d) though
6. _______ he is thin, he is strong.
   (a) But (b) As
   (c) Though (d) Because
7. Susie _______ phoned _______ wrote after she left home.
   (a) either, or (b) neither, nor
   (c) while, and (d) though, or
8. She had an unpleasant experience _______ she was in Thailand.
   (a) but (b) and
   (c) because (d) while
9. The committee rejected the proposal _______ they did not think it was practical.
   (a) or (b) but
   (c) though (d) because
10. Ankit welcomed his guests _______ off-ered them drinks.
    (a) and (b) while
    (c) until (d) as

III. Fill in the blanks with correct conjunction.

1. He said _____ was feeling much better.
   (a) he (b) that he
   (c) either could be used here
   (d) none of these
2. He disagreed with my comment _____ was better to start again.
   (a) it
   (b) that it
   (c) either could be used here
   (d) none of these
3. It annoys me _____ haven't phoned.
   (a) they
   (b) that they
   (c) either could be used here
   (d) none of these
4. I'm glad ___ have come.
   (a) you
   (b) that you
   (c) either could be used here
   (d) none of these
5. He replied _____ hadn't finished.
   (a) he
   (b) that he
   (c) Either could be used here
   (d) none of these
6. I thought _____ weren't coming.
   (a) you
   (b) that you
   (c) either could be used here
   (d) none of these
7. It was so nice _____ didn't want to leave.
   (a) I
   (b) that I
   (c) either could be used here
   (d) none of these
8. She shouted _____ couldn't hear us.
   (a) she
   (b) that she
   (c) Either could be used here
   (d) none of these
9. It looks lovely now _____ is out.
   (a) the cherry blossom
   (b) that the cherry blossom
   (c) Either could be used here
   (d) none of these

10. It's vital _____ gets done.
(a) it
(b) that it
(c) Either could be used here
(d) none of these

11. Wait here _____ I get back.
(a) as soon as
(b) until
(c) either could be used here
(d) none of these

12. I'll visit you _____ I have time.
(a) when
(b) whenever
(c) either could be used here
(d) none of these

13. We'll be ready ____ the time you get back.
(a) by (b) before
(c) after (d) none of these

14. We'll leave _____ we're ready.
(a) as soon as
(b) when
(c) either could be used here
(d) none of these

15. I'll be glad _____ it's finished.
(a) when (b) before
(c) after (d) none of these

16. We must finish it _____ we leave.
(a) before
(b) until
(c) either could be used here
(d) none of these

17. I hurt myself _____ I was playing tennis.
(a) whenever
(b) while
(c) either could be used here
(d) none of these

18. I'll give her the message _____ she arrives.
(a) a moment (b) the moment
(c) an moment (d) none of these

19. I'll be ready when she _____.
(a) arrives (b) will arrive
(c) shall arrive (d) none of these

20. I'll only pay you _____ you finish the work.
(a) if
(b) unless
(c) either could be used here
(d) none of these

21. We turned back ______ it was raining.
(a) because (b) because of
(c) because on (d) none of these

22. ______ I was tired, I managed to finish the work.
(a) Although (b) But
(c) Yet (d) none of these

23. I was tired, _____ I managed to finish the work
(a) although (b) but
(c) yet (d) none of these

24. I did it while he _____ away.
(a) was (b) was being
(c) was been (d) none of these

25. The Vaal River is one of the major rivers in South Africa but the runoff is not constant which means that large dams have to be built _______ store water for use.
(a) notwithstanding (b) regardless of
(c) so as to (d) thanks to

26. Due to _______ a lack of production ______ increasing housing prices, Liverpool is now ranked as one of the least affordable cities countrywide.
(a) neither / nor
(b) no sooner / than
(c) scarcely / before
(d) both / and

27. Mike has been told he will have to pay the fine ________ his high rank in the military.
(a) even if
(b) furthermore
(c) on grounds that
(d) despite

28. Some people believe vaccines overload our immune system, making it less able to react to other diseases ---- meningitis or AIDS, which are now threatening our health.
(a) but for (b) lest
(c) with the aim of (d) whereas

29. Continued high-blood pressure is dangerous _______ it can increase the risk of heart disease and stroke.
    (a) however
    (b) so that
    (c) as
    (d) no matter although

30. They like to keep their old houses rather than building the new ones _______ it is very hard and expensive to maintain them.
    (a) because
    (b) even though
    (c) on the contrary
    (d) on account of

31. The inhabitants of our village claim that pedestrians have no choice but to risk their lives crossing the dangerous road as there is _______ a pedestrian bridge _______ a crosswalk.
    (a) not only / but also
    (b) both / and
    (c) neither / nor
    (d) no sooner / than

32. _______ the Oscar Reward, the Cannes Film Festival is the biggest event which takes place in May in the South of France.
    (a) Except for
    (b) Such as
    (c) Lest
    (d) Unless

33. _______ vaccination has eliminated naturally occurring polio in North and South America, rare cases continue to occur in developing countries of Africa.
    (a) However
    (b) Although
    (c) As a result of
    (d) Hence

34. The economy in China is booming; ---- many foreign investors are planning to enter China's market.
    (a) nonetheless
    (b) even if
    (c) so as to
    (d) that's why

Phrasal Verbs

9

Phrasal verb is the name given to a verb which is composed of two or three words. One verb is combined with a preposition (like on, in, under) or an adverb (like up, down, away). Sometimes a phrasal verb can have a meaning that is very different to the meaning of at least one of those two or three words separately. Phrasal verbs are used more frequently in everyday speech than in formal, official writing or speaking.

Example:

a) Grow + up : The children are *growing up*. (Often this type of combination gives the verb a new meaning: Children are becoming big or children are getting older.)
b) Take + after : She *takes after* her mother.
c) Maria didn't know the word, so she *looked* it *up* in the dictionary.
d) Oh no, we've *run out* of milk! I'll have to buy some more.
e) Farmers have to *get up* early in the morning.

Types of Phrasal Verbs

There are five different types of phrasal verbs.

(i) Phrasal verbs which take objects and are separable
(ii) Phrasal verbs which take objects and are inseparable
(iii) Phrasal verbs which do not take objects (these are always inseparable)
(iv) Transitive phrasal verbs can be separable or inseparable.
(v) The intransitive phrasal verbs can also be separable or inseparable.

Intransitive Phrasal Verbs

Intransitive phrasal verbs have no direct object. (A direct object is "acted upon" by the verb).

Example:

a) I *woke up* at 10:30 AM.
b) You can *come over* to my house after school.
c) He's *going back* to Russia next month.

Transitive Phrasal Verbs

Transitive phrasal verbs have a direct object.

Example:

a) I'm going to *cut down* on fast food this year. (cut down on = reduce)
b) *Check out* that website – it's really great! (check out = look at, go to)

Separable and Inseparable Phrasal Verbs

If a phrasal verb is separable, it means you can separate the two words and put the direct object in the middle. If it is inseparable, then you can't do this.

Example:

a) Please *turn off* the TV. (Correct)
b) Please *turn* the TV *off*. (Correct)

I'll look after your dog while you're on vacation. (Correct)

I'll look your dog after while you're on vacation. (Incorrect)

Separable Phrasal Verbs

The object may come after the following phrasal verbs or it may separate the two parts:

Example:

(i) You have to *do* this paint job *over*.
(ii) You have to *do over* this paint job.

When the object of the following phrasal verbs is a pronoun, the two parts of the phrasal verb must be separated:

Example: You have to do it over.

The following are some separable phrasal verbs with their meaning and example.

Verb	Meaning	Example
blow up	explode	The terrorists tried to blow up the railroad station.
bring up	mention a topic	My mother brought up that little matter of my prison record again.
bring up	raise children	It isn't easy to bring up children nowadays.
call off	cancel	They called off this afternoon's meeting
do over	repeat a job	Do this homework over.
fill out	complete a form	Fill out this application form and mail it in.
fill up	fill to capacity	She filled up the grocery cart with free food.
find out	discover	My sister found out that her husband had been planning a surprise party for her.
give away	give something to someone else for free	The filling station was giving away free gas.
give back	return an object	My brother borrowed my car. I have a feeling he's not about to give it back.
hand in	submit something (assignment)	The students handed in their papers and left the room.
hang up	put something on hook or receiver	She hung up the phone before she hung up her clothes.
hold up	delay	I hate to hold up the meeting, but I have to go to the bathroom.
hold up	rob	Three masked gunmen held up the Security Bank this afternoon.
leave out	omit	You left out the part about the police chase down Asylum Avenue.
look over	examine, check	The lawyers looked over the papers carefully before questioning the witness. (They looked them over carefully.)
look up	search in a list	You've misspelled this word again. You'd better look it up.
make up	invent a story or lie	She knew she was in trouble, so she made up a story about going to the movies with her friends.
make out	hear, understand	He was so far away, we really couldn't make out what he was saying.
pick out	choose	There were three men in the line-up. She picked out the guy she thought had stolen her purse.
pick up	lift something off something else	The crane picked up the entire house. (Watch them pick it up.)
point out	call attention to	As we drove through Madhya Pradesh, Saurabh pointed out the major historical sites.

put away	save or store	(1) We put away money for our retirement. (2) She put away the cereal boxes.
put off	postpone	We asked the boss to put off the meeting until tomorrow. (Please put it off for another day.)
put on	put clothing on the body	I put on a sweater and a jacket. (I put them on quickly.)
put out	extinguish	The firefighters put out the house fire before it could spread. (They put it out quickly.)
read over	peruse	I read over the homework, but couldn't make any sense of it.
set up	to arrange, begin	My wife set up the living room exactly the way she wanted it. She set it up.
take down	make a written note	These are your instructions. Take them down before you forget.
take off	remove clothing	It was so hot that I had to take off my shirt.
talk over	discuss	We have serious problems here. Let's talk them over like adults.
throw away	discard	That's a lot of money! Don't just throw it away.
try on	put clothing on to see if it fits	She tried on fifteen dresses before she found one she liked.
try out	test	I tried out four cars before I could find one that pleased me.
turn down	lower volume	Your radio is driving me crazy! Please turn it down.
turn down	reject	He applied for a promotion twice this year, but he was turned down both times.
turn up	raise the volume	Grandpa couldn't hear, so he turned up his hearing aid.
turn off	switch off electricity	We turned off the lights before anyone could see us.
turn off	repulse	It was a disgusting movie. It really turned me off.
turn on	switch on the electricity	Turn on the CD player so that we can dance.
use up	exhaust, use completely	The gang members used up all the money and went out to rob some more banks.

Inseparable Phrasal Verbs (Transitive)

The part of the phrasal verb that carries the "verb-meaning" cannot be separated from the prepositions (or other parts) that accompany it: "Who will look after my estate when I'm gone?"

The following are some inseparable phrasal verbs with their meaning and example.

Verb	Meaning	Example
call on	ask to recite in class	The teacher called on students in the back row.
call on	visit	The minister to called on his counterpart.

get over	recover from sickness or disappointment	I got over the flu, but I don't know if I'll ever get over my broken heart.
go over	review	The students went over the material before the exam. They should have gone over it twice.
go through	use up; consume	(1) Their country went through most of its coal reserves in one year. (2) Did he go through all his money already?
look after	take care of	My mother promised to look after my dog while I was gone.
look into	investigate	The police will look into the possibilities of embezzlement.
run across	find by chance	I ran across my old roommate at the college reunion.
run into	meet	Manohar ran into his English professor in the hallway.
take after	resemble	My second son seems to take after his mother.
wait on	serve	It seemed strange to see my old boss wait on tables.

Three-Word Phrasal Verbs (Transitive)

The following are some three-word phrasal verbs with-their meaning and example.

Verb	Meaning	Example
break in on	interrupt (a conversation)	I was talking to Mom on the phone when the operator broke in on our call.
catch up with	keep abreast	After our month-long trip, it was time to catch up with the neighbours and the news around town.
check up on	examine, investigate	The boys promised to check up on the condition of the summer house from time to time.
come up with	to contribute (suggestion, money)	After years of giving nothing, the old man was able to come up with a thousand-dollar donation.
cut down on	curtail (expenses)	We tried to cut down on the money we were spending on entertainment.
drop out of	leave school	I hope none of my students drop out of school this semester.
get along with	have a good relationship with	I found it very hard to get along with my brother when we were young.
get away with	escape blame	Mayank cheated on the exam and then tried to get away with it.
get rid of	eliminate	The citizens tried to get rid of their corrupt mayor in the recent election.
get through with	finish	When will you ever get through with that program?

keep up with	maintain pace with	It's hard to keep up with the Joneses when you lose your job!
look forward to	anticipate with pleasure	I always look forward to the beginning of a new semester.
look down on	despise	It's typical of a country that the citizens look down on their geographical neighbours.
look in on	visit (somebody)	We were going to look in on my brother-in-law, but he wasn't home.
look out for	be careful, anticipate	Good instructors will look out for early signs of failure in their students
look up to	respect	First-graders really look up to their teachers.
make sure of	verify	Make sure of the student's identity before you let him into the classroom.
put up with	tolerate	The teacher had to put up with a great deal of nonsense from the new students.
run out of	exhaust supply	The runners ran out of energy before the end of the race.
take care of	be responsible for	My oldest sister took care of us younger children after Mom died.
talk back to	answer impolitely	The star player talked back to the coach and was thrown off the team.
think back on	recall	I often think back on my childhood with great pleasure.
walk out on	abandon	Her husband walked out on her and their three children.

Intransitive Phrasal Verbs

The intransitive phrasal verbs are not followed by an object: The following are some intransitive phrasal verbs with their meaning and example.

Verb	Meaning	Example
break down	stop functioning	That old car had a tendency to break down just when I needed it the most.
catch on	become popular	Popular songs seem to catch on in Mumbai first and then spread eastward.
come back	return to a place	Father promised that we would never come back to this horrible place.
come in	enter	They tried to come in through the back door, but it was locked.
come to	regain consciousness	He was hit on the head very hard, but after several minutes, he started to come to again.
come over	to visit	The children promised to come over, but they never do.

drop by	visit without appointment	We used to just drop by, but they were never home, so we stopped doing that.
eat out	dine in a restaurant	When we visited Paris, we loved eating out in the sidewalk cafes.
get by	survive	Uncle Abdul didn't have much money, but he always seemed to get by without borrowing money from relatives.
get up	arise	Grandmother tried to get up, but the couch was too low, and she couldn't make it on her own.
go back	return to a place	It's hard to imagine that we will ever go back to Romania.
go on	continue	He would finish one Dickens novel and then just go on to the next.
go on	happen	The cops heard all the noise and stopped to see what was going on.
grow up	get older	Charles grew up to be a lot like his father.
keep away	remain at a distance	The judge warned the stalker to keep away from his victim's home.
keep on (with gerund)	continue with the same	He tried to keep on singing long after his voice was ruined.
pass out	lose consciousness, faint	He had drunk too much; he passed out on the sidewalk outside the bar.
show off	demonstrate haughtily	Whenever he sat down at the piano, we knew he was going to show off.
show up	arrive	Day after day, Amit showed up for class twenty minutes late.
wake up	arouse from sleep	I woke up when the rooster crowed.

Word Order for Separable Phrasal Verbs

When the direct object is the specific name of a thing or person, it can be located after the phrasal verb or in the middle:

Example: I threw away the old pizza.

= I threw the old pizza away.

However, when the direct object is a pronoun (me, you, him, her, us, them, it), then it MUST go in the middle:

Example:

a) I threw it away. (Correct)
   I threw away it. (Incorrect)
   Here's an example with a person:

a) They'll pick up John from the airport.
   = They'll pick John up from the airport.
   = They'll pick him up from the airport.

b) They'll pick up him from the airport. (Incorrect)

Practice Exercise

I. Choose the correct phrasal verb in the following questions.

1. Could you turn _____ the TV? The soap opera is about to start.
   (a) back (b) on
   (c) off (d) out
2. There was nothing good on TV so I turned it _____ and went to bed.
   (a) off (b) up
   (c) in (d) down
3. The TV is too loud. Can you turn it _____ a bit?
   (a) up (b) out
   (c) off (d) down
4. The TV is too quiet. Can you turn it _____ a bit?
   (a) back (b) off
   (c) up (d) over
5. I′ve been looking _____ my car keys for half an hour. Have you seen them anywhere?
   (a) up (b) for
   (c) after (d) at
6. My mother has offered to look _____ the children, so we can go to the party.
   (a) for (b) into
   (c) at (d) after
7. If you don′t know what the word means, you'll have to look it _____ in the dictionary.
   (a) for (b) up
   (c) out (d) off
8. The meeting has been put _____ to Friday as so many people have got the flu.
   (a) up (b) in
   (c) back (d) out
9. The meeting has been brought _____ to Monday due to the seriousness of the situation.
   (a) on
   (b) out
   (c) down
   (d) forward
10. The company is taking _____ new workers to meet this projected demand.
    (a) at (b) on
    (c) up (d) over
11. Our alarm clock is set to go _____ at 6 a.m.
    (a) away (b) up
    (c) out (d) off
12. Gary asked Cynthia to marry him, but she turned him _____.
    (a) down (b) without
    (c) across (d) over
13. The emergency workers managed to put _____ the fire.
    (a) off (b) out
    (c) down (d) without
14. Everyone thought she was English, but she turned _____ to be Canadian.
    (a) up (b) off
    (c) by (d) out
15. The math teacher lets students chew gum in class, but the French teacher does not put _____ with it.
    (a) over (b) out
    (c) up (d) along
16. The university students want to do _____ with tuition, because they think education should be free.
    (a) away (b) out
    (c) up (d) off
17. Nelson is a creative liar who is always making _____ unusual excuses for not doing his work.
    (a) up (b) across
    (c) away (d) off
18. Paula always comes _____ as very sincere.
    (a) out (b) along
    (c) across (d) away
19. Tom and Carol often have heated arguments, but they always make _____ later.
    (a) down (b) away
    (c) up (d) along

20. We have to clean ______ the house before my parents arrive.
(a) down (b) away
(c) without (d) up

21. The police officer almost captured the criminals, but they managed to get ______.
(a) without (b) over
(c) along (d) away

22. I have come down with a cold, but I will get ______ it soon.
(a) over (b) up
(c) without (d) above

23. Robert was expected to arrive at 8 o'clock, but he didn't turn ______ until midnight.
(a) out (b) up
(c) off (d) with

24. Peter needs either to get a raise or to get a better job, because he can't get ______ on his current salary.
(a) by (b) out
(c) in (d) off

25. Manuela and Glenda didn't like each other at first, but now they get ______.
(a) over (b) across
(c) away (d) along

26. The plane is scheduled to take ______ at 7 a.m.
(a) away (b) to
(c) off (d) with

27. We need milk, but we can do ______ beer.
(a) without (b) along
(c) away (d) off

28. The wedding was originally scheduled for June 12, but it has been put ______ until September 24.
(a) out (b) away
(c) off (d) up

II. Fill in the blanks with phrasal verb taking one word from each group/box.

Get, give, look, put, stand, take, turn	After, on, off, out, up

1. I often use Wikipedia to______ information.
2. If you want to ______a bus in Delhi, you will have to queue.
3. Can I ___the TV? I want to watch the weather forecast.
4. It is very hard to ____ smoking.
5. It is so dark over here, you can really _____ your sunglasses now.
6. Shall I ____and offer my seat to the old lady?
7. With a few buckets of water, we _____the fire.
8. Who will_____ your cat when you're on holiday?
9. Would you like to ____your new dress today?
10. At the next stop, we have to ____the bus and walk along the street to the cinema.

III. Fill in the blanks with the best phrasal verb given in the box. Change the tense where required.

Die out, ask for, carry on, clean up, hold on, account for, call on, look after, run out, fall behind, talk over, wait for, hand in, feel up, take on, give away, run into, see off, hand round, wear away

1. You must _________ what you have done.
2. One must _________ with life even after having lost someone precious to them.
3. I asked Neema to ________ the cupboard.
4. Some tribal races have _________.
5. India has ________ in space technology.
6. I ________ all my money to the charity.
7. I __________ my job application.
8. Shital didn't ___________ for the dance, so she didn't go.
9. He was asked to ________ the pamphlets.
10. The principal ______ the teacher for the yearly meeting.
11. She ________ the CEO of the company.

12. ________, I'll come with you.
13. The nurse _______ me when I was ill.
14. They happened to _____ each other in the mall.
15. I ______ my friend ______ at the airport.
16. The teacher ______ another student.
17. The varnish will ______ soon.
18. We've _______ of sugar, rice, and vegetables.
19. The two captains met to _______ the sports events.
20. The owner of the restaurant _________us, when we went for dinner.

IV. Underline the phrasal verb in the following sentences.

1. The meeting will wind up in an hour.
2. The police called out to the drowning woman.
3. Those two are getting on great with each other.
4. The architect laid out the plans for the building.
5. She could not make out the meaning of the poem.
6. We had to move in to the new house in a day.
7. He's gone to see about the taxi.
8. All the tickets of the movie were sold out.
9. She works at a hospital.
10. You should be back by 10.

Punctuation

10

Punctuation is used to create sense, clarity and stress in the sentences. Punctuation marks are used to structure and organize writing, without punctuation what is being spoken or that which has or is being written will be meaningless. While speaking, we pause or change the tone of our voices to indicate an emphasis. While writing, we must use punctuation to indicate those points of emphasis.

Commas

Rule 1: Use commas to separate items in a list of three or more.

Remember that an "item" may refer to a noun, verb, or adjective phrase.

> **Note:** Usage of a comma to separate the second-to-last from the last item is optional.

Example: I need to buy eggs, milk, lettuce, and bread. (Correct)

Rule 2: Use a comma to separate independent clauses (complete thoughts) when they are joined by the following conjunctions: and, or, for, nor, so, but, yet

> **Note:** The comma should come before the conjunction.

Example: I want to buy the new jacket, but it is too expensive.

In this example, there are two independent clauses:

- "I want to buy the new jacket." (complete thought)
- "It is too expensive." (complete thought)

These clauses are separated by a comma before the conjunction "but".

Rule 3: Use a comma to separate a dependent clause (incomplete thought) from an independent clause (complete thought).

Example: When I get older, I will be able to drive.

If you are good, I will buy you a toy.

Without water, the plant will die.

Rule 4: Use a comma(s) to separate any word or phrase from the rest of the sentence that is not essential to the sentence's meaning. This phrase usually provides extra information about the subject.

Example:

a) My brother, a 26 year old male, is watching TV.

b) I am ready for my dad, a hard working man, to come home.

c) My mother, on the other hand, does not like chocolate.

Rule 5: Use a comma to separate a quotation from the rest of a sentence.

Example: "We need to buy more sugar," she said, "before it runs out!"

Rule 6: Use a comma to separate an introductory element from the rest of a sentence.

Example: Hi, how are you?

Rule 7: Use a comma to separate the name of a city from a country or state.

Example: I live in Chapel Hill, North Carolina.

Rule 8: Use a comma to separate the day of the week, the day of the month, and the year.

Example: Today is Thursday, April 18, 1943.

Semicolons

The semicolon has three primary functions:

☞ To combine closely related complete sentences (independent clauses) which are not joined by a conjunction.

Example: The man was wet; he was standing in the rain without an umbrella.

In this example, there are two complete sentences (independent clauses):

"The man was wet." (independent clause)

"He was standing in the rain without an umbrella." (independent clause)

☞ To separate complete sentences (independent clauses) that are joined by a conjunctive adverb.

Example: Jane likes fruit; however, she does not like apples.

In this example, there are two complete sentences (independent clauses):

"Jane likes fruit." (independent clause)

"She does not like apples." (independent clause)

☞ To separate items in a list when commas alone would be confusing.

Example: The school specializes in three fields of study: economics, the study of the economy; philosophy, the study of thought; and anthropology, the study of mankind.

Periods

The period has three primary functions:

☞ To show that a sentence has ended

Example: We are going to the mall today.

☞ To show that an abbreviation has ended

Example: We are shopping on State St. today.

☞ As a decimal point

Example: The shoes cost $ 42.99.

Apostrophes

The apostrophe has two primary functions:

❒ to show possession of a noun

❒ to show the omission of letters

To Show Possession of a Noun

☞ Add 's to the singular form of the word (even if it ends in -s).

Example:

a) I drive near the president's house every day.

b) I like James's car.

☞ Add ' to the end of plural nouns that end in -s.

Example: These are my sisters' dresses.

These are my friends' pencils.

☞ Add 's to the last noun to show joint possession of an object.

Example: We are at John and Anne's apartment.

Note: Apostrophes should not be used with possessive pronouns because possessive pronouns already show possession -- they don't need an apostrophe. His, her(s), its, my, mine, your(s), our(s), their(s) are all possessive pronouns.

Note: As a general rule, if the possessive noun is an inanimate object (not living, no causal agency) then no apostrophe is needed. There are exceptions to this rule, however.

Example: That is the door of the car. (Correct)

That is the car door. (Incorrect)

In the example, notice that the car does not need a possessive apostrophe because it is an inanimate object.

To Show the Omission of Letters and to form Contractions

☞ Apostrophes are used to show any omission of letters in a word.

☞ Apostrophes are also used to form contractions. A contraction is a combination of two words which results in a single word. The apostrophe is used where letters have been omitted. Contractions are common in speaking and in informal writing.

Example of contractions:

Affirmative contractions

❒ Pronoun + to be + would + will

I	:	I'm, I'd, I'll
You	:	you're, you'd, you'll
We	:	we're, we'd, we'll
They	:	they're, they'd, they'll
He	:	he's, he'd, he'll
She	:	she's, she'd, she'll
It	:	it's, it'd, it'll
There	:	there's ,there'd, there'll
That	:	that's, this'd, this'll

Note: The only time you need to use an apostrophe for "it is" is when forming the contraction "it's". "Its" (with no apostrophe) is used to show possession.

Negative contractions

Word Expression	Contraction	Word Expression	Contraction
do not	don’t	does not	doesn’t
did not	didn’t	is not	isn’t
are not	aren’t	was not	wasn’t
were not	weren’t	has not	hasn’t
have not	haven’t	had not	hadn’t
will not	won’t	would not	wouldn’t
cannot	can’t	could not	couldn’t
should	shouldn’t		

☞ Use apostrophes in the following sentences to make contractions.

Example: I am your friend.

I’m your friend.

Where is the book of John?

Where’s John’s book?

☞ **Question Mark [?]:** The question mark is used at the end of a sentence which is posed in a question format. Use the question mark at the end of all interrogative sentences. Do not use a question mark for reported questions. Long questions still need question marks. Question marks can sometimes appear within sentences.

Example: What are you doing there?

☞ **Exclamatory Mark [!]:** The exclamatory mark is used to express exasperation, astonishment, or surprise, or to emphasize a comment or a short, sharp phrase. In professional or everyday writing, exclamation marks are used sparingly at all. It is also used to mark a phrase as humorous, ironic or sarcastic.

Example: What a lovely flower it is!

☞ **Brackets (), [ ]:** Parentheses refers to round brackets () and square brackets [ ]. We normally refer to them as ‘round brackets’ or ‘square brackets’. Usually, we use square brackets [ ] for special purposes such as in technical manuals. Round brackets ( ), or ‘parentheses’ are used in a similar way to commas when we want to add further explanation, an afterthought, or comment that is to do with our main line of thought but distinct from it.

☞ **Hyphen [-]:** A hyphen joins two or more words together or parts of words together while avoiding confusion or ambiguity. Dashes can be used to add parenthetical statements or comments in much the same way as you would use brackets. They are the same signs, a hyphen has no spaces before or after while a dash does.

☞ **Quotation Marks [“”]:** Quotation marks are used when one is quoting from a text or reproducing work from another text into one’s own. They are also used when one is using direct speech.

Example: Ramesh said, “I have completed my homework”.

Practice Exercise

I. Select the correctly punctuated sentence.

1. Will your dad drive us to the museum or shall we take a bus?
   (a) Will your dad drive us to the museum, or shall we take a bus?
   (b) Will your dad, drive us to the museum, or shall we take a bus?
   (c) Will your dad drive us to the museum or, shall we take a bus?
   (d) Will your dad drive us to the museum or shall we take a bus?
2. After I had scraped the mud off my shoes I went indoors.
   (a) After I had scraped the mud, off my shoes, I went indoors.
   (b) After, I had scraped the mud off my shoes, I went indoors.
   (c) After I had scraped the mud off my shoes, I went indoors.
   (d) After I had scraped the mud off my shoes I went indoors.
3. I have already read the book that you chose for your report.
   (a) I have already read, the book that you chose for your report.
   (b) I have already read, the book that you chose, for your report.
   (c) I have already read the book that you chose, for your report.
   (d) I have already read the book that you chose for your report.
4. The principal entered the room and the students became silent.
   (a) The principal entered the room, and the students became silent.
   (b) The principal, entered the room, and the students became silent.
   (c) The principal entered the room, and the students, became silent.
   (d) The principal entered the room and the students became silent.
5. (a) Spain is a beautiful country; the beache's are warm, sandy and spotlessly clean.
   (b) Spain is a beautiful country: the beaches are warm, sandy and spotlessly clean.
   (c) Spain is a beautiful country, the beaches are warm, sandy and spotlessly clean.
   (d) Spain is a beautiful country; the beaches are warm, sandy and spotlessly clean.
6. (a) The children's books were all left in the following places: Mrs Smith's room, Mr Powell's office and the caretaker's cupboard.
   (b) The children's books were all left in the following places; Mrs Smith's room, Mr Powell's office and the caretaker's cupboard.
   (c) The childrens books were all left in the following places: Mrs Smiths room, Mr Powells office and the caretakers cupboard.
   (d) The children's books were all left in the following places, Mrs Smith's room, Mr Powell's office and the caretaker's cupboard.
7. (a) She always enjoyed sweets, chocolate, marshmallows and toffee apples.
   (b) She always enjoyed: sweets, chocolate, marshmallows and toffee apples.
   (c) She always enjoyed sweets chocolate marshmallows and toffee apples.
   (d) She always enjoyed sweet's, chocolate, marshmallow's and toffee apple's.
8. (a) Sarah's uncle's car was found without its wheels in that old derelict warehouse.
   (b) Sarah's uncle's car was found without its wheels in that old, derelict warehouse.
   (c) Sarahs uncles car was found without its wheels in that old, derelict warehouse.
   (d) Sarah's uncle's car was found without it's wheels in that old, derelict warehouse.
9. (a) I can't see Tim's car, there must have been an accident.
   (b) I cant see Tim's car; there must have been an accident.
   (c) I can't see Tim's car there must have been an accident.

(d) I can't see Tim's car; there must have been an accident.

10. (a) Paul's neighbours were terrible; so his brother's friends went round to have a word.
    (b) Paul's neighbours were terrible: so his brother's friends went round to have a word.
    (c) Paul's neighbours were terrible, so his brother's friends went round to have a word.
    (d) Paul's neighbours were terrible so his brother's friends went round to have a word.

11. (a) Tims gran, a formidable woman, always bought him chocolate, cakes, sweets and a nice fresh apple.
    (b) Tim's gran a formidable woman always bought him chocolate, cakes, sweets and a nice fresh apple.
    (c) Tim's gran, a formidable woman, always bought him chocolate cakes sweets and a nice fresh apple.
    (d) Tim's gran, a formidable woman, always bought him chocolate, cakes, sweets and a nice fresh apple.

12. (a) After stealing Tims car, the thief lost his way and ended up the chief constable's garage.
    (b) After stealing Tim's car the thief lost his way and ended up the chief constable's garage.
    (c) After stealing Tim's car, the thief lost his way and ended up the chief constable's garage.
    (d) After stealing Tim's car, the thief lost his' way and ended up the chief constable's garage.

13. (a) We decided to visit: Spain, Greece, Portugal and Italy's mountains.
    (b) We decided to visit Spain, Greece, Portugal and Italys mountains.
    (c) We decided to visit Spain, Greece, Portugal and Italy's mountains.
    (d) We decided to visit Spain Greece Portugal and Italy's mountains.

14. (a) That tall man, Paul's grandad, is this month's winner.
    (b) That tall man Paul's grandad is this month's winner.
    (c) That tall man, Paul's grandad, is this months winner.
    (d) That tall man, Pauls grandad, is this month's winner.

15. Which of the following sentences is correctly punctuated?
    (a) Many students prefer online classes to on-campus classes; however, on-campus classes do have the advantages of providing human contact and immediate feedback.
    (b) The study of writing can be quite rewarding; especially to those who actually write.
    (c) If good students study two hours for every hour they spend in class; they can expect to do well.
    (d) The professor was only a few minutes late; but the students had already left the classroom.

16. Which of the following sentences is correctly punctuated?
    (a) After studying the problem for several years, the college worked on a plan to address it.
    (b) After studying the problem, for several years the college worked on a plan to address it.
    (c) The college, after studying the problem for several years, worked on a plan to address it.
    (d) All three sentences are correctly punctuated with commas.

17. Which of the following sentences is correctly punctuated?
    (a) Professor Loren Pillar, Chair of the Animal Husbandry Department at Enormous State University recently resigned from his position as Director of Research for Global Dominance, a multi-national conglomerate that has come under criticism from animal-rights activists for animal experimentation.

(b) Professor Loren Pillar, Chair of the Animal Husbandry Department at Enormous State University recently resigned from his position as Director of Research for Global Dominance, a multi-national conglomerate that has come under criticism from animal-rights activists for animal experimentation.

(c) Professor Loren Pillar, Chair of the Animal Husbandry Department at Enormous State University, recently resigned from his position as Director of Research for Global Dominance, a multi-national conglomerate, that has come under criticism from animal-rights activists for animal experimentation.

(d) Professor Loren Pillar, Chair of the Animal Husbandry Department at Enormous State University, recently resigned from his position as Director of Research for Global Dominance, a multi-national conglomerate that has come under criticism from animal-rights activists for animal experimentation.

18. Which of the following sentences is correctly punctuated?
    (a) The student wrote that "Each of the experiments was successful."
    (b) The student wrote that, "Each of the experiments was successful."
    (c) The student wrote that each of the experiments was successful.
    (d) The student wrote "Each of the experiments was successful."

19. Which of the following sentences is correctly punctuated?
    (a) Only three social science disciplines are represented at our college - psychology, sociology, and anthropology.
    (b) Only three social science disciplines are represented at our college: psychology, sociology, and anthropology.
    (c) Only three social science disciplines - psychology, sociology, and anthropology - are represented at our college: .
    (d) All of the above sentences are punctuated corrrectly.

20. Which of the following comma rules is incorrect?
    (a) Place commas after introductory elements in sentences.
    (b) Place commas after items in a series.
    (c) Place a comma before coordinating conjunctions that join independent clauses.
    (d) Set off restrictive, essential elements with commas.

II. Punctuate the following sentences.

1. Why are you not resting
2. I just came back from the theatre
3. Don't be such an idiot
4. Where are the apples kept
5. How could you do that to a good friend
6. Rani went and bought the ice-cream
7. I hope you succeed in life
8. Robert Browning is a famous poet
9. Why is it taking so long
10. When will we be reaching Dehradun

III. Punctuate and make use of capital letters (where required) in the passage.

Kunal is one of the most laid-back people i know he is tall and slim with black hair and he always wears a T-shirt and black jeans his jeans have holes in them and his converse boots are scruffy too he usually sits at the back of the class and he often seems to be sleepy however when the exam results are given out he always gets an "A" i don't think hes as lazy as he appears to be

IV. Use appropriate punctuation marks in the following sentences.

1. We had spent a greal deal of time in France, so the kids enjoyed its natural beauty.
2. Some people work best in the mornings others do better in the evenings
3. What are you doing next weekend
4. Mother had to go into hospital she had heart problems
5. Did you understand why I was upset
6. It is a fine idea let us hope that it is going to work

7. We will be arriving on Monday morning at least I think so
8. A textbook can be a wall between teacher and class
9. The girls father sat in a corner
10. In the words of Murphys Law Anything that can go wrong will go wrong
11. A grandparent job is easier than a parents
12. It looks as if the sun goes around the earth but in reality the earth goes round the sun
13. He neither smiled spoke nor looked at me
14. Long ago in a distant country there lived a beautiful princess
15. It was my aunt who took Shiv yesterday and not my father16. Deepika was invited to the party but she was ill so Lara went instead of her
17. Sorry to disturb you could I speak to you for a moment
18. Is it any use to expect them to be on time
19. Jai going to sleep during the wedding was rather embarrassing
20. Having lost all my money I went home

Tenses

11

Kinds of Tense

Introduction

Tense is an effect of time on verb. There are three main tense. All tense can be either statements or questions.

The table below contains the various tenses that a verb can be used in to indicate the time when or action takes place.

The 3 main tenses are Past, Present and Future. Each of these is further classified into 4 categories as shown below:

Past Tense	Present	Future
Simple past	Simple present	Simple future
Past continuous	Present continuous	Future continuous
Past perfect	Present perfect	Future perfect
Past perfect continuous	Present perfect continuous	Future perfect continuous

There are four present tense forms in English:

Present simple:	I work.
Present continuous:	I am working.
Present perfect:	I have worked.
Present perfect continuous:	I have been working.

We use these forms:

☞ To talk about the present:

Example: He works at McDonald's. He has worked there for three months now.

He is working at McDonald's. He has been working there for three months now.

London is the capital of Britain.

Present Simple

The present tense is the base form of the verb; e.g., I work in Delhi.

But the third person (she/he/it) adds an -s; e.g., She works in Delhi.

Use

We use the present tense to talk about:

☞ Something that is true in the present:

Example: I'm nineteen years old.

He lives in Meerut.

☞ Something that happens again and again in the present:

Example: I play football every weekend.

We use words like sometimes, often. always, and never (adverbs of frequency) with the present tense:

Example: I sometimes go to the cinema.

She never plays football.

☞ Something that is always true:

Example: The adult human body contains 206 bones.

Light travels at almost 300,000 kilometres per second.

☞ Something that is fixed in the future.

Example: The school term starts next week.

The train leaves at 19:45 this evening.

☞ For interrogatives and negatives

Example: Do you play the piano?

Where do you live?

Where does he come from?

Why do they not work?

☞ With the present tense, we use do and does to make questions. We use does for the third person (she/he/it) and we use do for the others. We use do and does with question words like where, what and why. But look at the following questions beginning with who:

Example: Who plays football at the weekend?

Who works at City Hospital in Delhi?

☞ With the present tense we use do and does to make negatives. We use does not (doesn't) for the third person (she/he/it) and we use do not (don't) for the others.

Example: I like tennis, but I don't like football. (don't = do not)

I don't play the piano, but I play the guitar.

They don't work at the weekend.

Present Continuous

The present continuous tense is formed from the present tense of the verb ***be*** and the present participle (***-ing*** form) of a verb:

Use

1. We use the present continuous tense to talk about the present:

☞ For something that is happening at the moment of speaking:

Example: I'm just leaving work. I'll be home in an hour.

Please be quiet. The children are sleeping.

☞ For something which is happening before and after a given time:

Example: At eight o'clock we are usually having breakfast.

When I get home the children are doing their homework.

☞ For something which we think is temporary:

Example: I'm working in Chennai for the last two weeks.

☞ For something which is new and contrasts with a previous state:

Example: These days most people are using email instead of writing letters.

What sort of clothes are teenagers wearing nowadays? What sort of music are they listening to?

☞ To show that something is changing, growing or developing:

Example: The climate is changing rapidly.

Your English is improving.

☞ For something which happens again and again:

Example: They are always arguing.

Rama is always laughing.

Note: We normally use always with this use.

2. We use the present continuous tense to talk about the future:

☞ For something which has been arranged or planned:

Example: Sudha is going to a new school next term.

What are you doing next week?

Present Perfect and Present Perfect Continuous

The present perfect is formed from the present tense of the verb have and the past participle of a verb:

The present perfect continuous is formed with have/has been and the -ing form of the verb:

Use

We use the present perfect tense:

☞ For something that started in the past and continues in the present:

Example: They've been married for nearly fifty years.

She has lived in Ashram all her life.

Note: We normally use the present perfect continuous for this:

She has been living in Ashram all her life.

It's been raining for hours.

☞ For something we have done several times in the past and continue to do:

Example: I've played the guitar ever since I was a teenager.

I've been watching that programme every week.

We often use a clause with since to show when something started in the past:

Example: They've been staying with us since last week.

I have worked here since I left school.

I've been watching that programme every week since it started.

Note: We often use the adverb ever to talk about experience up to the present:

Example: My last birthday was the worst day I have ever had.

Note: We use "never" for the negative form:

Example: Have you ever met Mr. Shastri?

Yes, but I've never met his wife.

☞ For something that happened in the past but is important at the time of speaking:

Example: I can't get in the house. I've lost my keys.

I'm tired out. I've been working all day.

☞ We use the present perfect of be when someone has gone to a place and returned:

Example: A: Where have you been?

B: I've just been out to the supermarket.

A: Have you ever been to San Francisco?

B: No, but I've been to Los Angeles.

☞ But when someone has not returned we use have/has gone:

Example: A: Where is Maria? I haven't seen her for weeks.

B: **She's gone to** Paris for a week. She'll be back tomorrow.

We often use the present perfect with time adverbials which refer to the recent past:

just; only just; recently;

Example: Scientists have recently discovered a new breed of peas.

We have just got back from our holidays.

☞ Or adverbials which include the present:

Ever (in questions); so far; until now; up to now; yet (in questions and negatives)

Example: Have you ever seen a ghost?

Where have you been up to now?

Have you finished your homework yet?

No, so far I've only done my history.

Warning:

☞ We do not use the present perfect with an adverbial which refers to past time which is finished:

Example: I have seen that film yesterday.

We have just bought a new car last week.

When we were children we have been to California.

☞ But we can use it to refer to a time which is not yet finished:

Example: Have you seen Laxmi today?

We have bought a new car this week.

Past Tense

The past tense in English is used:

☞ To talk about the past

☞ To talk about hypotheses – things that are imagined rather than true.

☞ For politeness.

There are four past tense forms i n English:

Past simple:	I worked
Past continuous:	I was working
Past perfect:	I had worked
Past perfect continuous:	I had been working

We use these forms:

☞ To talk about the past:

Example: He worked at McDonald's. He had worked there since July.

He was working at McDonald's. He had been working since July.

☞ To refer to the present or future in conditions:

Example: He could get a new job if he really tried.

I would always help someone who really needed help.

I wish it wasn't so cold.

☞ In conditions, hypotheses and wishes, if we want to talk about the past, we always use the past perfect:

Example: I would have helped him if he had asked.

I wish I hadn't spent so much money last month.

☞ We can use the past forms to talk about the present in a few polite expressions:

Example: Excuse me, I was wondering if this was the train for York.

I just hoped you would be able to help me.

Past Simple

Forms

With most verbs the past tense is formed by adding -ed:

call → called; like → liked; want → wanted; work → worked

But there are a lot of irregular past tenses in English. Here are the most common irregular verbs with their past tenses:

Base Form	Irregular Past Tense Form
be	was/were
begin	began
break	broke
bring	brought
buy	bought
build	built
choose	chose
come	came
cost	cost
cut	cut
do	did

Base Form	Irregular Past Tense Form
draw	drew
drive	drove
eat	ate
feel	felt
find	found
get	got
give	gave
go	went
have	had
hear	heard
hold	held

Base Form	Irregular Past Tense Form
keep	kept
know	knew
leave	left
lead	led
let	let
lie	lay
lose	lost
make	made
mean	meant
meet	met
pay	paid
put	put
run	ran
say	said
sell	sold

Base Form	Irregular Past Tense Form
send	sent
set	set
sit	sat
speak	spoke
spend	spent
stand	stood
take	took
teach	taught
tell	told
think	thought
understand	understood
wear	wore
win	won
write	wrote

Use

We use the past tense to talk about:

☞ Something that happened once in the past:

Example: I met my wife in 1983.

We went to Spain for our holidays.

They got home very late last night.

☞ Something that happened again and again in the past:

Example: When I was a boy I walked a mile to school every day.

We swam a lot while we were on holiday.

They always enjoyed visiting their friends.

☞ Something that was true for some time in the past:

Example: I lived abroad for ten years.

He enjoyed being a student.

She played a lot of tennis when she was younger.

☞ We often use phrases with ago with the past tense:

Example: I met my wife a long time ago.

Past Continuous

The past continuous is formed from the past tense of be with the -ing form of the verb:

We use the past continuous to talk about the past:

☞ For something which continued before and after another action:

Example: The children were doing their homework when I got home.

As I was watching television the telephone rang.

☞ This use of the past continuous is very common at the beginning of a story:

Example: Last week as I was driving to work...

☞ For something that happened before and after a particular time:

Example: It was eight o'clock. I was writing a letter.

☞ To show that something continued for some time:

Example: My head was aching.

Everyone was shouting.

☞ For something that was happening again and again:

Example: I was practising every day, three times a day.

They were always quarrelling.

☞ With verbs which show change or growth:

Example: The children were growing up quickly.

My hair was going grey.

The town was changing quickly.

Past Perfect

We use the verb had and the past participle for the past perfect:

Example: I had finished the work.

She had gone.

The past perfect continuous is formed with had been and the -ing form of the verb:

Example: I had been finishing the work.

The past perfect is used in the same way as the present perfect, but it refers to a time in the past, not the present. We use the past perfect tense:

☞ For something that started in the past and continued up to a given time in the past:

Example: She didn't want to move. She had lived in London all her life.

We normally use the past perfect continuous for this:

a) She didn't want to move. She had been living in London all her life.

b) Everything was wet. It had been raining for hours.

☞ For something we had done several times up to a point in the past and continued to do after that point:

Example:

a) He had written three books and he was working on another one.

b) I had been watching the programme every week, but I missed the last episode.

We often use a clause with since to show when something started in the past:

Example:

a) They had been staying with us since the previous week.

b) I had been watching that programme every week since it started, but I missed the last episode.

☞ When we are reporting our experience and including up to the (then) present:

Example: My eighteenth birthday was the worst day I had ever had.

☞ For something that happened in the past but is important at the time of reporting:

Example: I couldn't get into the house. I had lost my keys.

We use the past perfect to talk about the past in conditions, hypotheses and wishes:

Example: I would have helped him if he had asked.

I wish I hadn't spent so much money last month.

Future Tense

An action that is going to take place in future will be written in future tense. It is of four types:-

a) Simple future tense
b) Future continuous tense
c) Future perfect tense
d) Future perfect continuous tense.

a) The Simple Future Tense:- It is used:

i) To express an indefinite supposed action or activity in the future time

Example: Sheena will perform on stage.

ii) To express determination, promise, order or command.

Example: Raghav will work hard to get a scholarship.

iiii) To express a natural phenomenon.

Example: Glaciers will melt due to global warming.

iv) To express expected or supposed main action.

Example: If I go to Amritsar, I shall bring a sweater for you.

b) The Future Continuous Tense:- It is used:

i) To express an continuity of a supposed or expected action in future

Example: We shall be waiting for the train to arrive

ii) To denote the possible continuity of a habit.

Example: Mother will be doing her daily household chores.

iiii) To indicate the continuity of a supposed or expected action in the future when the second action takes place.

Example: When I reach home, my mother will be waiting for me at her door.

c) The Future Perfect Tense:- It is used

i) To express the completion of an action supposed or expected to take place in the future time

Example: The passengers will have arrived on time to board the train.

ii) To express an action which states earlier but is still expected to continue in the future time

Example: We shall have travelled for three hours when we reach Agra.

d) The Future Perfect Continuous Tense:- It is used:

To express an action which will begin beore a definite moment in the future, will continue upto that moment & will be in progress even at that moment.

Example: Tomorrow at this time we will have been driving to Munnar for three hours.

Practice Exercise

Fill in blanks with the correct form of verb.

1. Although the police __________ every precaution, the robber managed to escape.
   (a) take (b) takes
   (c) has taken (d) had taken
2. The boys ______ television every night unless they have homework.
   (a) watch (b) watches
   (c) watched (d) watching
3. Maria ______ an appointment to see the doctor. It is at 10.00 am. tomorrow.
   (a) make (b) makes
   (c) made (d) has made
4. They ______ when they are ready.
   (a) come (b) came
   (c) will come (d) have come
5. Reena ______ watching horror films although she has nightmares afterwards.
   (a) like (b) likes
   (c) liked (d) will like
6. It ______ every afternoon for the past week. The weather forecast predicts rain for next week too.
   (a) is raining
   (b) was raining
   (c) has been raining
   (d) had been raining
7. I ______ the door before I realized that the keys were inside the house.
   (a) lock (b) locked
   (c) has locked (d) had locked
8. When Sally ______ her first pay, she bought presents for her parents.
   (a) receive (b) received
   (c) has received (d) had received
9. It's lovely to wake up in the morning and ______ birds singing.
   (a) hear (b) hears
   (c) heard (d) hearing
10. Shivam ______ $80.00 for that bag.
    (a) pay (b) paid
    (c) pays (d) paying
11. When I went back to my hometown three years ago, I found that a lot of changes ______.
    (a) are taken place
    (b) were taken place
    (c) have taken place
    (d) had taken place
12. Look ! A hamster ______ by a cat.
    (a) is chased
    (b) is being chased
    (c) was being chased
    (d) has been chased
13. I'm sorry the house is not available any longer. It ______ to a timber tycoon.
    (a) is sold
    (b) was being sold
    (c) has been sold
    (d) will be sold
14. Ai Ling ______ to Manhattan in 1997.
    (a) is transferred
    (b) was transferred
    (c) has been transferred
    (d) should be transferred
15. Passengers ______ to smoke in the train.
    (a) are not allowed
    (b) was not allowed
    (c) had not allowed
    (d) will not allow
16. Firemen who battled the fire reported that it_____ under control after forty minutes.
    (a) is brought
    (b) was brought
    (c) can be brought
    (d) has been brought
17. The students ______ to leave the building immediately.
    (a) ordered
    (b) will order
    (c) have ordered
    (d) have been ordered

18. In future, famous singers ______ to perform at charity concerts.
(a) are invited
(b) were invited
(c) has been invited
(d) will be invited

19. The roof may have been leaking for the past few weeks but you do not have to worry about it any longer. It ______ now.
(a) was repaired
(b) is repairing
(c) has repaired
(d) is being repaired

20. The price ______, but I doubt whether it will remain so.
(A) went down (B) will go down
(C) has gone down (D) was going down

21. My mother ______ biscuits from the shop once a week.
(a) is buying
(b) has bought
(c) buys
(d) will have bought

22. The groom, together with his parents, ______ the guests.
(a) is greeting (b) have greeted
(c) are greeting (d) were greeting

23. None of the new equipment ______ yet.
(a) has arrived (b) have arrived
(c) were arriving (d) are arriving

24. ______ she ______ a lot of friends at the party?
(a) Does, makes (b) Did, make
(c) Did, made (d) Do, make

25. Nobody ______ the telephone an hour ago.
(a) is using (b) were using
(c) was using (d) has used

26. If I ______ some money I would not have to borrow now.
(a) am saving (b) have saved
(c) saved (d) had saved

27. A river ______ downstream.
(a) flows (b) will flow
(c) is flowing (d) was flowing

28. She ______ a maid by next year.
(a) employs
(b) employed
(c) has employed
(d) will have employed

29. He ______ never ______ since he nearly ______.
(a) has ... swum, drowned
(b) had ... swum, was drowning
(c) was ... swimming, drowned
(d) did ... swum, had drowned

30. We ______ jungle-trekking.
(a) are disliking
(b) have disliked
(c) dislike
(d) were disliking

Conditionals

12

Conditional tenses are used to speculate about what could happen, what might have happened, and what we wish would happen. In English, most sentences using the conditional contain the word *if*. Much usage is referred to as "the unreal past" because we use a past tense but we are not actually referring to something that happened in the past. There are five main ways of constructing conditional sentences in English. In all cases, these sentences are made up of an *if* clause and a main clause. In many negative conditional sentences, there is an equivalent sentence construction using "unless" instead of 'if'.

Types of Conditional Sentences

Conditional sentence type	Usage	If clause verb tense	Main clause verb tense
Zero	General truths	Simple present	Simple present
Type 1	A possible condition and its probable result	Simple present	Simple future
Type 2	A hypothetical condition and its probable result	Simple past	Present conditional or Present continuous conditional
Type 3	An unreal past condition and its probable result in the past	Past perfect	Perfect conditional
Mixed type	An unreal past condition and its probable result in the present	Past perfect	Present conditional

The Zero Conditional

The zero conditional is used for when the time being referred to is **now or always** and the situation is **real and possible**. The zero conditional is often used to refer to general truths. The tense in both parts of the sentence is the simple present. In zero conditional sentences, the word "if" can usually be replaced by the word "when" without changing the meaning.

Example:

If clause	Main clause
If + simple present	**simple present**
If you heat ice	it melts.
If it rains	the grass gets wet.

Type 1 Conditional

The type 1 conditional is used to refer to the **present or future** where the **situation is real**. The type 1 conditional refers to a possible condition and its probable result. In these sentences the if clause is in the simple present, and the main clause is in the simple future.

Example:

If clause	Main clause
If + simple present	**simple future**
If you don't hurry	you will miss the train.
If it rains today	you will get wet.

Type 2 Conditional

The type 2 conditional is used to refer to a time that is **now or any time**, and a situation that is **unreal**. These sentences are not based on fact. This types of conditional are used to refer to a hypothetical condition and its probable result. In these conditional sentences, the 'if clause' uses the simple past, and the main clause uses the present conditional.

If clause	Main clause
If + simple past	**present conditional or present continuous conditional**
If you went to bed earlier	you would not be so tired.
If it rained	you would get wet.
If I spoke Italian	I would be working in Italy.

Type 3 Conditional

The type 3 conditional is used to refer to a time that is **in the past**, and a situation that is **contrary to reality**. The facts they are based on are the opposite of what is expressed. The type 3 conditional is used to refer to an unreal past condition and its probable past result. In these conditional sentences, the if clause uses the past perfect, and the main clause uses the perfect conditional.

If clause	Main clause
If + past perfect	**perfect conditional or perfect continuous conditional**
If you had studied harder	you would have passed the exam.
If it had rained	you would have gotten wet.
If I had accepted that promotion	I would have been working in Milan.

Mixed Type Conditional

The mixed type conditional is used to refer to a time that is **in the past**, and a situation that is **ongoing into the present**. The facts they are based on are the opposites of what is expressed. The mixed type conditional is used to refer to an unreal past condition and its probable result in the present. In mixed type conditional sentences, the if clause uses the past perfect, and the main clause uses the present conditional.

If clause	Main clause
If + past perfect or simple past	**present conditional or perfect conditional**
If I had worked harder at school	I would have a better job now.
If we had looked at the map	we wouldn't be lost.
If you weren't afraid of spiders	you would have picked it up and put it outside.

Verbs in Time Clauses and if Clauses

☞ In clauses with time words like ***when***, ***after***, ***until*** we often use the **present tense** form to talk about the future:

Example: I'll come home **when I finish work**.

You must wait here **until your father comes**.

☞ In conditional clauses with ***if*** or ***unless*** we often use the **present tense** forms to talk about the future:

Example: We won't be able to go out **if it is raining**.

I will come tomorrow **unless I have to look after** the children.

☞ We do not normally use ***will*** in clauses with ***if*** or with **time words**:

Example: I'll come home when I ~~will~~ **finish** work.

We won't be able to go out if it ~~will rain~~. **rains**.

☞ But we can use *will* if it means a **promise** or **offer**:

Example: I will be very happy if you **will** come to my party.

We should finish the work early if Rohit **will** help us.

'If' Clauses and Hypotheses

Some clauses with ***if*** are like hypotheses, so we use **past tense** forms to talk about the present and future.

☞ For something that **has not happened** or **is not happening**:

We use the past tense forms to talk about the **present** in clauses with ***if***:

Example: He could get a new job if he really **tried**.

If I **had** his address I could write to him.

☞ For something that we believe or know **will not happen**:

We use the past tense forms to talk about the **future** in clauses with **if**:

Example: We would go by train if it **wasn't** so expensive

I would look after the children for you at the weekend if **I was** at home.

☞ To make suggestions about **what might happen**:

Example: If he **came** yesterday we could borrow his car.

If we **invited** John, Mary would bring Angela.

☞ When we are talking about something which did **not** happen **in the past**, we use the **past perfect** in the ***if*** clause and a **modal** verb in the main clause:

Example: If you had seen him you could have spoken to him.

If I had got the job we would be living in Delhi.

☞ If the **main clause** is about the **past**, we use a **modal** with ***have***:

Example: If you had seen him you could have spoken to him.

If you had invited me I might **have** come.

☞ If the **main clause** is about the **present**, we use a present tense form or a **modal without have**:

Example: If I had got the job, we **would be living** in Delhi now.

If you had done your homework, you **would know** the answer.

Wishes

We use **past tense forms** to talk about wishes: We use past tense modals ***would*** and ***could*** to talk about wishes for the **future**:

Example: I don't like my work. **I wish I could** get a better job.

That's a dreadful noise. **I wish it would** stop.

☞ We use **past tense** forms to talk about wishes for the **present**:

Example: I don't like this place. **I wish I lived** in somewhere more interesting.

These seats are very uncomfortable. **I wish we were travelling** first class.

John wishes he wasn't so busy.

I wish it wasn't so cold.

☞ We use the **past perfect** to talk about wishes for the **past**:

Example: I wish I had worked harder when I was at school.

Mary wishes she had listened to what her mother told her.

Hypotheses (Things That We Imagine)

☞ We use **present tense forms** after phrases like ***what if***, ***in case*** and ***suppose*** to talk about the **future** if we think it is **likely to happen**:

Example: Those steps are dangerous. **Suppose someone has** an accident.

We should leave home early **in case we are** late.

☞ We use a **past tense** form to talk about the **future** after ***suppose*** and ***what if*** to suggest something is **not likely** to happen:

Example: It might be dangerous. **Suppose they got** lost.

What if he lost his job? What would happen then?

☞ We use modals ***would***, ***could*** for a hypothesis about the **future**:

Example: We can't all stay in a hotel. **It would be** very expensive.

Drive carefully. **You could have** an accident.

☞ We use ***would*** in the main clause and the ***past*** in a subordinate clause to talk about the **imagined future**:

Example: **I would always help** someone who really **needed** help.

I would always help someone **if they really needed** it.

☞ We use modals with ***have*** to talk about something that **did** not **happen in the past**:

Example: I did not see Mary, or **I might have spoken** to her.

Why didn't you ask me? **I could have told** you the answer.

Practice Exercise

Fill in the blanks with correct form of tense/verb given in bracket. Mind the position of the if-clause and negations.

1. If I ________(go) to Delhi, I'll visit the zoo.
2. If it ________(rain), we'd be in the garden.
3. If you _______(worn) a lighter jacket, the car driver would have seen you earlier.
4. We ________(watch) TV tonight if Sohan hadn't bought the theatre tickets.
5. She wouldn't have had two laptops if she ________(sign) the contract.
6. If I was/were a millionaire, I ________(live) in Beverly Hills.
7. You would save energy if you ________ (switch of) the lights more often.
8. If we had read the book, we________ (understand) the film.
9. My sister could score better on the test if the teacher______(explain) the grammar once more.
10. They ________(arrive) on time if they hadn't missed the train.
11. If it rains, the boys ______(play) hockey.
12. If he ________(grow) his own vegetables, he wouldn't have to buy them.
13. Gaurav ________(see) the Red Ford if he travelled to Delhi.
14. Would you go out more often if you_____ (do) so much in the house?
15. She wouldn't have yawned the whole day if she ________(stay up) late last night.
16. If you ________(wait) a minute, I'll come with you.
17. If we arrived at 10, we________(miss) presentation.
18. We ________(help) John if we'd known about his problems.
19. If they ________(use) new batteries, their camera would have worked correctly.
20. If I went anywhere, it ________(be) New Zealand.
21. If you like, you ________(stay) for two days.
22. If I ________(see) the film in the cinema, I wouldn't have watched it on TV again.
23. If the parents bought the cat, their children ________(be) very happy.
24. Metal ________(expand) if you heat it.
25. He ________(receive) my e-mail if he'd been online yesterday evening.
26. They'd have been able to return the bottle if they ________(tear off) the labels.
27. If she ________(tidy) up her room, she must find the receipt.
28. What________(do) if you had a million dollars.
29. Where would you live if you ________ (be) younger.
30. If you ________(wait) for a little moment, I'll tell the doctor you are here.

Voice

13

Voice is the form of verb, which expresses whether the person or thing denoted by the subject does something or something is done to it.

There are two kinds of voices:

(i) Active voice

(ii) Passive voice

Example: Reeta writes a letter. (Active voice)

A letter is written by Reeta. (Passive voice)

Verbs are either used in active or passive voice. In the active voice, the subject and verb relationship is straightforward: the subject is a doer. In the passive voice, the subject of the sentence is not a doer. It is shown with 'by + doer' or is not shown in the sentence.

Active and Passive Voice

If you are a speaker of English, you may experience situations where you have to use both forms of tenses i.e. active form and passive form.

Active Voice

In active sentences, the subject is active and performs the actions.

Example: The cow (Subject) is eating (Verb) grass (Object) (Active Voice)

Passive Voice

In passive sentences, the subject is no longer active or the subject is acted upon by the verb.

Example: Grass (Subject) is being eaten (Verb) by the cow (Object)—Passive Voice

Basic Rules of Passive Voice

1. Change the object into subject. If there is a pronoun of object case, convert that as follows:

Passive	Active
Me	I
You	You
Her	She
Them	They
Us	We
Him	He
It	It
Whom	Who

2. Change the subject into object. And use 'by' before the object. If there is a pronoun of nominative case, convert it as follows:

Passive	Active
I	by me
You	by you
She	by her
They	by them
We	by us
He	by him
It	by it
Who	by whom

Main points on active voice and passive voice:

- First of all, find subject, object and the main verb i.e. find SVO .
- Convert the object into subject.
- Use the suitable helping verb or auxiliary verb according to the tense. If helping verb is given, use verb as it is. But note that the helping verb used should be according to the object.
- Convert the verb into past participle or 3rd form of the verb.
- Use the preposition 'by'.
- Convert the subject into object.

Active and Passive Voice with Tenses

Simple Present Tense	
Active Voice	**Passive Voice** (is, am, are + 3rd verb)
He **lights** the candle.	The candle **is** lit by him.
He **does not light** the candle.	The candle **is not** lit by him.
Do you **eat** meat?	**Is** meat **eaten** by you?
Present Continuous Tense	
Active Voice	**Passive Voice** (is, am, are + being + 3rd verb)
I **am driving** a car.	A car **is being driven** by me.
I **am not driving** a car.	A car **is not being driven** by me.
Am I **driving** a car?	**Is** a car **being driven** by me?
Present Perfect Tense	
Active Voice	**Passive Voice** (has, have + been + 3rd verb)
She **has stolen** my book.	My book **has been stolen** by her.
She **has not stolen** my book.	My book **has not been stolen** by her.
Has she **stolen** my book?	**Has** my book **been stolen** by her?
Simple Past Tense	
Active Voice	**Passive Voice** (was, were + 3rd verb)
She **finished** work.	Work **was finished** by her.
She did not **finish** work.	Work **was not finished** by her.
Did she **finish** work?	**Was** work **finished** by her?
Past Continuous Tense	
Active Voice	**Passive Voice** (was, were + being + 3rd verb)
He **was revising** his books.	His books **were being being revised** by him.
He **was not revising** his books.	His books **were not being revised** by him.
Was he **revising** his books?	**Were his** books **being revised** by him?
Past Perfect Tense	
Active Voice	**Passive Voice** (had + been + 3rd verb)
I **had completed** the assignment.	The assignment **had been completed** by me.
I **had not completed** the assignment.	The assignment **had not been completed** by me.
Have I completed the assignment?	**Has** the assignment **been completed** by me?

Simple Future Tense	
Active Voice	**Passive Voice** (will, shall + be + 3rd verb)
My uncle **will** pay my tuition fee.	My tuition fee **will be paid** by my uncle.
My uncle **will not** pay my tuition fee.	My tuition fee **will not be paid** by my uncle.
Will my uncle pay my tuition fee?	**Will** my tuition fee **be paid** by my uncle?
Future Perfect Tense	
Active Voice	**Passive Voice** (will, shall + have been + 3rd verb)
We **shall have done** our home-work.	Our home -work **shall have been done** by us.
We **shall not have done** our home-work.	Our home -work **shall not have been done** by us.
Shall We **have done** our home –work?	**Shall** our home -work **have been done** by us?

Note: In Present perfect continuous tense, Past perfect continuous tense, Future perfect continuous tense, Future continuous tense, we use the same sentence in passive voice. It means these tenses cannot be changed in passive form.

Active and Passive Voice with Modals

Modals	Auxiliary Verb in Passive Voice	Active Voice	Passive Voice
Can/ Could	Can/Could + be + 3rd verb	I **can solve** these sums.	These sums **can be solved** by me.
		I **cannot solve** these sums.	These sums **cannot be solved** by me.
		Can I **solve** these sums?	**Can** these sums **be solved** by me?
Has to/ Have to	Has to/ Have to + 3rd verb	He has to complete his assignment.	His assignment has to be completed by him?
Must	Must + 3rd verb	You **must learn** this book.	This book **must be learnt** by you.
May	May + be + 3rd verb	I **may buy** the book.	The book **may be bought** by me.
Might	Might + be + 3rd Verb	They **might play** chess.	Chess **might be played** by them.
Should	Should + be + 3rd verb	Students **should** learn all lessons.	All lessons **should be learnt** by students.

Active and Passive Voice with Imperative Sentences

In these sentences we express command, order, advice, and request.

Rules

1. Lets + new object + be/Not be +past participle or 3rd form.
2. For sentences containing, request, advice and order, we will use **you are requested to, advised to** and **ordered to**.

Note: Always remove please and kind if they are given in the sentence.

Active Voice	Passive Voice
Shut the door.	**Let** the door **be shut**.
Post the letter at once.	**Let** the letter **be posted** at once.
Always **speak** the truth.	**Let** the truth always **be spoken**.
Do not starve the cow.	**Let** the cow **not be starved**.
Let him **help** his brother.	**Let** his brother **be helped** by him.
Clean your room.	**Let** your room **be cleaned**.
Learn your lesson.	**Let** your lesson **be learnt**.
Please do me a favour tonight	**You are requested to** do me a favour tonight.
Get out of my house.	**You are ordered to** get out of my house.
Kindly do not smoke in public place.	**You are requested not to** smoke in public place

Practice Exercise

I. Fill in the blanks with suitable active and passive verb forms.

1. This house ———————— in 1970 by my grandfather.
   (a) Built (b) Was built
   (c) Was build (d) Has built
2. The robbers ———————— by the police.
   (a) Have arrested
   (b) Have been arrested
   (c) Was arrested
   (d) Had arrested
3. We ———————— for the examination.
   (a) Have preparing
   (b) Are preparing
   (c) Had preparing
   (d) Have been prepared
4. It ———————— since yesterday.
   (a) Is raining
   (b) Has been raining
   (c) Have been raining
   (d) Was raining
5. I ———————— for five hours.
   (a) Have been working
   (b) Has been working
   (c) Was working
   (d) Am working
6. The students ———————— to submit their reports by the end of this week.
   (a) Have asked (b) Are asked
   (c) Has asked (d) Are asking
7. She ———————— for a while.
   (a) Are ailing
   (b) Is ailing
   (c) Has been ailing
   (d) Have been ailing
8. The teacher ———————— the student for lying.
   (a) Has been punished
   (b) Punished
   (c) Is punished
   (d) Was punished
9. I ———————— to become a successful writer.
   (a) Have always wanted
   (b) Am always wanted
   (c) Was always wanted
   (d) Am always wanting
10. The inmates of the juvenile home ———————— well by their caretakers.
    (a) Were not being treated
    (b) Were not treating
    (c) Have not being treated
    (d) Was not being treated
11. As the patient could not walk he ———————— home in a wheel chair.
    (a) Has carried
    (b) Has been carried
    (c) Was carried
    (d) Was carrying
12. The injured ———————— to the hospital in an ambulance.
    (a) Were taking (b) Was taking
    (c) Were taken (d) Have taken

II. Choose the option which best expresses the given sentence in Passive/Active voice.

1. You can play with these kittens quite safely.
   (a) These kittens can played with quite safely.
   (b) These kittens can play with you quite safely.
   (c) These kittens can be played with you quite safely.
   (d) These kittens can be played with quite safely.
2. A child could not have done this mischief.
   (a) This mischief could not be done by a child.
   (b) This mischief could not been done by a child.
   (c) This mischief could not have been done by a child.
   (d) This mischief a child could not have been done.

3. James Watt discovered the energy of steam.
   (a) The energy of steam discovered James Watt.
   (b) The energy of steam was discovered by James Watt.
   (c) James Watt was discovered by the energy of steam.
   (d) James Watt had discovered energy by the steam.
4. She makes cakes every Sunday.
   (a) Every Sunday cakes made by her.
   (b) Cakes are made by her every Sunday.
   (c) Cakes make her every Sunday.
   (d) Cakes were made by her every Sunday.
5. She spoke to the official on duty.
   (a) The official on duty was spoken to by her.
   (b) The official was spoken to by her on duty.
   (c) She was spoken to by the official on duty.
   (d) She was the official to be spoken to on duty.
6. The doctor advised the patient not to eat rice.
   (a) The patient was advised by the doctor not to eat rice.
   (b) The patient was advised by the doctor that he should not eat rice.
   (c) The patient was being advised by the doctor that he should not rice by the doctor.
   (d) The patient has been advised not to eat rice by the doctor.
7. I cannot accept your offer.
   (a) Your offer cannot be accepted by me.
   (b) I cannot be accepted by your offer.
   (c) The offer cannot be accepted by me.
   (d) Your offer cannot be accepted.
8. You should open the wine about three hours before you use it.
   (a) Wine should be opened about three hours before use.
   (b) Wine should be opened by you three hours before use.
   (c) Wine should be opened about three hours before you use it.
   (d) Wine should be opened about three hours before it is used.
9. They will inform the police.
   (a) The police will be informed by them.
   (b) The police will inform them.
   (c) The police are informed by them.
   (d) Informed will be the police by them.
10. Why do you tell a lie?
   (a) Why a lie told by you?
   (b) Why is a lie be told by you?
   (c) Why is a lie told by you?
   (d) Why is a lite being told you?
11. You will praise her very much.
   (a) She will praised very much by you.
   (b) She will be praised very much by you.
   (c) She will being praised very much by you.
   (d) She will been praised very much by you.
12. I take exercise daily.
   (a) Exercise are taken daily by me.
   (b) Exercise is taken daily by me.
   (c) Exercise is being taken daily by me.
   (d) Exercise is been taken daily by me.
13. She will invite me.
   (a) I shall be invited by her.
   (b) I will invited by her.
   (c) I shall being invited by her.
   (d) I will been invited by her.
14. Did you visit a zoo?
   (a) Was a zoo being visited by you?
   (b) Was a zoo be visited by you?
   (c) Was a zoo been visited by you?
   (d) Was a zoo visited by you?
15. Our task had been completed before sunset.
   (a) We completed our task before sunset.
   (b) We have completed our task before sunset.
   (c) We complete our task before sunset.
   (d) We had completed our task before sunset.
16. The boy laughed at the beggar.
   (a) The beggar was laughed by the boy.
   (b) The beggar was being laughed by the boy.
   (c) The beggar was being laughed at by the boy.
   (d) The beggar was laughed at by the boy.

17. The boys were playing Cricket.
    (a) Cricket had been played by the boys.
    (b) Cricket has been played by the boys.
    (c) Cricket was played by the boys.
    (d) Cricket was being played by the boys.
18. They drew a circle in the morning.
    (a) A circle was being drawn by them in the morning.
    (b) A circle was drawn by them in the morning.
    (c) In the morning a circle have been drawn by them.
    (d) A circle has been drawing since morning.
19. They will demolish the entire block.
    (a) The entire block is being demolished.
    (b) The block may be demolished entirely.
    (c) The entire block will have to be demolished by the
    (d) The entire block will be demolished.

III. Rewrite the following sentences in active voice.

1. The building was damaged by the fire.
2. By whom were you taught French?
3. You will be given a ticket by the manager.
4. The streets were thronged with spectators.
5. We will be blamed by everyone.
6. The trees were blown down by the wind.
7. The thieves were caught by the police.
8. The letter was posted by Alice.
9. We were received by the hostess.
10. The snake was killed with a stick.

IV. Rewrite the following sentences in passive voice.

1. He opens the door.
2. We set the table.
3. She pays a lot of money.
4. I draw a picture.
5. They wear blue shoes.
6. They don't help you.
7. He doesn't open the book.
8. You do not write the letter.
9. Does your mum pick you up?
10. Does the police officer catch the thief?

◆◆◆

Reported Speech

14

The manner of expressing the words of speaker is called narration or reported speech. We can express the words of a speaker in two ways : direct way and indirect way.

Reported speech is divided into **direct speech** and **indirect speech**.

Direct Speech

Direct speech repeats, and/or quotes the exact words spoken. When one uses direct speech in writing, one places the words spoken between quotation marks (“ ”) and there is no change in these words. One may be reporting something that’s being said right now.

Example: Sarla said, “What time will you be at home?” and I said, “I don’t know.”

Indirect Speech

Reported or indirect speech is usually used to talk about the past, so one normally changes the tense of the words of speaker. Reporting verbs change to ‘said’, ’told’, ‘asked’, and the word ‘that’ is used to introduce the reported words. Inverted commas are not used.

Example: Suman said, “I saw him.” (Direct speech)

Suman said that she had seen him. (Indirect speech).

‘That’ may be omitted: She told him that she was happy. She told him she was happy.

Tips on Reported Speech

☞ Use ‘said’ when there is no indirect object: He *said* that he was tired.

☞ Always use ‘tell’ when you say who was being spoken to (i.e. with an indirect object)

Example: He *told* me that he was tired.

☞ Use these verbs ‘Talk’ and ‘speak’ to describe the action of communicating

Example: He *talked* to us. She was *speaking* on the telephone.

Note: Use the above verbs with ‘about’ to refer to what was said

Example: He talked (to us) about his parents.

Rules of Changing Direct Speech into Indirect Speech

1. Remove comma and inverted commas.
2. Put “that” between the reporting and reported speeches. (it is optional to put “that” between both speeches)
3. Change the pronoun of the direct speech according to the rules.
4. Change the tense of the direct speech appropriately according to rules.
5. Change the words expressing nearness in time or places of the direct speech into its appropriate words expressing distance.

Change in Tenses

Rules	Direct Speech	Indirect Speech
Simple Present changes to Simple Past	“I always drink coffee”, she said	She said that she always drank coffee.
Present Continuous changes to Past Continuous	“I am reading a book”, he explained.	He explained that he was reading a book
Present Perfect changes to Past Perfect	She said, “He has finished his work”	She said that he had finished his work.

Present Perfect Continuous changes to Past Perfect Continuous	"I have been to Spain", he told me.	He told me that he had been to Spain.
Simple Past changes to Past Perfect	"Bill arrived on Saturday", he said.	He said that Bill had arrived on Saturday.
Past Perfect changes to Past Perfect (No Change)	"I had just turned out the light," he explained.	He explained that he had just turned out the light.
Past Continuous changes to Past Perfect Continuous	"We were living in Paris", they told me.	They told me that they had been living in Paris.
Future changes to Present Conditional	"I will be in Geneva on Monday", he said	He said that he would be in Geneva on Monday.
Future Continuous changes to Conditional Continuous	She said, "I'll be using the car next Friday."	She said that she would be using the car next Friday.

Note: ❒ The past perfect and past perfect continuous tenses do not change.

❒ The tense of Reported Speech does not change if the reported speech is a universal truth though its reporting verb belongs to past tense.

Example: The teacher said that the sun rises in the east.

Changes in Modals

Rules	Direct Speech	Indirect Speech
CAN changes into COULD	He said, "I can drive a car".	He said that he could drive a car.
MAY changes into MIGHT	He said, "I may buy a computer"	He said that he might buy a computer.
MUST changes into HAD TO	He said, "I must work hard"	He said that he had to work hard.
Note: The models Would, Could, Might, Should, Ought to do not change.		
Would	They said, "we would apply for a visa"	They said that they would apply for visa.
Could	He said, "I could run faster"	He said that he could run faster.
Might	John said, "I might meet him".	John said that he might meet him.
Should	He said, "I should avail the opportunity"	He said that he should avail the opportunity.
Ought to	He said to me, "you ought to wait for him"	He said to me that I ought to wait for him.

Changes for Imperative Sentences

Imperative sentences consist any of these four things:

Most commonly used words to join clauses together are ordered, requested, advised and suggested. Forbid(s)/ forbade is used for the negative sentences.

Mood of sentence in Direct Speech	Reporting verb in Indirect Speech
Order	ordered
Request	requested / entreated
Advice	advised / urged
Never	told, advised or forbade (No need of "not" after "forbade")
Direction	directed
Suggestion	suggested to
Warning	warned
(If a person is addressed directly)	called

Changes for Exclamatory Sentences

Rules for conversion:

1. Exclamatory sentence changes into assertive sentence.
2. Interjections are removed.
3. Exclamation mark changes into full stop.
4. Question words like, 'what' and 'how' are removed and before the adjective of reported speech we put 'very'
5. Changes of 'tenses', 'pronouns' and 'adjectives' will be according to the previous rules.

Mood of sentence in Direct Speech	Reporting verb in Indirect Speech
Sorrow in reported speech	Exclaimed with sorrow/ grief OR exclaimed sorrowfully or cried out
Happiness in reported speech	exclaimed with joy/ delight OR exclaimed joyfully
Surprise in reported speech	exclaimed with surprise/ wonder/ astonishment"
Appreciation and it is being expressed strongly	applauded

Changes for Interrogative Sentences

Rules for conversion:

Changes	Direct Speech	Indirect Speech
Reporting Verb	said/ said to	Asked, enquired or demanded.
Joining Clause	If sentence begins with auxiliary verb	joining clause should be if or whether.
	If sentence begins with "wh' questions	then no conjunction is used as "question-word" itself act as joining clause/word
Punctuation	Question Mark	Full Stop
Helping Verbs	sentences expressing positive feeling	do/does is removed from sentence.
	if 'No' is used in interrogative sentences	do/does is changed into did.
	Did or has/have	Had

Note: Helping verbs (is, am, are, was, were) are used after the subject.

Change in Words Showing Nearness

The words expressing nearness in time or places are generally changed into words expressing distance.

Direct Speech	Indirect Speech
Here	There
Today	That day
This morning	That morning
Yesterday	The day before
Tomorrow	The next day
Next week	The following week
next month	The following month
Now	Then
Ago	Before
Thus	So
Last Night	The night before
This	That
These	Those
Hither	Thither
Hence	Thence
Come	Go

Change in Pronouns

The pronouns of the Direct Speech are changed where necessary, according to their relations with the reporter and his hearer, rather than with the original speaker. If we change direct speech into indirect speech, the pronouns will change in the following ways.

Rule	Direct Speech	Indirect Speech
The first person of the reported speech changes according to the subject of reporting speech.	Abhay says, "I am in tenth class."	Abhay says that he is in tenth class.
The second person of reported speech changes according to the object of reporting speech.	He says to them, "You have completed your job."	He tells them that they have completed their job.
The third person of the reported speech doesn't change.	Mansi says, "She is in tenth class."	Mansi says that she is in tenth class.

Practice Exercise

I. Choose the option which best expresses the given sentence in Indirect/Direct speech.

1. "If you don't keep quiet I shall shoot you", he said to her in a calm voice.
   (a) He warned her to shoot if she didn't keep quiet calmly.
   (b) He said calmly that I shall shoot you if you don't be quiet.
   (c) He warned her calmly that he would shoot her if she didn't keep quiet.
   D. Calmly he warned her that be quiet or else he will have to shoot her.
2. I told him that he was not working hard.
   (a) I said to him, "You are not working hard."
   (b) I told to him, "You are not working hard."
   (c) I said, "You are not working hard."
   (d) I said to him, "He is not working hard."
3. His father ordered him to go to his room and study.
   (a) His father said, "Go to your room and study."
   (b) His father said to him, "Go and study in your room."
   (c) His father shouted, "Go right now to your study room"
   (d) His father said firmly, "Go and study in your room."
4. He said to his father, "Please increase my pocket-money."
   (a) He told his father, "Please increase the pocket-money"
   (b) He pleaded his father to please increase my pocket money.
   (c) He requested his father to increase his pocket-money.
   (d) He asked his father to increase his pocket-money.
5. She said that her brother was getting married.
   (a) She said, "Her brother is getting married."
   (b) She told, "Her brother is getting married."
   (c) She said, "My brother is getting married."
   (d) She said, "My brother was getting married."
6. He exclaimed with joy that India had won the Sahara Cup.
   (a) He said, "India has won the Sahara Cup"
   (b) He said, "India won the Sahara Cup"
   (c) He said, "How! India will win the Sahara Cup"
   (d) He said, "Hurrah! India has won the Sahara Cup"
7. The little girl said to her mother, "Did the sun rise in the East?"
   (a) The little girl said to her mother that the sun rose in the East.
   (b) The little girl asked her mother if the sun rose in the East.
   (c) The little girl said to her mother if the sun rises in the East.
   (d) The little girl asked her mother if the sun is in the East.
8. The man said, "No, I refused to confess guilt."
   (a) The man emphatically refused to confess guilt.
   (b) The man refused to confess his guilt.
   (c) The man told that he did not confess guilt.
   (d) The man was stubborn enough to confess guilt.
9. Nita ordered her servant to bring her cup of tea.
   (a) Nita told her servant, "Bring a cup of tea."
   (b) Nita said, "Bring me a cup of tea."
   (c) Nita said to her servant, "Bring me a cup of tea."
   (d) Nita told her servant, "Bring her that cup of tea."
10. My cousin said, "My room-mate had snored throughout the night."
   (a) my cousin said that her room-mate snored throughout the night.
   (b) my cousin told me that her room-mate snored throughout the night.
   (c) my cousin complained to me that her room-mate is snoring throughout the night.
   (d) my cousin felt that her room-mate may be snoring throughout the night.

11. "Please don't go away", she said.
    (a) She said to please her and not go away.
    (b) She told me to go away.
    (c) She begged me not to go away.
    (d) She begged that I not go away.
12. She said to her friend, "I know where is everyone"
    (a) She told that she knew where was everyone.
    (b) She told her friend that she knew where everyone was.
    (c) She told her friend that she knew where is everyone.
    (d) She told her friend that she knows where was everyone.

II. Fill in the blanks with the correct option.

1. I told him _____ do it.
   (a) to not (b) to don't
   (c) not to (d) don't
2. He asked us _____ show our passports.
   (a) if (b) to
   (c) for
3. She asked us if we _____ finished the work on Monday.
   (a) have (b) had
   (c) Either could be used here.
4. She asked us _____ on time.
   (a) to be (b) for being
5. She asked if she _____ leave early.
   (a) can (b) could
6. They asked me _____ going to the party.
   (a) that I was (b) if I was
7. He told me _____ my father.
   (a) phone (b) to phone
8. She said that no one _____ to the meeting last week.
   (a) has come (b) had come
9. She told me _____ she wasn't going to come.
   (a) that (b) if
   (c) Either could be used here.
10. He asked me what I _____ if I failed to get the job.
    (a) would do (b) would have done
11. He told me he ___ be here by three o'clock at the latest and it's half past already.
    (a) will
    (b) would
    (c) Either could be used here.
12. She promised she _____ do it by the end of the week and then let me down.
    (a) will
    (b) would
    (c) Either could be used here.
13. She said it _____ raining when she got here.
    (a) already started
    (b) had already started
    (c) Either could be used here.
14. She explained how _______ do it.
    (a) to
    (b) I should
    (c) Either could be used here.
15. He said he _____ her before.
    (a) didn't meet
    (b) hadn't met
    (c) Either could be used here.

III. Complete the sentences using reported speech.

1. John said, "I love this town."
   John said ....
2. "Do you like soccer ?" He asked me.
   He asked me ....
3. "I can't drive a lorry," he said.
   He said ....
4. "Be nice to your brother," he said.
   He asked me
5. "Don't be nasty," he said.
   He urged me ....
6. "Don't waste your money" she said.
   She told the boys ....
7. "What have you decided to do?" she asked him.
   She asked him ....
8. "I always wake up early," he said.
   He said ....

9. "You should revise your lessons," he said.

   He advised the students ....

10. "Where have you been?" he asked me.

    He wanted to know ....

IV. Change the following sentences to indirect speech.

1. "Where is my jacket?" she asked.
2. "How are you?" Naina asked us.
3. He asked, "Do I have to do it?"
4. "Where have you been?" the mother asked her daughter.
5. "Which dress do you like most?" she asked her friend.
6. "What are they doing?" she asked.
7. "Are you going to the cinema?" he asked me.
8. The teacher asked, "Who speaks English?"
9. "How do you know that?" she asked me.
10. "Has Priyanka talked to Kunal?" my friend asked me.

V. Change the following sentences to Direct speech.

1. He said that he liked that song.
2. She asked me where my sister was.
3. She said that she didn't speak Assamese.
4. They asked me to say hello to Satya.
5. He said that the film had begun at seven o'clock.
6. She told the boys not to play on the grass.
7. She asked him where he had spent his money.
8. He said that he never made mistakes.
9. He wanted to know if she knew Dr. Roy.
10. The stuntman advised the audience not to try that at home.

Concord

15

Subject and Verb must agree with each other in number (singular or plural). If the subject is singular, the verb must also be singular. If the subject is plural, the verb must be plural.

Example: A student reads the lesson.

Students read the lesson.

A singular subject (*she, Bill, car*) takes a singular verb (*is, goes, shines*), whereas a plural subject takes a plural verb.

Example: The list of items is on the desk.

If you know that *list* is the subject, then you will choose *is* for the verb.

Rules of Subject Verb Agreement

1. Subjects and verbs must agree in number. This is the cornerstone rule that forms the background of the concept.

Example: The *dog growls* when he is angry. The *dogs growl* when they are angry.

2. Don't get confused by the words that come between the subject and verb; they do not affect agreement.

Example: The *dog*, who is chewing on my jeans, *is* usually very good.

3. Prepositional phrases between the subject and verb usually do not affect agreement.

Example: The *colours* of the rainbow *are* beautiful.

4. When sentences start with "there" or "here," the subject will always be placed after the verb, so care needs to be taken to identify it correctly.

Example: There *is* a problem with the balance sheet. Here *are* the papers you requested.

5. Subjects don't always come before verbs in questions. Make sure you accurately identify the subject before deciding on the proper verb form to use.

Example: Does the *dog* usually *eat* grass? Where *are* the *pieces* of this puzzle.

6. If two subjects are joined by *and*, they typically require a plural verb form.

Example: The cow and the pig *are jumping* over the moon.

7. The verb is singular if the two subjects separated by *and* refer to the same person or thing.

Example: *Red beans and rice is* my mom's favourite dish.

8. If one of the words *each, every, or no* comes before the subject, the verb is singular.

Example: No *smoking or drinking is* allowed. Every *man and woman is* required to check in.

9. If the subjects are both singular and are connected by the words *or, nor, neither/nor, either/or*, and *not only/but also* the verb is singular.

Example: *Jessica or Christian is* to blame for the accident.

10. The only time when the object of the preposition factors into the decision of plural or singular verb forms is when noun and pronoun subjects like some, half, none, more, all, etc. are followed by a prepositional phrase. In these sentences, the object of the preposition determines the form of the verb.

Example: All of the *chicken* is gone. All of the *chickens* are gone.

11. The singular verb form is usually used for units of measurement or time.

Example: Four *quarts of oil was* required to get the car running.

12. If the subjects are both plural and are connected by the words *or, nor, neither/nor, either/or*, and *not only/but also*, the verb is plural.

Example: *Dogs and cats are* both available at the pound.

13. If one subject is singular and one plural and the words are connected by the words *or, nor,*

neither/nor, either/or, and *not only/but also*, you use the verb form of the subject that is nearest the verb.

Example: Either the *bears* or the *lion has* escaped from the zoo. Neither the *lion* nor the *bears have* escaped from the zoo.

14. Indefinite pronouns typically take singular verbs. *

Example: *Everybody wants* to be loved.

15. * Except for the pronouns (few, many, several, both, all, some) that always take the plural form.

Example: *Few were* left alive after the flood.

16. If two infinitives are separated by *and* they take the plural form of the verb.

Example: *To walk and to chew gum require* great skill.

17. When gerunds are used as the subject of a sentence, they take the singular verb form of the verb; but, when they are linked by *and*, they take the plural form.

Example: *Standing* in the water *was* a bad idea. *Swimming* in the ocean and *playing drums are* my hobbies.

18. Collective nouns like herd, senate, class, crowd, etc. usually take a singular verb form.

Example: The *herd* is stampeding.

19. Titles of books, movies, novels, etc. are treated as singular and take a singular verb.

Example: *The Burbs is* a movie starring Tom Hanks.

20. Final Rule – Remember, only the subject affects the verb!

Practice Exercise

Choose the correct sentence/option in which the subjects and verbs agree.

1. (a) At the end of the story, they was living happily ever after.
   (b) At the end of the story, they were living happily ever after.
   (c) At the end of the story, they were living happily ever after.
   (d) At the end of the story, they was living happily ever after.
2. (a) Al and Eli go to the beach to surf with their friends.
   (b) Al and Eli go to the beach to surf with his friends.
   (c) Al and Eli goes to the beach to surf with their friends.
   (d) Al and Eli goes to the beach to surf with their friends.
3. (a) When Al and Eli arrive, they find that their friends has waxed their boards.
   (b) When Al and Eli arrive, they find that their friends has waxed their boards.
   (c) When Al and Eli arrive, they find that his friends have waxed their boards.
   (d) When Al and Eli arrive, they find that their friends have waxed their boards.
4. (a) A group of children from that school are not being cooperative.
   (b) A group of children from that school is not being cooperative.
   (c) A group of children from that school is not being cooperative.
   (d) A group of children from that school are not being cooperative.
5. (a) Unless our staff members do really cooperate, we will not meet our goals.
   (b) Unless our staff members really do cooperate, we will not meet our goals.
   (c) Unless our staff members do really cooperate we will not meet our goals.
   (d) Unless our staff members really do cooperate we will not meet our goals.
6. (a) Either Gary or I am responsible, for allocating the funds.
   (b) Either Gary or I are responsible, for allocating the funds.
   (c) Either Gary or I am responsible for allocating the funds.
   (d) Either Gary or I are responsible for allocating the funds.
7. (a) Neither she nor they were willing to predict the election results.
   (b) Neither she nor they was willing to predict the election results.
   (c) Neither she nor they was willing to predict, the election results.
   (d) Neither she nor they were willing to predict, the election results.
8. (a) Nora is one of the candidates who are worthy of my vote.
   (b) Nora is one of the candidates who is worthy of my vote.
   (c) Nora is one of the candidates who are worthy of my vote.
   (d) Nora is one of the candidates, who is worthy of my vote.
9. (a) Nora, of all the candidates who are running is the best.
   (b) Nora, of all the candidates who are running, is the best.
   (c) Nora, of all the candidates who is running, is the best.
   (d) Nora, of all the candidates who is running, is the best.
10. (a) My problem, which is minor in comparison with others exists because I dropped out of high school.
    (b) My problem which is minor in comparison with others, exist because I dropped out of high school.
    (c) My problem, which is minor in comparison with others, exists because I dropped out of high school.
    (d) My problem, which is minor in comparison with others, exist because I dropped out of high school.

11. (a) His dogs, which is kept outside, bark all day long.
    (b) His dogs, which is kept outside, bark all day long.
    (c) His dogs, which are kept outside bark all day long.
    (d) His dogs, which are kept outside, bark all day long.
12. (a) There's three strawberries left.
    (b) There's three strawberries left.
    (c) There is three strawberries left.
    (d) There are three strawberries left.
13. (a) Here is the reports from yesterday.
    (b) Here are the reports from yesterday.
    (c) Here are the reports, from yesterday.
    (d) Here is the reports from yesterday.
14. (a) Some of my goals has yet to be met.
    (b) Some of my goals has yet to be met.
    (c) Some of my goals have yet to be met.
    (d) Some of my goals are yet to be met.
15. (a) All of my goals is being met and surpassed.
    (b) All of my goals are been met and surpassed.
    (c) All of my goals are being met and surpassed.
    (d) All of my goals is being met and surpassed.
16. (a) None of this is your business.
    (b) None of these is your business.
    (c) None of this are your business.
    (d) None of this are your business.
17. (a) None of them are coming tonight home.
    (b) None of them are coming home tonight.
    (c) None of them is coming home tonight.
    (d) None of them is coming home tonight.
18. (a) One-third of the city are experiencing tonight a blackout.
    (b) One-third of the city are experiencing a blackout tonight.
    (c) One-third of the city is experiencing, a blackout tonight.
    (d) One-third of the city is experiencing a blackout tonight.
19. (a) One-third of the people is suffering.
    (b) One-third of the people, are suffering.
    (c) One-third of the people are suffering.
    (d) One-thirds of the people is suffering.
20. (a) When she talks, everyone listens.
    (b) When she talks, everyone listen.
    (c) When she talks everyone listen.
    (d) When she talks everyone listens.
21. (a) Neither the farmers nor the farm workers is willing to settle the strike.
    (b) Neither the farmer nor the farm workers are willing to settle the strike.
    (c) Neither the farmers nor the farm workers are willing to settle the strike.
    (d) Neither the farmer nor the farm workers is willing to settle the strike.
22. (a) Neither Darren nor Ida is capable of such a crime.
    (b) Neither Darren nor Ida are capable of such a crime.
    (c) Neither Darren nor Ida is capable of such crime.
    (d) Neither Darren nor Ida are capable of such crime.

Question Forms

16

Questions are asked when one needs to acquire some knowledge or needs to know something. One needs to know how to frame questions that way.

Types of Questions

There are four basic types of questions:

Yes/No Questions

Sometimes, the only answer that we need to know is YES or NO.

Example: Question: Can you drive?

Answer: No, I can't.

Question-Word Questions

Sometimes, we want more than just a YES or NO for an answer. While asking for information, we usually place a question word at the beginning of the sentence. The question-word indicates the information that we want, for example: where (place), when (time), why (reason), who (person).

Example: Question: Where do you live?

Answer: In Mumbai.

Choice Questions

Sometimes, we give our listener a choice. We ask them to choose between two possible answers. So their answer is (usually) already in the question.

Example: Question: Do you want tea or coffee?

Answer: Coffee, please.

Opinion Questions

Sometimes, we want our listener's advice or opinion on something. The question normally contains the topic we want their opinions on. These answers are usually longer than the other and can stretch into discussions. They normally have the word opinion and synonyms for it in the question.

Example: Question: What are the remedial measures for global warming?

Answer: Global warming is defined as the increase in temperature of earth. ....

Practice Exercise

I. Rearrange the following to form a correct question.

1. what done you have would?
2. going do we tomorrow to are what?
3. were her words what last?
4. do we shall what?
5. better could done what they have?
6. eaten what we would have?
7. have points scored when will they three?
8. should start when we?
9. to must bed night tomorrow we go when?
10. would you when started have to get ready?
11. be ready report will when the?
12. had seen when you him last?
13. dine shall tonight we where?
14. will age where have 65 been by he?
15. would have you washed car where gotten your?
16. if 100 where go would had you you dollars?
17. all cookies where gone have the?
18. to play baseball where tonight going they are?
19. do would you why that?
20. them why should help we?
21. playing why street you all the in were?
22. would gotten he have a car new why?
23. to do why we have grass the mow?
24. criminal shouldn't commited crime the have why the?
25. be coming will who the for reunion family?
26. be who first Mars walk the to on will?
27. been who a league game has major to soccer?
28. glasses were whose wearing you?
29. done who better a could have job?
30. shall appoint as president who we next the?

II. Name the type of questions in the following sentences.

1. Can you swim?
2. Did he go to work or to school?
3. Has your class finished?
4. Where is my pen?
5. Who did you visit?
6. Why didn't he go to work?
7. Shall we go to your place or mine?
8. When will Lucy arrive?
9. Who called here so late?
10. What do you think about the movie?

III. Write questions for these answers.

1. **Ans:** She is opening a present.
   Q: ______________________________
2. **Ans:** The boys are hiding under Anita's bed.
   Q: ______________________________
3. **Ans:** My sister prefers porridge for breakfast.
   Q: ______________________________
4. **Ans:** On Thursday Prasad has Sociology, History and Maths.
   Q: ______________________________
5. **Ans:** Yesterday Anil and Anu went to the swimming pool.
   Q: ______________________________
6. **Ans:** The plane is landing at the airport.
   Q: ______________________________

Collocations

17

Collocations are the words that are normally paired together to make a new meaning completely different from the ones the words possess individually. It's like a phrase but not quite. Neither word can be substituted as most probably it will cease to have meaning. Like 'fast food', one can't make it 'quick food' but 'fast food' means the food that is served very quickly and can be taken away to be eaten in the street.

Kinds of Collocations

There are mainly seven types of collocations based on their formation.

(i) **Adverb + adjective:** completely satisfied (NOT downright satisfied)

(ii) **Adjective + noun:** excruciating pain (NOT excruciating joy)

(iii) **Noun + noun:** a surge of anger (NOT a rush of anger)

(iv) **Noun + verb:** lions roar (NOT lions shout)

(v) **Verb + noun:** commit suicide (NOT undertake suicide)

(vi) **Verb + expression with preposition:** burst into tears (NOT blow up in tears)

(vii) **Verb + adverb:** wave frantically (NOT wave feverishly)

Here're some more examples to learn how to use collocations in sentences.

1. adverb + adjective

Example: Invading (to enter forcefully as an enemy) that country was an *utterly stupid* thing to do.

We entered a *richly decorated* room.

2. adjective + noun

Example: The doctor ordered him to take *regular exercise*.

The Titanic sank on its *maiden voyage*.

3. noun + noun

Example: Let's give Mr Jones a *round of applause*.

The *ceasefire agreement* came into effect at 11am.

4. noun + verb

Example: The *lion* started *to roar* when it heard the dog barking.

Snow was falling as our *plane took off*.

5. verb + noun

Example: The prisoner was hanged for *committing murder*.

I always try to *do my homework* in the morning, after *making my bed*.

6. verb + expression with preposition

Example: We had to return home because we had *run out of money*.

At first her eyes were *filled with horror*, and then she burst into tears.

7. verb + adverb

Example: She *placed* her keys *gently* on the table and sat down.

Mary *whispered softly* in John's ear.

Tips to Learn Collocations

Collocations cannot be derived based on a formula, these have to be learnt. A few tips to learn collocations are following.

1. Try to be aware of collocations, and recognize them when you see or hear them.
2. Treat collocations as single blocks of language instead of separate words, like they're one phrase.
3. When you learn a new word, write down other words that collocate with it.

4. Read as much as possible. Reading is an excellent way to learn vocabulary and collocations.
5. Revise and practice using new collocations in context after learning them.
6. Learn collocations in groups that work for you. Learn them by topic such as time, number, weather, money, family or by a particular word such as take action, take a chance, take an exam etc.).

Note: You can find information on collocations in any good learner's dictionary. Specialized dictionaries of collocations may also be helpful.

Practice Exercise

I. Fill in the blanks with the correct collocation/option.

1. My grandfather was a _______ smoker, so few people were surprised when he died of oral cancer.
   (a) serial (b) heavy
   (c) big (d) none of these
2. She was a _______ wife who loved her husband more than anything else in the whole universe.
   (a) devoted (b) sincere
   (c) intelligent (d) none of these
3. I always avoid his company because he is a terrible _________.
   (a) bore (b) nuisance
   (c) guy (d) none of these
4. It is a golden ____________ if you miss it, you will regret it.
   (a) chance (b) opportunity
   (c) offer (d) none of these
5. She seemed quite interested in buying that house, but at the last moment, she changed her ______.
   (a) mind (b) thoughts
   (c) offer (d) none of these
6. Although I was _________annoyed by her attitude, I said nothing.
   (a) moderately (b) lightly
   (c) slightly (d) none of these
7. Could you ______the oil?
   (a) inspect (b) check
   (c) test (d) none of these
8. Raghav needs to take a _________ before he falls ill.
   (a) Vacation (b) Break
   (c) Holiday (d) none of these
9. We were ____ on time for the show.
   (a) Bang (b) Right
   (c) Not (d) none of these
10. You should _____ you respect to your seniors.
    (a) Give (b) Have
    (c) Pay (d) none of these

II. Find the correct answer from the options given below.

1. He spoke English with a ______ French accent.
   (a) average (b) careless
   (c) widespread (d) pronounced
   (e) chronic
2. His new novel has met with ______ acclaim.
   (a) careless (b) dreadful
   (c) great (d) pronounced
   (e) wholehearted
3. We need to make sure that there is enough ______ accommodation to house all the delegates.
   (a) careless (b) dreadful
   (c) yellow (d) luxury
   (e) wholehearted
4. He gave us a ______ account of all that you had achieved over there.
   (a) ready (b) yellow
   (c) careless (d) luxury
   (e) glowing
5. Could you please give me an ______ account?
   (a) itemised (b) dreadful
   (c) great (d) luxury
   (e) glowing
6. We need to crack down hard on the ______ abuse of drugs.
   (a) average (b) outright
   (c) widespread (d) frenetic
   (e) careless
7. He was able to predict what was going to happen with ______ accuracy.
   (a) itemised (b) uncanny
   (c) careless (d) luxury
   (e) glowing
8. They've made some highly ______ accusations about us.
   (a) itemised (b) uncanny
   (c) damaging (d) luxury
   (e) glowing

9. We need to find a new site with _________ access to the European motorway network.
   (a) ready (b) outright
   (c) widespread (d) pronounced
   (e) wholehearted
10. This will probably be the ___________ achievement of her career.
   (a) itemised (b) uncanny
   (c) damaging (d) crowning
   (e) glowing
11. I did all the groundwork on this project but he only gave me a ______ acknowledgment in his report.
   (a) itemised (b) uncanny
   (c) damaging (d) crowning
   (e) grudging
12. I don't know him very well. He's just a ______ acquaintance.
   (a) casual (b) uncanny
   (c) damaging (d) crowning
   (e) grudging
13. We're fighting for the ______ abolition of the death penalty.
   (a) average (b) outright
   (c) decisive (d) frenetic
   (e) chronic
14. I'm afraid he was involved in a ______ accident.
   (a) ready (b) dreadful
   (c) widespread (d) pronounced
   (e) wholehearted
15. He invited me around to see his ______ acquisition, a new BMW.
   (a) casual (b) latest
   (c) damaging (d) crowning
   (e) grudging
16. We need to take some ______ action before it is too late.
   (a) casual
   (b) latest
   (c) decisive
   (d) crowning
   (e) grudging
17. He wasn't particularly good. He was of about ______ ability.
   (a) average (b) latest
   (c) decisive (d) frenetic
   (e) chronic
18. I don't think we can succeed without the ______ acceptance of the unions.
   (a) average (b) polite
   (c) careless (d) pronounced
   (e) wholehearted
19. There is always a lot of ______ activity going on but nothing much seems to get done!
   (a) careless (b) latest
   (c) yellow (d) frenetic
   (e) grudging
20. I'm afraid her husband has got a ______ addiction to gambling.
   (a) careless (b) latest
   (c) decisive (d) frenetic
   (e) chronic
21. We need to carry out a detailed ______ of the project before we go any further.
   (a) amount (b) analysis
   (c) alarm (d) alternative
   (e) ambition
22. The news of the merger and the threat of job losses has caused considerable ______ among the work force.
   (a) allusion
   (b) allowance
   (c) alarm
   (d) applause
   (e) application
23. If we let the unions decide everything, there will be complete ______. It just won't work.
   (a) amount (b) analysis
   (c) anarchy (d) alternative
   (e) ambition
24. I think he had been very unhappy for some time. He suddenly exploded with pent-up ______ and was completely out of control.
   (a) amount (b) analysis
   (c) anarchy (d) anger
   (e) ambition

25. David has a different way of looking at the world. He always sees things from an unusual _______ .
(a) amount (b) analysis
(c) anarchy (d) anger
(e) angle

26. Deborah and Simon can't stand each other. There is deep _______ between them.
(a) animosity (b) analysis
(c) anarchy (d) anger
(e) angle

27. Everybody knows it already but there will be a formal _______ later this morning.
(a) animosity (b) announcement
(c) anarchy (d) anger
(e) angle

28. I don't know what she earns exactly but I do know it is a vast _______.
(a) amount (b) allowance
(c) alarm (d) alternative
(e) ambition

29. In the factory, men are getting paid more than women and we need to do away with this _______.
(a) animosity (b) announcement
(c) anomaly (d) anger
(e) angle

30. I expect you to give me a straight _______ to this.
(a) animosity (b) announcement
(c) anomaly (d) answer
(e) angle

31. In costing this, I think we need to make generous _______ for the probable delays in getting planning permission.
(a) allusion (b) allowance
(c) appetite (d) applause
(e) application

32 I think we should look round for a feasible _______ .
(a) allusion
(b) allowance
(c) alarm
(d) alternative
(e) application

33. I think you need to make a full _______ to her for your sexist behaviour.
(a) animosity
(b) announcement
(c) anomaly
(d) answer
(e) apology

34. He made an emotional _______ to keep his job but he'd made too many mistakes and I had to let him go.
(a) appeal (b) announcement
(c) anomaly (d) answer
(e) apology

35. We didn't think she would come and so we were delighted when she put in an unexpected _______ at our party.
(a) appeal (b) appearance
(c) anomaly (d) answer
(e) apology

36 He seems to be devoured by overwhelming _______ .
(a) allusion (b) allowance
(c) alarm (d) alternative
(e) ambition

37. Microhard seem to have a healthy _______ for taking over innovative companies.
(a) appeal (b) appearance
(c) appetite (d) answer
(e) apology

38. In his speech he made a flattering _______ to your work.
(a) allusion (b) appearance
(c) appetite (d) applause
(e) application

39. The announcement was made to deafening _______ .
(a) appeal (b) appearance
(c) appetite (d) applause
(e) apology

40. If you want the job, you're going to have to put in a formal _______ .
(a) appeal (b) appearance
(c) appetite (d) applause
(e) application

41. I'm an ______ admirer of your work.
(a) ardent (b) triumphant
(c) stale (d) considerable
(e) cast-iron

42. This new process is a ______ advance in technology.
(a) ardent (b) significant
(c) stale (d) considerable
(e) cast-iron

43. He knows the interviewer already and that will give him an ______ advantage over me.
(a) ardent (b) significant
(c) unfair (d) considerable
(e) cast-iron

44. I wouldn't upset him. He can be a ______ adversary.
(a) ardent (b) significant
(c) unfair (d) dangerous
(e) cast-iron

45. He gave me some ______ advice and I took it.
(a) ardent (b) significant
(c) unfair (d) dangerous
(e) blunt

46. We know very little about this. We need to bring in an ______ adviser to help us.
(a) outside (b) significant
(c) unfair (d) dangerous
(e) blunt

47. I don't like this at all. It's a really ______ affair.
(a) outside (b) ugly
(c) unfair (d) dangerous
(e) blunt

48. It's not a very challenging job. I only have to deal with ______ affairs.
(a) outside (b) ugly
(c) everyday (b) dangerous
(e) blunt

49. They don't always agree but I think there is a bond of ______ affection between them.
(a) outside (b) ugly
(c) everyday (d) deep
(e) blunt

50. It seems no time at all since I started work and here I am at ______ age.
(a) outside (b) ugly
(c) everyday (d) deep
(e) retirement

Jumbled Words

18

Jumbled words are words with their letters mixed up so that their meaning is unrecognizable. It's a word puzzle which tests the dexterity of one's mind as well the vocabulary one possesses. The best way to deal with such a problem is to have a good vocabulary.

Here are some guidelines one can follow while trying to un-jumble or unscramble words:

- ☞ Look for common letter combinations, such as 'th', 'ly' and 'sh'. When you see two letters that look like they may go together, put them side by side and try to arrange the rest of the letters around them to form a word.
- ☞ Count the number of vowels and consonants. If there are more vowels, then the word is likely to begin with one of them. Try different arrangements of letters with each vowel at the front of the word until you find a word that makes sense.
- ☞ Write the letters down using a different pattern to help your brain see the letters in a new way. Sometimes seeing things in a new way presents an answer you could not see before.
- ☞ You can also write the letters down like the numbers on the face of a clock. For some people, displaying the letters in this way can help them to see the word clearly.
- ☞ Take your time and allow your brain to think and process what it sees. If you move too quickly, your brain is less likely to see anything other than the order printed on the page.
- ☞ Practice as much as possible. The more you practice on how to unscramble words, the easier it will be for you to learn them. Once your brain is used to the process, you can find words with minimal effort.
- ☞ Lastly, read a lot. Reading will help to improve your vocabulary. Therefore, make sure you read anytime you can.

Practice Exercise

Un-jumble the following words.

1. Scblemra
2. Bcealan
3. Ursenive
4. Psorrofes
5. Atlntisa
6. Adisepar
7. Stentatem
8. perienexce
9. Ofngfspri
10. Ovaterco
11. Gouslori
12. Chdil
13. stijufy
14. Ealqu
15. Sifpecic
16. Echnri
17. Avuentred
18. Deebat
19. Fusamo
20. Nalatur
21. Ellc
22. Feli
23. Crbaaeti
24. Ieulontov
25. Osirecmcop
26. Vusir
27. Gnsoiram
28. Oninclg
29. Ngee
30. Eocgylo
31. Ngeeyr
32. Oroemmcsho
33. Patln
34. Giunf
35. Tobioislg
36. Imaanl
37. Thogrw
38. Oislfs
39. Tprinoe
40. Csnlueu
41. Laek
42. Oldg
43. Cavolno
44. Aktqurahee
45. Tanminuo
46. Virer
47. Stedre
48. Oncae
49. Krco
50. Trewa
51. Teer
52. Vala
53. Ocnttinen
54. Mamag
55. Sterof
56. Greiecb
57. Asrgs
58. Lios
59. Rian
60. Roldw

Synonyms and Antonyms

19

Synonym

Synonyms are words or phrases which have the same or nearly the same meaning as other words or phrases in the same language:

Example: The words 'allure' and 'entice' are synonyms.

Antonym

An antonym is a word which means the opposite of another word. Antonyms are also called opposites. Synonyms and opposites are helpful to enrich vocabulary and learn language skills.

Example: Opposite of "origin" is "remnant".

Examples:

Word	Synonyms	Antonyms
abandon	desert, forsake	keep
abbreviate	shorten, condense	lengthen, increase
ability	skill, aptitude	incompetence, inability
able	capable, qualified	incapable
above	overhead	below
abundant	ample, sufficient	scanty, insufficient
accurate	correct, right	wrong
achieve	accomplish, attain	fail
active	energetic, animated, lively	lethargic, idle, sluggish
adamant	firm, unyielding	maneuverable, yielding
add	increase, total	subtract, decrease, reduce
adequate	sufficient, enough, ample	insufficient, sparse
adjourn	postpone, recess	recommence, continue
adult	grown-up	child
advocate	support, recommend	oppose
after	following, next	before
afraid	frightened, scared	courageous, brave
aggressive	assertive, pushy, militant	passive, peaceful
aid	help, assist	hinder
always	forever	never
amateur	beginner, novice	professional
ambitious	aspiring, driven	lazy, indifferent

antagonize	provoke, embitter	soothe, tranquilize
apparent	obvious, evident	hidden, obscure
approve	accept, ratify, endorse	disapprove, censure
arrive	reach, come	depart, leave
arrogant	haughty, stuck-up	humble, modest
artificial	fake, synthetic	real, authentic
ask	question, inquire	answer
atrocious	dreadful, contemptible, vile	kind, wonderful
authentic	genuine, real, factual	false, artificial
average	ordinary, fair	unusual, exceptional
awful	dreadful, atrocious	pleasant
awkward	clumsy, uncoordinated	graceful
ban	prohibit, forbid, outlaw	allow, permit
barren	unproductive, infertile	fertile, productive
bashful	shy, timid	outgoing, assured
beautiful	pretty, attractive, lovely	ugly
before	prior, earlier	after, behind
beginning	start, initiate	finish, end
believe	trust, accept	doubt, distrust
below	under, lower	above
beneficial	helpful, useful, advantageous	harmful, adverse
best	finest, choice	worst
birth	beginning	death, end
blend	combine, mix	separate
bottom	base, foundation	top
brave	courageous, bold, heroic	cowardly, timid
break	fracture, burst	repair, heal
brief	short, concise	long
broad	wide, expansive	narrow
busy	active, occupied, working	idle, inactive
buy	purchase	sell
calm	quiet, tranquil, still	excited, turbulent
capture	apprehend, seize, arrest	free, release
care	concern, protection	neglect

careful	cautious, watchful	careless, reckless
cease	stop, discontinue	continue, recommence
certain	positive, sure, definite	uncertain, unsure
charming	delightful, appealing, enchanting	obnoxious, gross, vulgar
chilly	cool, nippy	warm
chubby	plump, pudgy	thin, skinny
clarify	explain, simplify	confuse
close	shut, fasten	open
close	near, imminent	far
coarse	bumpy, rough	fine, smooth
colossal	enormous, immense, mammoth	tiny, insignificant, trivial
combine	blend, unite, join	separate
comical	amusing, funny, humorous	tragic, sorrowful
complex	complicated, intricate	simple
competent	capable, qualified	incompetent, inept
comprehend	understand, grasp	confuse, misinterpret
complete	conclude, finish	incomplete
complex	complicated, intricate	simple
compress	crush, condense, squeeze	expand
concrete	real, tangible, solid	abstract, flimsy
concur	agree, cooperate	disagree
condemn	censure, denounce	approve
condense	compress, concentrate	expand, enlarge
confess	admit, acknowledge	deny
confine	contain, enclose, restrain	free, release
conflict	oppose, differ, clash	agree
conflict	fight, battle, struggle	peace, harmony
conform	comply, submit	dissent, dispute
confuse	complicate, muddle, jumble	clarify
congested	overcrowded, stuffed	empty, unfilled
connect	join, link, attach	separate, disconnect
conscientious	scrupulous, virtuous	neglectful, careless
conscious	aware, cognizant	unaware, unconscious

consecutive	successive, continuous	interrupted
conservative	cautious, restrained	radical, extreme
considerate	thoughtful, sympathetic, mindful	thoughtless, selfish
constantly	always, continually	scarcely, seldom
contaminate	pollute, defile, infect	purify
contented	satisfied, pleased	dissatisfied, unhappy
continue	persist, persevere	discontinue, stop
convalesce	recuperate, recover, heal	relapse
convenient	handy, accessible	inconvenient
conventional	customary, traditional	unusual
correct	accurate, right, proper	wrong, incorrect
courage	bravery, valor	cowardice
courteous	polite, civil	rude
cover	conceal, hide	expose
cozy	comfortable, snug, homey	uncomfortable
cranky	cross, irritable	good-humoured
crazy	insane, daft, mad	sane
cruel	mean, heartless, ruthless	kind, humane
cry	sob, weep	laugh
dally	loiter, linger	rush
damage	hurt, impair, harm	remedy, repair
dangerous	unsafe, hazardous, perilous	safe
daring	bold, audacious	cautious
dark	dismal, black	light
dawn	daybreak, sunrise	evening
dead	lifeless, deceased	alive, active
decay	rot, spoil	bloom, flourish
deduct	subtract, remove	add
defend	protect, shield	attack, assault
defy	resist, challenge	obey, comply
delicate	fragile, dainty	sturdy
demolish	destroy, wreck	restore
denounce	blame, censure, indict	commend

dense	thick, heavy, compressed	sparse, empty
depart	leave, exit	arrive, come
deposit	store, place	withdraw
desolate	barren, forsaken	dense, verdant
despise	hate, detest, loathe	love
destitute	poor, penniless	wealthy
destroy	ruin, wreck, devastate	restore
detach	separate, unfasten, remove	attach
deter	hinder, prevent	encourage
determined	sure, convinced, resolute	doubtful
die	expire, perish	live
different	distinct, unlike	same, alike
difficult	hard, challenging	easy
dilute	weaken, thin	strengthen, concentrated
diminish	curtail, lessen, decrease	increase, amplify
dirty	soiled, messy	clean
disagree	differ, dispute	agree
dispute	debate, oppose	agree
diverse	different, distinct	same, similar
divide	separate, split	unite
docile	tame, gentle	wild, stubborn
dormant	sleeping, inactive	awake, active
doubt	mistrust, dispute	believe
drab	dull, lifeless	bright
drastic	severe, extreme, tough	mild, moderate
dreadful	terrible, unpleasant	splendid, super
dry	arid, parched	wet
dubious	doubtful, questionable	certain
dull	blunt, dreary	sharp, bright
dumb	stupid, dense	smart
early	premature, beforetime	late
easy	simple	hard
eccentric	peculiar, unusual	normal
ecstasy	joy, rapture, elation	sadness, depression

empty	drain, unload	fill
encourage	promote, support, urge	discourage
enemy	opponent, foe	ally, friend
enjoy	like, appreciate	dislike, hate
enlarge	expand, magnify	reduce, shrink
enormous	vast, immense, colossal	tiny, microscopic
enough	sufficient, ample, plenty	insufficient
entirely	wholly, completely, solely	partly
eternal	always, perpetual, everlasting	temporary, passing
evident	apparent, obvious, clear	doubtful, vague
evil	bad, wrong, wicked	good
exceptional	remarkable, outstanding	ordinary, commonplace
excite	arouse, provoke, incite	compose, calm
exhilarated	overjoyed, ecstatic, elated	depressed, dejected, sad
explicit	exact, distinct, unmistakable	indefinite, unclear
exquisite	delightful, charming, lovely	revolting, repulsive
exterior	outside, outer	interior
extravagant	extreme, excessive, luxurious	meagre
fabulous	marvelous, amazing	unexciting
face	confront, meet	avoid
fair	honest, just, impartial	unjust, unfair
fake	imitation, phony, artificial	real, genuine
false	incorrect, untrue	true
fancy	elaborate, ornate, fussy	simple, plain
fantastic	incredible, outrageous	ordinary, usual
fast	rapid, quick, swift	slow
fat	chubby, plump, stout	thin
fatal	deadly, mortal, killing	safe, unharmed
fatigue	tire, exhaust	fresh, new
feasible	possible, attainable, practical	impossible
feeble	weak, frail	strong
ferocious	fierce, savage, brutal, savage	tame, gentle
fertile	fruitful, productive	unproductive, barren
few	less	many

fiction	fantasy, untruth, myth	truth
fill	load, pack	empty
fix	mend, repair	break
flaw	defect, fault, blemish	perfection
flimsy	frail, fragile, delicate	sturdy, strong
flippant	impudent, sassy	polite, respectful
fluid	liquid	solid
foe	enemy, adversary, opponent	friend
follow	succeed, trail	lead, precede
forbid	prohibit, ban, bar	encourage
forgive	pardon, excuse, absolve	punish, penalise
former	previous, earlier	latter
fraction	part, portion, segment	whole
frank	candid, straightforward, blunt	evasive
frenzy	fury, rage	serenity, calmness
fresh	unused, new	old, stale
friend	comrade, buddy	enemy
frigid	freezing, frosty	warm, hot
frivolous	trivial, unimportant, silly	important, serious
front	fore	back
full	packed, stuffed	empty
furious	angry, enraged, infuriated	calm, placid
future	coming, tomorrow	past
gain	acquire, obtain, receive	lose
gallant	chivalrous, stately	ungentlemanly, timid
gather	collect, accumulate, compile	scatter, disperse
gaudy	showy, garish, vulgar	tasteful, refined
gaunt	scrawny, skinny, thin	overweight, plump
generous	giving, selfless, big-hearted	selfish, stingy
gentle	tender, mild	rough, harsh
genuine	real, authentic, sincere	fake, phony
gigantic	immense, colossal, enormous	tiny, minute
give	donate, present, offer	take, receive
glad	happy, pleased, delighted	sad, unhappy

gloomy	dark, dismal, depressing	cheery, bright
glorious	splendid, magnificent, superb	terrible, awful
good	nice, fine, well-behaved	bad, awful
gorgeous	ravishing, dazzling, stunning	hideous, unattractive
gratitude	thankfulness, appreciation	ungratefulness
great	outstanding, remarkable	insignificant, unimportant
handy	useful, convenient, skillful	inconvenient, inept
hard	firm, solid, difficult	soft, easy
hate	loathe, detest	love
help	aid, assist	hinder, thwart
high	elevated, lofty	low
hold	grasp, grip, retain	release, discharge
honest	truthful, sincere, frank	untruthful, insincere
hospitable	welcoming, cordial, gracious	rude, unfriendly
hostile	antagonistic, aggressive, militant	friendly, cordial
huge	vast, immense, great	small, tiny
humble	modest, unpretentious	vain, showy
humiliate	embarrass, disgrace, dishonour	honour, dignify
identical	alike, duplicate	different, varied
idle	inactive, lazy	busy, ambitious
ignorant	uninformed, unaware	knowledgeable
immaculate	spotless, pure	dirty, filthy
immature	childish, inexperienced	mature, adult
immune	resistant, exempt	susceptible
impartial	neutral, unbiased, fair	prejudiced
impatient	eager, anxious, intolerant	patient
imperative	compulsory, crucial, mandatory	unnecessary, optional
imperfect	marred, defective, faulty	perfect, flawless
impetuous	impulsive, rash, reckless	restrained, careful
important	significant, meaningful	unimportant, meaningless
independent	self-reliant, autonomous	dependent, unsure
inferior	lesser, substandard	superior
infuriate	enrage, agitate, provoke	soothe, clam

ingenious	clever, creative, original	unoriginal, dull
innocent	guiltless, blameless	guilty
insane	crazy, deranged, mad	sane
insufficient	inadequate, deficient	adequate, enough
intelligent	bright, sensible, rational	ignorant, dense
interesting	provocative, engrossing	dull, boring
intermittent	sporadic, periodic	regular, continual
internal	inner, inside	external, outer
intolerant	bigoted, prejudiced	understanding, accepting
intriguing	fascinating, enthralling	uninteresting, dull
irrelevant	inappropriate, unrelated	relevant, pertinent, applicable
irritate	annoy, agitate, provoke	soothe, calm
join	connect, unite, link	separate, disconnect, detach
jolly	merry, jovial, joyful	sad, grim, glum
jubilant	overjoyed, delighted, elated	dejected, depressed
keep	save, protect, guard	discard, lose
kind	considerate, tender, thoughtful	mean, cruel, inconsiderate
lament	mourn, grieve	rejoice, celebrate
large	big, massive, huge	small, little
last	final, end	first, beginning
least	fewest, minimum, smallest	most, maximum
legible	readable, clear	illegible, unreadable
lenient	lax, unrestrained, easy	harsh, strict
listless	lethargic, tired	active, energetic
logical	sensible, sane, rational	illogical, unreasonable
long	lengthy	short
loose	slack, limp	tight
lure	attract, seduce, entice	repel
luxurious	extravagant, elegant	meagre, scanty
magnify	expand, enlarge, exaggerate	reduce, minimize
mandatory	required, compulsory	optional, obligatory
manoeuvre	manipulate, handle, scheme	straight forward
maximum	greatest, uppermost, highest	minimum, least
meager	scanty, sparse, poor	abundant, generous

mean	unkind, malicious, nasty	pleasant, nice
mediocre	fair, moderate	outstanding
mend	repair, fix	break
migrant	drifting, traveling, transient	stationary, immovable
militant	combative, aggressive, warlike	peaceful
minor	lesser, inferior, secondary	major
mirth	merriment, fun, laughter	gloom, sadness
mischievous	naughty, impish	well-behaved, angelic
misfortune	hardship, catastrophe, mishap	good luck, fortune
mobile	moveable, changeable	immobile, stationary
moderate	temperate, lenient, medium	extreme, harsh
momentous	important, powerful, outstanding	unimportant, insignificant
monotonous	boring, tedious dreary, humdrum	interesting
moral	ethical, virtuous, righteous	immoral, unethical
morbid	appalling, awful, ghastly	pleasant
morose	gloomy, sullen, moody, glum	cheerful, optimistic
mourn	grieve, lament, bemoan	rejoice
mysterious	elusive, occult, secret	obvious, known
naughty	bad, disobedient, wrong	good, appropriate
neat	clean, orderly, tidy	sloppy, disorderly
negligent	careless, derelict, inattentive	conscientious, careful
nervous	ruffled, flustered, perturbed	composed, calm
neutral	impartial, unprejudiced	prejudiced, partial
new	unused, fresh, modern	old, antique
nice	pleasing, desirable, fine	unpleasant, naughty
nonchalant	indifferent, lackadaisical, blase	concerned, apprehensive
normal	ordinary, typical, usual	abnormal, unusual
numerous	several, abundant, considerable	few, scanty
obey	mind, heed, comply	disobey, resist
oblivious	unconscious, preoccupied, dazed	mindful, aware
obnoxious	offensive, abominable, repulsive	pleasant, pleasing
observe	examine, study, scrutinize	ignore, disregard

obsolete	extinct, dated, antiquated	stylish, vogue, current
obstinate	stubborn, bullheaded, adamant	maneuverable, flexible
odd	peculiar, weird, strange	usual, ordinary
offend	displease, affront, disgust	please, delight
ominous	threatening, menacing	fortuitous
opaque	obscure, murky, unclear	transparent, clear
open	begin, unfold, originate	close
opponent	enemy, rival, foe	ally, friend
optimistic	hopeful, confident	pessimistic
optional	voluntary, elective	required
ordinary	usual, average	unusual, remarkable
outrageous	preposterous, shocking	warranted, acceptable
outstanding	extraordinary, distinguished	insignificant, inconsequential
painstaking	meticulous, precise, fastidious	careless, negligent
passive	compliant, submissive, yielding	forceful
past	former, previous, preceding	future
patience	tolerance, perseverance	impatience
peculiar	weird, bizarre	normal, conventional
perfect	flawless, accurate	imperfect, faulty
permanent	enduring, lasting	temporary, changing
perpetual	eternal, endless, incessant	short-lived, fleeting
persuade	convince, influence	dissuade, deter
plausible	believable, reasonable, logical	unbelievable
plentiful	ample, enough, abundant	scarce, insufficient
pliable	supple, flexible, compliant	rigid, closed-minded
polite	gracious, refined, courteous	rude, discourteous
poor	destitute, needy, impoverished	rich, wealthy
portion	part, segment, piece	whole, total
possible	conceivable, feasible, plausible	impossible, unachievable
precarious	dangerous, uncertain, shaky	sure, safe
precious	cherished, valuable, prized	cheap, worthless
prejudiced	biased, opinionated, influenced	impartial
premature	early, hasty	late, delayed
premeditated	planned, intended, calculated	spontaneous, accidental

preserve	uphold, guard, save	destroy, neglect
pretty	lovely, beautiful, attractive	homely, unattractive
prevalent	customary, widespread	uncommon, unusual
prevent	thwart, prohibit, hinder	permit, allow
probable	likely, apt, liable	improbable, doubtful
proficient	skilled, adept, competent	inefficient, inept
profit	gain, earnings, benefit	loss
prohibit	forbid, bar, restrict	allow, permit
prominent	distinguished, eminent	unknown, not renowned
prompt	punctual, timely	late, slow
prosperous	thriving, successful, flourishing	unsuccessful, fruitless
proud	arrogant, elated	modest, ashamed
push	shove, propel	pull
qualified	competent, suited, capable	unfit, unsuited
question	interrogate, inquire, ask	answer
quiet	silent, hushed, tranquil	noisy, rowdy
quit	cease, stop, withdraw	continue, remain
racket	noise, commotion, disturbance	peace, quiet
radiant	luminous, shining, lustrous	dim, not
raise	hoist, elevate	illuminated lower
ratify	approve, confirm, endorse	veto, refuse
rational	logical, level-headed, sensible	irrational, crazy
ravage	devastate, ruin, damage	restore, revitalize
raze	destroy, demolish	build, construct
recreation	amusement, pleasure, pastime	work, labour
reduce	lessen, decrease, diminish	increase, enlarge, amplify
refute	contradict, dispute	agree, concur
regular	routine, customary, steady	irregular, abnormal
regulate	control, oversee, handle	decontrol
relentless	persistent, merciless, unyielding	lenient, sympathetic
relevant	pertinent, suitable, apropos	irrelevant, insignificant
reliable	trustworthy, steadfast, stable	undependable, unreliable
reluctant	unwilling, hesitant	willing, accommodating
remote	secluded, isolated, distant	close, accessible

repulsive	hideous, offensive, gruesome	pleasing, alluring
reputable	honorable, upstanding, honest	dishonest, untrustworthy
resist	oppose, withstand, defy	comply, conform
retaliate	avenge, revenge, reciprocate	accept
reveal	show, disclose, divulge	hide, conceal
ridiculous	nonsensical, foolish, preposterous	sensible, believable
risky	hazardous, perilous, chancy	safe, sound
rowdy	boisterous	well-mannered, genteel
rude	impolite, discourteous	polite, mannerly
sad	unhappy, dejected, gloomy	happy, glad
same	identical, alike, equivalent	different, diverse
savage	uncivilized, barbarous	civilized, gentle, tame
save	preserve, conserve, keep	spend, discard
scarce	scanty, rare, sparse	plentiful, abundant
scrawny	skinny, gaunt, spindly	husky, chubby
scrupulous	meticulous, ethical, fastidious	unethical, careless
seize	apprehend, grab, snatch	release, free
separate	divide, segregate, partition	unite, join
serene	peaceful, tranquil, calm	disturbed, upset
serious	grave, solemn, pensive	flighty, fickle
shrewd	clever, cunning, crafty	unthinking, careless
shy	bashful, timid	bold, aggressive
sick	ill, ailing	well, healthy
slim	slender, thin, svelte	stout, stocky
sluggish	listless, lethargic, inactive	quick, speedy
small	little, insignificant, trivial	large, important
smooth	slick, glossy, level	rough
sociable	friendly, cordial, gregarious	unfriendly, aloof
sorrow	woe, anguish, grief	joy, ecstasy
special	exceptional, notable, particular	ordinary, usual
spontaneous	instinctive, automatic, natural	planned, rehearsed
stable	steady, unchanging, settled	unsettled
stationary	fixed, immobile, firm	movable, portable

stimulate	rouse, stir, motivate	stifle, suppress
stop	quit, cease, terminate	start, begin
strenuous	vigorous, laborious	effortless, easy
strict	stringent, severe, stern	lenient
strong	powerful, mighty, potent	weak
stupid	unintelligent, dense, foolish	knowledgeable, smart
subsequent	following, succeeding, latter	preceding, previous
successful	thriving, prosperous, triumphant	failing, unsuccessful
sufficient	ample, enough, adequate	lacking, insufficient
superb	magnificent, exquisite	inferior, mediocre
suppress	restrain, inhibit, squelch	foster, encourage
surplus	excess, additional, extra	lack, deficit
swift	fast, speedy, hasty	slow, sluggish
synthetic	man-made, artificial	natural
tall	high, lofty	short
tangible	concrete, definite	vague, ambiguous
taut	tense, tight, stiff	relaxed
tender	delicate, gentle, affectionate	harsh, rough
terrible	dreadful, horrible, vile	wonderful, superb
thaw	melt, defrost	freeze
thrifty	economical, frugal, prudent	wasteful, extravagant
thrive	prosper, flourish, develop	fail, fade, shrivel
total	whole, entire, complete	partial
trivial	insignificant, worthless	important, crucial
turbulent	tumultuous, blustering, violent	clam, peaceful
turmoil	commotion, disturbance, fracas	quiet, tranquility
unbiased	impartial, unprejudiced, fair	prejudiced, partial
upset	perturb, ruffle, agitate	soothe, calm
urgent	crucial, important, imperative	unimportant, trivial
vacant	unoccupied, empty	filled, occupied
vague	unclear, obscure, indistinct	clear, definite
valiant	courageous, brave, heroic	cowardly, fearful
vibrate	shake, quiver, tremble	firm, steady
vicious	malicious, spiteful, ferocious	kind, humane

victory	triumph, win, success	defeat
virtuous	moral, righteous, angelic	sinful, wicked
vulgar	offensive, uncouth, coarse	refined, tasteful
wealth	riches, prosperity, assets	poverty
weary	tired, fatigued, lethargic	energetic, lively
wholehearted	earnest, sincere	insincere
wild	uncivilized, savage, reckless	tame, calm
win	triumph, succeed, prevail	lose
wise	knowing, scholarly, smart	dull, uneducated
wonderful	marvelous, incredible, splendid	ordinary, blah
worn	used, impaired, old	new, fresh
wrong	incorrect, untrue, mistaken	correct, right
yield	produce, bear, provide	keep, retain
zenith	peak, pinnacle, apex	bottom, base

Practice Exercise

I. Choose the correct synonym of the underlined word from the options.

1. I am <u>terrible</u> at mathematics.
   (a) good (b) awful
   (c) brilliant (d) none of these
2. I found several spelling <u>mistakes</u>.
   (a) errors (b) corrections
   (c) difficult (d) none of these
3. Mr. Singh <u>required</u> five visas made for the family trip for abroad.
   (a) took (b) wanted
   (c) needed (d) none of these
4. He tried to <u>remember</u> a poem.
   (a) write (b) rewrite
   (c) recollect (d) none of these
5. He used <u>unlawful</u> methods to become rich.
   (a) illegal (b) right
   (c) roundabout (d) none of these
6. Kings are always associated with <u>courage</u>.
   (a) nobility (b) bravery
   (c) riches (d) none of these
7. Rita was <u>content</u> only after she got her ice-cream.
   (a) happy (b) satisfied
   (c) quiet (d) none of these
8. His <u>statement</u> accounted to slander.
   (a) truth (b) lies
   (c) libel (d) none of these
9. Non-biodegradable matter is <u>useless</u> in this day and age.
   (a) worthless (b) useful
   (c) annoying (d) none of these
10. It was <u>forbidden</u> to go into the forest.
    (a) fine (b) un-allowed
    (c) prohibited (d) none of these

II. Directions: Pick out the nearest correct meaning or synonym of the word given is capital letters.

1. GERMINATE
   (a) decay (b) breed
   (c) produce (d) sprout
2. EFFICACY
   (a) delicacy (b) ruthlessness
   (c) efficiency (d) solemnity
3. MAGNATE
   (a) tycoon (b) senior executive
   (c) non-magnetic (d) symbolic
4. FACET
   (a) sweet (b) tap
   (c) deceit (d) aspect
5. PERNICIOUS
   (a) deadly (b) curious
   (c) gorgeous (d) expensive
6. PERSUADE
   (a) assure (b) opinionated
   (c) convince (d) cheat
7. FORTIFY
   (a) topple (b) destroy
   (c) reproduce (d) strengthen
8. PHENOMENAL
   (a) incidental (b) eventful
   (c) natural (d) extraordinary
9. PARADIGM
   (a) solution (b) model
   (c) discovery (d) invention
10. HONORARY
    (a) honest (b) dignified
    (c) unpaid (d) praiseworthy
11. FACULTY
    (a) privilege (b) desire
    (c) branch (d) ability
12. FORESEE
    (a) contemplate (b) visualise
    (c) assume (d) hypothesis
13. ANNEX
    (a) add (b) low
    (c) copy (d) initial
14. MENAGE
    (a) suffocation
    (b) system
    (c) law
    (d) household

15. DILEMMA
(a) darkness (b) freedom
(c) trap (d) confusion

16. RIGMAROLE
(a) short-cut
(b) lengthy procedure
(c) unnecessary burden
(d) happy responsibility

17. TRANSCEND
(a) lower (b) climb
(c) energise (d) cross

18. IMPERATIVE
(a) order (b) command
(c) suggestion (d) necessity

19. EXEMPT
(a) duty (b) provide
(c) relieve of (d) forgive

20. INFIRMITY
(a) disease (b) malady
(c) weakness (d) slimness

21. IMMINENT
(a) eminent (b) immediate
(c) future (d) impending

22. CHASTE
(a) filthy (b) lewd
(c) immoral (d) noble

23. FASCINATE
(a) captivate (b) irritating
(c) fashionable (d) impulsive

24. CURVATURE
(a) angularity (b) straightness
(c) short-cut (d) streamline

25. SUMMIT
(a) base (b) slope
(c) declivity (d) peak

26. WEAN
(a) introduce (b) withdraw
(c) detach (d) alienate

27. MENDACIOUS
(a) irritating (b) misleading
(c) provocative (d) untruthful

28. OSTRACISED
(a) hated
(b) shut out from the society
(c) criticised
(d) applauded by the majority

29. SPURIOUS
(a) false (b) harmful
(c) poisonous (d) foreign

30. OBNOXIOUS
(a) clever (b) shrewd
(c) disagreeable (d) outdated

31. PERNICIOUS
(a) radical (b) baneful
(c) scientific (d) negative

32. RECTIFY
(a) to command (b) to correct
(c) to destroy (d) to build

33. CORDON
(a) pile of logs
(b) heavy cloak
(c) line of people placed as guard
(d) none of these

34. CONCERT
(a) beauty (b) power
(c) agreement (d) none of these

35. MITIGATE
(a) to heal
(b) soothen
(c) to pardon
(d) to send on a mission

36. DEVOID
(a) evasive (b) hopeless
(c) lacking (d) stupid

37. RESOLVED
(a) summarised (b) dispelled
(c) determined (d) hanged

38. APPOSITE
(a) appropriate (b) foolish
(c) painful (d) none of these

39. BUOYANT
(a) childlike (b) sturdy
(c) brisk (d) light-hearted

40. INFIRM
(a) sturdy (b) anxious
(c) patient (d) feeble

41. INTELLECT
(a) rationality (b) imbecility
(c) insanity (d) reverie

42. MANIAC
(a) lunatic (b) deft
(c) sober (d) dunce

43. OMEN
(a) augury (b) superstition
(c) imagery (d) imagination

44. SPECTACLE
(a) pageant (b) show
(c) mystification (d) panorama

45. TURBULENCE
(a) treachery (b) triumph
(c) commotion (d) overflow

46. DEFER
(a) discourage (b) minimize
(c) postpone (d) estimate

47. ADAGE
(a) proverb (b) youth
(c) supplement (d) hardness

48. ENSUE
(a) compel (b) plead
(c) remain (d) follow

49. ZENITH
(a) lowest point (b) middle
(c) compass (d) summit

50. HYPOTHETICAL
(a) magical (b) theoretical
(c) visual (d) two-faced

51. SUPERFICIAL
(a) shallow (b) aged
(c) unsually fine (d) proud

52. DISPARAGE
(a) separate (b) belittle
(c) compare (d) imitate

53. LUDICROUS
(a) profitable (b) ridiculous
(c) excessive (d) undesirable

54. INTREPID
(a) moist (b) rude
(c) tolerant (d) fearless

55. FILCH
(a) hide (b) steal
(c) swindle (d) covet

56. URBANE
(a) well-dressed (b) friendly
(c) polished (d) prominent

57. DECANT
(a) bisect (b) pour off
(c) speak widly (d) bequeath

58. ANTITHESIS
(a) contract (b) examination
(c) conclusion (d) opposite

59. HAVOC
(a) festival (b) sea battle
(c) disease (d) ruin

60. REJUVENATE
(a) reply (b) judge
(c) renew (d) age

61. VERBATIM
(a) word for word (b) in secret
(c) at will (d) in summary

62. ENTICE
(a) inform (b) attract
(c) observe (d) disobey

63. ACCLAIM
(a) discharge (b) divide
(c) excel (d) applaud

64. SOLILOQUY
(a) figure of speech
(b) isolated position
(c) historical incident
(d) monologue

65. STUPEFY
(a) lie (b) make dull
(c) talk nonsense (d) overread

66. ADMONISH
(a) polish (b) distribute
(c) escape (d) caution

67. ATROPHY
(a) wither (b) grow
(c) soften (d) spread

68. COMPREHEND
(a) agree (b) reprieve
(c) settle (d) understand

69. SUFFICE
(a) endure (b) be adeqaute
(c) annex (d) eat up

70. PERSONABLE
(a) self-centred (b) initimate
(c) attractive (d) sensitive

71. ANALOGY
(a) similarity (b) distinction
(c) transposition (d) variety

72. INTRIGUE
(a) request (b) poison
(c) plot (d) veto

73. DEBONAIR
(a) gay (b) extravagant
(c) corrupt (d) healthful

74. PONDEROUS
(a) conceited (b) heavy
(c) shameless (d) abundant

75. CHARGIN
(a) delight (b) caution
(c) deceit (d) vexation

76. DEFAMATION
(a) slander (b) debt
(c) infeciton (d) deterioration

77. APLOMB
(a) caution (b) shortsightedness
(c) timidity (d) self-assurance

78. FORTITUDE
(a) wealth
(b) loudness
(c) courage
(d) luck

79. MERCENARY
(a) poisonous
(b) unworthy
(c) serving only for pay
(d) luring by false charms

80. DEIFY
(a) face (b) worship
(c) flatter (d) challenge

81. TYRANNY
(a) misrule (b) power
(c) madness (d) cruelty

82. CONNOISSEUR
(a) ignorant (b) interpreter
(c) delinquent (d) lover of art

83. WRATH
(a) jealousy (b) hatred
(c) anger (d) violence

84. REBATE
(a) loss (b) refund
(c) compensation (d) discount

85. PROLIFIC
(a) plenty (b) competent
(c) fertile (d) predominant

86. AFFABLE
(a) friendly (b) cheerful
(c) helpful (d) neutral

87. EXORBITANT
(a) odd (b) ridiculous
(c) excessive (d) threatening

88. TERRIFIC
(a) big (b) excellent
(c) tragic (d) terrible

89. ABNEGATION
(a) self-denial (b) self-sacrifice
(c) self-praise (d) self-criticism

90. AFFLUENT
(a) prosperous (b) poor
(c) talkative (d) close

91. INFREQUENT
(a) never (b) usual
(c) rare (d) sometimes

92. MASSACRE
(a) stab (b) slaughter
(c) murder (d) assassinate

93. DISTINGUISH
(a) darken (b) abolish
(c) differentiate (d) confuse

94. GRATIFY
(a) frank (b) appreciate
(c) pacify (d) indulge

95. TERMINATE
(a) suspend (b) dismiss
(c) end (d) interrupt

96. OBJECT
(a) disobey (b) challenge
(c) deny (d) disapprove

97. ADVERSITY
(a) crisis (b) misfortune
(c) failure (d) helplessness

98. STUBBORN
(a) easy (b) obstinate
(c) willing (d) pliable

99. TACITURNITY
(a) reserve (b) hesitation
(c) changeableness (d) dumbness

100. BLITHE
(a) graceful (b) joyous
(c) giddy (d) other worldly

101. ELICIT
(a) induce (b) extract
(c) divulge (d) instil

102. PORTRAY
(a) communicate (b) paint
(c) express (d) draw

103. ARTIFACT
(a) synthetic (b) man-made
(c) natural (d) exact copy

104. PILFER
(a) destroy (b) damage
(c) steal (d) snatch

105. LETHAL
(a) dreary (b) dreadful
(c) deadly (d) strange

106. TEDIOUS
(a) painful (b) troublesome
(c) lengthy (d) tiresome

107. OBSCENE
(a) objectionable (b) indecent
(c) displeasing (d) condemnable

108. UNIFORMITY
(a) routine (b) continuity
(c) stability (d) constistency

109. MYSTIQUE
(a) fame (b) reputation
(c) admirable quality (d) popularity

110. RESILIENT
(a) flexible (b) proud
(c) separable (d) rigid

111. DUBIOUS
(a) straight (b) sincere
(c) zig zag (d) doubtful

112. CAVIL
(a) appreciate (b) amuse
(c) quibble (d) munch

113. RESTITUTE
(a) help (b) avenge
(c) revenge (d) repair

114. RETRIBUTION
(a) contempt (b) revenge
(c) punishment (d) discount

115. INTRINSIC
(a) introvert (b) intricate
(c) complicated (d) secret

116. APPRAISAL
(a) estimation (b) praise
(c) approval (d) investigation

117. LUMINARY
(a) bright (b) lightning
(c) famous (d) dashing

118. STRINGENT
(a) shrill (b) regorous
(c) dry (d) strained

119. JEREMAI
(a) friction (b) incident
(c) trouble (d) accident

120. WHIMPER
(a) prevent (b) cry
(c) instigate (d) pacify

121. HARASS
(a) grieve (b) injure
(c) excite (d) annoy

122. GADFLY
(a) harror (b) naisance
(c) gain (d) blessing

123. HYBRID
(a) unusual (b) hackneyed
(c) pedigreed (d) crossbred

124. MAIM
(a) disfigure (b) slit
(c) severe (d) slash

125. EXCRUCIATE
(a) refifne (b) torture
(c) extract (d) imprison

126. OUTRE
(a) fair (b) traditional
(c) real (d) eccentric

127. ASSIMILATE
(a) absorb (b) arrange
(c) receive (d) assemble

128. COTERIE
(a) mob (b) group
(c) family (d) institution

129. OBEISANCE
(a) insult (b) obedience
(c) indifference (d) disrespect

130. FATIGUE
(a) weariness (b) sweating
(c) tension (d) drowsiness

131. PERFIDY
(a) debauchery (b) deceit
(c) treachery (d) conceit

132. MASTICATE
(a) devour (b) drink
(c) chew (d) swallow

133. BIZARRE
(a) colourful (b) strange
(c) exotic (d) comical

134. ZENITH
(a) top (b) bright
(c) wonderful (d) smart

135. CURSORY
(a) penetrating (b) informal
(c) superficial (d) angry

136. DISMAL
(a) deformed (b) impolite
(c) bleak (d) watery

137. NEMESIS
(a) punishment (b) victory
(c) adventure (d) reward

138. CONNIVE
(a) threaten (b) shield
(c) instigate (d) disregard

139. ERSATZ
(a) liveliness (b) imitation
(c) freshness (d) pleasure

140. ANNOTATION
(a) translation (b) prologue
(c) quip (d) explanatory note

141. EXACERBATE
(a) irritate (b) enlighten
(c) aggravate (d) exaggerate

142. THRIVE
(a) hurt (b) persuade
(c) push (d) flourish

143. VAPID
(a) virtuous (b) vital
(c) priceless (d) dull

144. FRANTIC
(a) urgent (b) excited
(c) novel (d) painful

145. EGREGIOUS
(a) social (b) shocking
(c) common (d) plain

146. MAMMOTH
(a) greedy (b) wild
(c) straight (d) huge

147. HUMDRUM
(a) thoughtful (b) musical
(c) unnatural (d) commonplace

148. MANIA
(a) fame (b) greatness
(c) fear (d) illusion

149. OBLOQUY
(a) lethargy (b) burial service
(c) verbal abuse (c) vulgar joke

150. ENTHRAL
(a) inspire (b) charm
(c) glorify (d) annoy

151. BAFFLE
(a) insult (b) frustrate
(c) defame (d) antagonise

152. DAUNT
(a) detain (b) annoy
(c) abuse (d) intimidate

153. BEHOLDEN
(a) upright (b) lovable
(c) grateful (d) obliged

154. SOLICIT
(a) beseech (b) require
(c) claim (d) demand

155. CLUMSY
(a) adroit (b) dexterous
(c) rough (d) ungraceful

156. FRICASSEE
(a) grill (b) decorate
(c) stew (d) to baste

157. HINDER
(a) create (b) protect
(c) vindicate (d) impede

158. ABIDE
(a) hold (b) encourage
(c) accept (d) comment

159. MONOLITHIC
(a) short-sighted (b) black & white
(c) repetitive (d) very large

160 . SYMBIOSIS
(a) transformation (b) close association
(c) cure- all (d) similarity

161. EGRESSION
(a) digression (b) effusion
(c) departure (d) hostility

162. PERNICIOUS
(a) relevant (b) vigilant
(c) destructive (d) minute care

163. IRRUPTION
(a) hate (b) bursting in
(c) interference (d) altercation

164. ECHELON
(a) rank (b) opponent
(c) follower (d) identity

165. PREVARICATE
(a) anticipate (b) lie
(c) delay (d) authentiacate

166. EXUDE
(a) ooze (b) wither
(c) over flow (d) evaporate

167. PRECARIOUS
(a) brittle (b) perilous
(c) critical (d) cautious

168. MALAISE
(a) stagnation (b) spite
(c) curse (d) sickness

169. VOGUE
(a) fashion (b) rejection
(c) order (d) satisfaction

170. IMPREGNATE
(a) conceal (b) suffer
(c) affect (d) conclude

171. DELEGATE
(a) officer (b) participant
(c) member (d) representative

172. ABANDON
(a) admit (b) refrain
(c) abstain (d) forsake

173. AVER
(a) assert (b) confess
(c) impress (d) trust

174. YAW
(a) dedicate (b) soar
(c) arouse (d) drift

175. DELECTABLE
(a) attractive (b) delightful
(c) desirable (d) delicate

176. HINDER
(a) obstruct (b) challenge
(c) damage (d) ruin

177. REITERATE
(a) reassess (b) rewrite
(c) repeat (d) stutter

178. FEIGN
(a) pretend (b) attend
(c) condemn (d) condone

179. VITUPERATE
(a) appreciate (b) abuse
(c) appraise (d) encourage

180. NAUSEATE
(a) tempt (b) sicken
(c) despise (d) detest

181. INIQUITOUS
(a) unequal (b) curious
(c) biased (d) wicked

182. ECSTATIC
(a) animated (b) enraptured
(c) bewildered (d) fitful

183. REPLENISH
(a) fill (b) supply
(c) provide (d) restore

184. WALLOW
(a) luxuriate (b) suffer
(c) sacrifice (d) prosper

185. INNATE
(a) unique (b) important
(c) inborn (d) essential

186. FURTIVE
(a) baffling (b) fleeing
(c) hasty (d) stealthy

187. ACCOLADE
(a) welcome (b) award
(c) affection (d) arrival

188. INDIGENCE
(a) poverty (b) prosperity
(c) suffering (d) scarcity

189. DISTINCTION
(a) degree (b) difference
(c) diffusion (d) disagreement

190. STALEMATE
(a) deadly (b) dead-end
(c) deadlock (d) dead-drunk

191. REQUITE
(a) repay (b) demand
(c) refuse (d) requisition

192. COMPENDIUM
(a) glossary (b) reference
(c) index (d) summary

193. OVERSTRUNG
(a) active (b) energetic
(c) concerned (d) too sensitive

194. FRATERNISE
(a) associate (b) organise
(c) expel (d) cheat

195. CATALOGUE
(a) menu (b) record
(c) list (d) pamphlet

196. OVERSTRUNG
(a) concerned (b) active
(c) sensitive (d) energetic

197. GREGARIOUS
(a) sociable (b) turbulent
(c) pugnacious (d) clumsy

III. Directions: Pick out the opposite meaning or antonym of the word given in capital letters.

1. PROCLAIM
(a) denounce (b) pretend
(c) attend (d) distend

2. SUMPTUOUS
(a) irritable (b) meagre
(c) fancy (d) sad

3. FEIGN
(a) condone (b) attend
(c) willing (d) original

4. INSIPID
(a) witty (b) meagre
(c) wily (d) lucid

5. SALUBRIOUS
(a) sticky (b) soft
(c) famous (d) malaise

6. REFULGENT
(a) angry (b) dull
(c) sad (d) lament

7. INNOCUOUS
(a) offensive (b) harmless
(c) organic (d) anger

8. AFFECTATION
   (a) sincerity (b) humility
   (c) stirring (d) affluent
9. LUMINOUS
   (a) dark (b) ludicrous
   (c) unsteady (d) provoking
10. INTRICACY
   (a) ornate (b) simplicity
   (c) distance (d) cordiality
11. AMELIORATE
   (a) amend (b) gyrate
   (c) sweeten (d) worsen
12. LACKADAISICAL
   (a) abundant (b) energetic
   (c) theatrical (d) actual
13. CAPRICIOUS
   (a) thoughtful (b) specious
   (c) carcinogenic (d) capacious
14. PERFIDIOUS
   (a) loyal (b) treacherous
   (c) religious (d) humane
15. ENNUI
   (a) sticky (b) activity
   (c) start (d) yearly
16. LASCIVIOUS
   (a) devout (b) fluid
   (c) chaste (d) stable
17. CONSCIENTIOUS
   (a) cruel (b) licentious
   (c) careless (d) whip
18. PERIGEE
   (a) apogee (b) hybrid
   (c) descent (d) night
19. FLUCTUATE
   (a) conceive (b) stabilise
   (c) energise (d) emancipate
20. RADICAL
   (a) superficial (b) slow
   (c) narrow (d) simple
21. ACCORD
   (a) concord (b) policy
   (c) dissent (d) act
22. HAPLESS
   (a) lucky (b) kind
   (c) helpful (d) futile
23. FRIVOLOUS
   (a) trivial (b) significant
   (c) fearless (d) permissive
24. INTEGRAL
   (a) minor (b) major
   (c) essential (d) independent
25. HOLISTIC
   (a) negative (b) piecemeal
   (c) impure (d) inadequate
26. EXTENSION
   (a) diminution (b) condensation
   (c) deletion (d) subtraction
27. INDIGENTLY
   (a) richly (b) awfully
   (c) completely (d) diligency
28. AUDACITY
   (a) quivering (b) patricide
   (c) bravado (d) cowardice
29. ELEVATION
   (a) depression (b) deflation
   (c) depreciation (d) recession
30. PROFANE
   (a) pious (b) kitten
   (c) energy (d) wild
31. UNFATHOMABLE
   (a) comprehensible (b) sinkable
   (c) uncomfortable (d) infallible
32. TERMINATION
   (a) endeavouring (b) beginning
   (c) amendment (d) phasing
33. INSPIRED
   (a) discouraged (b) extracted
   (c) negated (d) admired
34. PARTICIPATE
   (a) precipitate (b) change
   (c) disengage (d) boycott
35. EGALITARIAN
   (a) unequal (b) socialist
   (c) capitalist (d) liberal

36. DEFICIENCY
(a) abundance (b) deficit
(c) ill (d) profit

37. FLOURISH
(a) improve (b) retard
(c) hamper (d) stop

38. VENEER
(a) exterior (b) interior
(c) impression (d) armour

39. DICTATORSHIP
(a) democracy (b) tyranny
(c) aristocracy (d) self-rule

40. EVENTUALLY
(a) primarily (b) resultantly
(c) initially (d) objectively

41. PHENOMENAL
(a) ordinary (b) experiential
(c) natural (d) spiritual

42. NONCHALANT
(a) fearful (b) cowardly
(c) patriotic (d) excited

43. ABOMINATE
(a) love (b) loathe
(c) abhor (d) despise

44. INGENUOUS
(a) cunning (b) stupid
(c) naive (d) young

45. EGREGIOUS
(a) notorious (b) splendid
(c) abortive (d) maturity

46. DISSIPATE
(a) waste (b) conserve
(c) organise (d) unite

47. STURDY
(a) important (b) rich
(c) weak (d) vigorous

48. SACROSANCT
(a) irreligious (b) unethical
(c) irreverent (d) open

49. CELIBATE
(a) reprobate (b) prodigal
(c) profligate (d) married

50. OBSOLETE
(a) rare (b) useless
(c) recent (d) conducive

51. MAGNANIMOUS
(a) small (b) generous
(c) naive (d) selfish

52. EVACUATE
(a) admit (b) emerge
(c) abandon (d) invade

53. SANGUINE
(a) bloody (b) thin
(c) happy (d) gloomy

54. CORPULENT
(a) sallow (b) co-operative
(c) enterprising (d) emaciated

55. OCCIDENTAL
(a) oriental (b) accidental
(c) coincidental (d) confidential

56. FLACCID
(a) upright (b) taut
(c) rough (d) even

57. NEPOTISM
(a) midnight (b) partiality
(c) impartiality (d) chauvinism

58. ABSTEMIOUS
(a) fastidious (b) punctilious
(c) dissipated (d) prodigal

59. CHIMERICAL
(a) numerical (b) real
(c) obvious (d) heavenly

60. VERBOSE
(a) laconic (b) talkative
(c) vent (d) suspense

61. DIMINUTIVE
(a) enlarged (b) bright
(c) small (d) admonitory

62. IMMUNITY
(a) obligatory (b) impassive
(c) impervious (d) susceptibility

63. AMALGAMATE
(a) synthesise (b) bubble
(c) separate (d) moderate

64. CAPTIOUS
(a) capable (b) detailed
(c) tolerant (d) classical

65. MANIFOLD
(a) hidden (b) enrolled
(c) simple (d) exact

66. WARP
(a) plush (b) web
(c) alienate (d) straighten

67. JOCOSE
(a) dull (b) humorous
(c) regulated (d) brief

68. PAMPER
(a) neglect (b) scold
(c) scorn (d) discourage

69. NEGLIGENCE
(a) diligence (b) punctuality
(c) integrity (d) meticulousness

70. INSTANTLY
(a) repeatedly (b) lately
(c) immediately (d) slowly

71. OBVIOUSLY
(a) obscurely (b) surely
(c) indefinitely (d) certainly

72. EXTRAORDINARY
(a) exceptional (b) unusual
(c) dull (d) plain

73. SPREAD
(a) express (b) prohibit
(c) contain (d) contradict

74. PROHIBIT
(a) grant (b) agree
(c) permit (d) accept

75. RUTHLESS
(a) gracious (b) compassionate
(c) generous (d) malicious

76. CHAGRIN
(a) tempt (b) ascetic
(c) swollen (d) pleased

77. BEGET
(a) forget (b) fade
(c) harm (d) abort

78. AUSTERE
(a) painful (b) comfortable
(c) lavish (d) plentiful

79. APPROPRIATE
(a) unqualified (b) unskilled
(c) unable (d) unsuitable

80. WILD
(a) arrogant (b) humble
(c) tamed (d) rude

81. SUBSERVIENT
(a) aggressive (b) straightforward
(c) dignified (d) supercilious

82. CONFESS
(a) deny (b) refuse
(c) contest (d) contend

83. ENGAGE
(a) abstain (b) liberate
(c) release (d) join

84. JUDICIOUS
(a) imprudent (b) silly
(c) separation (d) sagacious

85. UPROARIOUS
(a) tumultuous (b) upright
(c) posture (d) calm

86. GRATEFUL
(a) quick (b) beholden
(c) unappreciative (d) convincing

87. TOIL
(a) laborious task (b) sloth
(c) strive (d) vivid

88. INDISCRIMINATE
(a) promiscuous (b) selective
(c) undistinguished (d) broad

89. FICKLE
(a) steadfast (b) independent
(c) unwise (d) esoteric

90. TARDY
(a) sluggish (b) dilatory
(c) reluctant (d) prompt

91. FABLE
(a) truth (b) fact
(c) reality (d) actuality

92. AFFECTIONATE
(a) cold (b) indifferent
(c) hostile (d) unfriendly

93. ERUDITE
(a) ignorant (b) unknown
(c) illiterate (d) unfamiliar

94. PRETENTIOUS
(a) unassuming (b) calm
(c) secretive (d) cowardly

95. POLTROON
(a) plutocrat (b) hero
(c) amateur (d) partisan

96. ABOLISH
(a) remove (b) reside
(c) confront (d) establish

97. RETALIATION
(a) disintegration (b) wholesale
(c) admonition (d) reconciliation

98. ABET
(a) aid (b) risk
(c) pacify (d) prevent

99. REPREHENSIBLE
(a) commendable (b) fearful
(c) ignorant (d) culpable

100. SEDATE
(a) addicted (b) excited
(c) shy (d) inebriate

101. ABATE
(a) gamble (b) dilute
(c) increase (d) discourage

102. MOROSE
(a) docile (b) boorish
(c) diffuse (d) cheerful

103. SALIENT
(a) emphatic (b) striking
(c) important (d) incline

104. PRECEPT
(a) discernment (b) instruction
(c) important (d) incline

105. PALPABLE
(a) innovative (b) fresh
(c) imaginary (d) creative

106. MALIGNANT
(a) swallow (b) prune
(c) benign (d) virulent

107. POLEMIC
(a) aggressive attack (b) warlike
(c) logically argued (d) controversial

108. DELIRIOUS
(a) large (b) calm
(c) insane (d) responsive

109. JUVENILE
(a) mature (b) youthful
(c) blind (d) control

110. MORIBUND
(a) restored (b) healthy
(c) wholesome (d) growing

111. ANALYSIS
(a) synthesis (b) substitution
(c) emphasis (d) replacement

112. GENUINE
(a) innocent (b) spurious
(c) real (d) plutonic

113. DISSENT
(a) ascent (b) accent
(c) agreement (d) convergence

114. DEFICIT
(a) implicit (b) explicit
(c) surplus (d) superfluous

115. RETREAT
(a) advance (b) recede
(c) entice (d) caputre

116. AUTONOMY
(a) submissiveness (b) dependence
(c) subordination (d) slavery

117. SHALLOW
(a) high (b) hidden
(c) deep (d) hollow

118. OVERT
(a) deep (b) shallow
(c) secret (d) unwritten

119. SYNTHETIC
(a) cosmetic (b) plastic
(c) affable (d) natural

120. PRECARIOUS
(a) dangerous (b) safe
(c) cautious (d) easy

121. DEEP
(a) elementary (b) superficial
(c) shallow (d) perfunctory

122. LEND
(a) hire (b) pawn
(c) cheat (d) borrow

123. PAUCITY
(a) surplus (b) scarcity
(c) presence (d) richness
(e) want

124. MINOR
(a) heavy (b) tall
(c) major (d) big

125. APPROPRIATE
(a) unskilled (b) unsuitable
(c) unqualified (d) unable

126. OPAQUE
(a) misty (b) covered
(c) clear (d) transparent

127. RUTHLESS
(a) mindful (b) compassionate
(c) majestice (d) merciful

128. VIOLENT
(a) tame (b) humble
(c) gentle (d) harmless

129. DEARTH
(a) extravagance (b) scarcity
(c) abundance (d) sufficiency

130. TRANSPARENT
(a) coloured (b) childlike
(c) opaque (d) imminent

131. EXHIBIT
(a) conceal (b) prevent
(c) withdraw (d) concede

132. HAUGHTY
(a) pitiable (b) scared
(c) humble (d) cowardly

133. VIRTUE
(a) vice (b) fraud
(c) wickedness (d) crime

134. ACQUITTED
(a) entrusted (b) convicted
(c) burdened (d) freed

135. LACONIC
(a) prolix (b) profligate
(c) prolifie (d) bucolic

136. ABSOLUTE
(a) scarce (b) limited
(c) prolific (d) bucolic

137. MAGNIFY
(a) induce (b) diminish
(c) destroy (d) shrink

138. BOOST
(a) hinder (b) obstruct
(c) discourage (d) rebuke

139. SMOOTH
(a) ugly (b) awkward
(c) hard (d) rough

140. BASE
(a) roof (b) height
(c) top (d) climax

141. MOIST
(a) parched (b) dry
(c) hard (d) crisp

142. DEMON
(a) charitable (b) kind-hearted
(c) angel (d) fair-minded

143. DELETE
(a) impound (b) insert
(c) inspire (d) injure

144. ONEROUS
(a) straight-forward (b) easy
(c) complex (d) plain

145. BRIDGE
(a) divide (b) bind
(c) release (d) open

146. ATTRACT
(a) repulse (b) reject
(c) repel (d) distract

147. GRATUITY
(a) annuity (b) stipend
(c) discount (d) wages

148. KNOWLEDGE
(a) ignorance (b) illiteracy
(c) foolishness (d) backwardness

149. NADIR
(a) progress (b) liberty
(c) zenith (d) modernity

150. FOREIGNER
(a) national (b) stranger
(c) native (d) alien

151. LANGUID
(a) smart (b) energetic
(c) fast (d) ferocious

152. STRINGENT
(a) magnanimous (b) lenient
(c) vehement (d) general

153. ALIENATE
(a) gather (b) identify
(c) assemble (d) unite

154. MALICIOUS
(a) boastful (b) indifferent
(c) kind (d) generous

155. SPURIOUS
(a) false (b) genuine
(c) simple (d) systematic

156. LISSOME
(a) ungainly (b) huge
(c) pungent (d) crude

157. HINDRANCE
(a) agreement (b) cooperation
(c) persuasion (d) aid

158. JEER
(a) mourn (b) praise
(c) mock (d) sneer

159. PROHIBIT
(a) accept (b) permit
(c) agree (d) grant

160. ROUGHLY
(a) exactly (b) completely
(c) pointedly (d) largely

161. MISERLY
(a) generous (b) liberal
(c) spend thrift (d) charitable

162. DENSITY
(a) brightness (b) clarity
(c) intelligence (d) rarity

163. CONTENTED
(a) rash (b) narrow-minded
(c) gloomy (d) disappointed

164. CONCEAL
(a) unfold (b) reveal
(c) open (d) discover

165. SELDOM
(a) rarely (b) laily
(c) often (d) never

166. PERTINENT
(a) indifferent (b) detached
(c) determined (d) irrelevant

167. AMICABLE
(a) cunning (b) shy
(c) hostile (d) crazy

168. CLARITY
(a) exaggeration (b) candour
(c) confusion (d) reserve

169. SUPERFICIAL
(a) artificial (b) deep
(c) shallow (d) real

170. COMMEND
(a) suspend (b) admonish
(c) hate (d) dislike

171. DAUNTLESS
(a) cautious (b) thoughtful
(c) weak (d) adventurous

172. EXODUS
(a) restoration (b) return
(c) home-coming (d) influx

173. INNOCENT
(a) sinful (b) guilty
(c) deadly (d) corruption

174. DEAR
(a) cheap (b) worthless
(c) free (d) priceless

175. APPOSITE
(a) inappropriate (b) intemperate
(c) inconsistent (d) irregular

176. JETTISON
(a) rejoice (b) surrender
(c) accept (d) defend

177. SCOLD
(a) enamour (b) rebuke
(c) criticise (d) praise

178. PODGY
(a) short (b) thin
(c) weak (d) slim

179. VIRTUOUS
(a) scandalous (b) vicious
(c) wicked (d) corrupt

180. GRIM
(a) serious (b) satisfying
(c) delightful (d) painful

181. DEPLETE
(a) refund (b) replenish
(c) fulfil (d) recover

182. CONSPICUOUS
(a) indifferent (b) harmless
(c) insignificant (d) unknown

183. CONFESS
(a) deny (b) refuse
(c) contest (d) contend

184. HOARD
(a) deposit
(b) supply
(c) satisfy
(d) accumulate

185. PROVOCATION
(a) destruction (b) peace
(c) pacification (d) vocation

186. FACT
(a) fable (b) story
(c) illusion (d) fiction

187. NATIVE
(a) alien (b) foreigner
(c) newcomer (d) stranger

188. MODICUM
(a) simplicity (b) a large amount
(c) brazenness (d) immodestry

189. MASK
(a) deface (b) injure
(c) expose (d) hit

190. FICKLE
(a) diseased (b) fast
(c) constant (d) quick

191. CHOICE
(a) refusal (b) dilemma
(c) harm (d) approval

192. DAINTY
(a) splendid (b) aggressive
(c) vigorous (d) towering

193. NIMBLE
(a) giant (b) clumsy
(c) quick (d) frank

194. RESERVED
(a) likeable (b) talkative
(c) popular (d) companionable

Homophones and Homonyms

20

Homophone

A homophone is a word that sounds the same but is different in meaning. Phonetically, these words are alike but their meanings and spellings are completely different. The best method to learn homophones is to read books and to have a dictionary and thesaurus at hand and to flip through them from time to time.

Example: Peace: We all hope for world *peace*.

Piece: May I have a *piece* of cake?

What one should be careful of when using homophones:

Some of the most commonly used homophones create the most common grammatical mistakes in the English language. Homophones are a little confusing at first, but learning how to properly use homophones will help you to:

- Avoid making common English grammatical mistakes
- Have confidence in your English
- Improve your overall understanding of the English language.

These are a few common homophones which are generally confused.

Example: Their, there, they're

Two, to, too

As they are used so often and day to day that many people tend to confuse them but continuous practice and hard-work would help eliminate these problems.

Homonym

Homonyms are the words that may be spelt the same and may even be phonetically similar but have different meanings. Homophones fall under the category of homonyms; this means that all homophones could be homonyms but no homonym can be a homophone because of the difference in spelling.

Example: The *clear* water helped him *clear* his eyes of dust.

Difference between Homonym and Homophone

There is a fundamental difference between a homophone and a homonym.

Example:

Homonym	Homophone
Multiple meaning words	*Words that sound alike*
the *spruce* tree... to *spruce* up... (to make clean and neat	*addition* for math *edition* of a book
suit yourself... wore *a suit*...	I want *to* go I like it *too* One plus one is *two*
weigh on the *scale*... *scale* the wall...	*capital* building state *capital*
the price is *fair*... go to the *fair*...	Pick a *flower* Bake with *flour*

Practice Exercise

I. Choose the correct homophone from the options to fill in the blanks.

1. There was a _______ of buffaloes in the field.
   (a) Herd (b) Heard
2. A _________ saved the people of the village from a monster.
   (a) Night (b) Knight
3. The_______ of the ship was broken, they had no hope of surviving without it at sea.
   (a) Massed (b) Mast
4. The students _________ the courage up to ask the teacher for a free period.
   (a) Mustard (b) Mustered
5. The man's voice grew _______ as he directed everyone away from the fire.
   (a) Hoarse (b) Horse
6. The weak are always _______ on by the strong.
   (a) Preyed (b) Prayed
7. The ______ of the nobleman died for want of food.
   (a) Serf (b) Surf
8. The court ______ the husband's right over the building the couple had owned together.
   (a) Waived (b) Waved
9. They were dealing with _____ issues concerning life and death.
   (a) Dual (b) Duel
10. An _____ passes by quicker than one thinks.
    (a) Our (b) Hour

II. Fill in the blanks with the correct option/ homophone.

1. I didn't ____ what she said.
   (a) hear (b) here
2. They forgot to take ____ printouts.
   (a) there (b) their
   (c) they're (d) none of these
3. Venison is the meat from a ____.
   (a) dear (b) deer
4. The house is by the ____.
   (a) see (b) sea
5. She held the ____ in her hand.
   (a) reigns (b) rains
   (c) reins (d) none of these
6. They tried to ____ the painting.
   (a) steel (b) steal
7. He had to ____ the button on.
   (a) sow (b) sew
8. I hope the ____ is fine.
   (a) weather (b) whether
9. He was a medieval ____.
   (a) night (b) knight
10. The building ____ is huge.
    (a) site (b) sight
11. She's as mad as a March ____.
    (a) hair (b) hare
12. She gave him a ____ of her mind.
    (a) peace (b) piece
13. He ____ a snowball at the police officer.
    (a) threw (b) through
14. It's a ____ of time.
    (a) waist (b) waste
15. They didn't ____ us of the danger.
    (a) warn (b) worn
16. They read the poems ____.
    (a) allowed (b) aloud
17. It's made from wheat ____.
    (a) flower (b) flour
18. They've got a ____ at the Ritz.
    (a) suit (b) suite
    (c) sweet (d) none of these
19. On the ____, I enjoyed it.
    (a) whole (b) hole
20. It's not much ____ to go.
    (a) father (b) farther
21. You're no ____ of mine!
    (a) sun (b) son
22. He's the ____ to the throne.
    (a) air (b) heir
23. The tea's a bit ____.
    (a) weak (b) week

24. She's the _____ owner.
(a) soul (b) sole
25. The book is _____ back at the library in two weeks.
(a) dew (b) due
26. You slow a car with the _____.
(a) brake (b) break
27. The negative feeling you get when you do something wrong is _____.
(a) gilt (b) guilt
28. The cyclist was ______ very fast.
(a) peddling
(b) pedalling/pedaling
29. It was _____ madness.
(a) sheer (b) shear
30. The eagle is a bird of _____.
(a) prey (b) pray
31. Could you _____ the film for a minute?
(a) paws (b) pause
32. After standing for an hour in the heat, he _____.
(a) feinted (b) fainted
33. Don't tell them anything- they're not very _____.
(a) discrete (b) discreet
34. He's very old-fashioned and _____.
(a) stayed (b) staid
35. Floating _____ are used to help boats navigate.
(a) boys (b) buoys
(c) bouys (d) none of these
36. He's very _____ and worries about his appearance all the time.
(a) vein
(b) vane
(c) vain
(d) none of these
37 They took blood from my _____.
(a) vane (b) vein
(c) vain (d) none of these
38. I am an innocent ____ in all of this.
(a) pawn (b) porn
39 That's a _____ tree.
(a) beach (b) beech
40. We have to make sure the timing's right- we must be in _____.
(a) sink (b) sync

III. Fill in the blanks with the correct option/ homonym.

1. The burning candle created a pleasant _____ in the room.
(a) sent (b) cent
(c) scent (d) none of these
2. We're going to Prague in the spring. Can you recommend some interesting _____?
(a) sites (b) sights
(c) cites (d) none of these
3. If we're taking the subway, I'll need to borrow some money for the _____.
(a) faire (b) fare
(c) fair (d) none of these
4. Jimmy wants to be president one day. In fact, Bill Clinton is his _____.
(a) idyll (b) idle
(c) idol (d) none of these
5. Congratulations! I heard you won a gold _____ in the swimming competition.
(a) meddle (b) medal
(c) metal (d) none of these
6. Please don't _____ in my business. If I need your advice, I'll ask for it!
(a) medal (b) metal
(c) meddle (d) none of these
7. Would you like a piece of fruit? Perhaps a _____?
(a) pear (b) pair
(c) pare (d) none of these
8. Henry VIII's _____ lasted for 38 years.
(a) rain (b) reign
(c) rein (d) none of these
9. They're going to ____ several houses to clear the land for a shopping mall.
(a) raise
(b) raze
(c) rays
(d) none of these

10. Wow! You made that jacket yourself? I didn't even know you could ____.
(a) sew (b) so
(c) sow (d) none of these

11. I'll need your help in making the lasagna. Would you please ____ the cheese?
(a) grate (b) great

12. Mike was sent to the _____ office for misbehaving.
(a) principal's (b) principle's

13. What kind of fish would you like – salmon or ____?
(a) soul (b) sole

14. They sell beautiful _____ from Italy at the Metropolitan Museum gift shop.
(a) stationary (b) stationery

15. Jennifer played the ____ of Elizabeth Bennet in her school production of Pride and Prejudice.
(a) roll (b) role

16 After speaking for three hours at the conference, Joe was feeling a little _______.
(a) hoarse (b) horse

17. Mary didn't win a medal. She came in _____.
(a) fourth (b) forth

18. The Panama Canal is a stunning ____ of engineering.
(a) feet (b) feat

19. This interesting new study looks at the ____ of a positive attitude on health.
(a) affects (b) effects

20. Student _____ meetings are held every Friday afternoon.
(a) council (b) counsel

21. She worked at two part time jobs to pay off her student ___.
(a) loan (b) lone

22. The businessman ___ his flight so he had to call his office.
(a) missed (b) mist

23. It is important to ___ your children when they do good work.
(a) praise (b) prays
(c) preys (d) none of these

24. Clothes that are in ___ are not always suitable to my taste.
(a) stile (b) style

25. The pulmonary ___ carries blood from the heart to the lungs.
(a) vain (b) vane
(c) vein (d) none of these

26. She bought twelve, consumed ___ and had four donuts leftover.
(a) ate (b) eight

27. Cotton, straw and hay can be stored in a bundle called a ___.
(a) bail (b) bale

28. Trans-Pacific flights usually carry two different flight ___.
(a) crews (b) cruise

29. Chuck heard his team mates ___ when his shot missed the goal.
(a) groan (b) grown

30. She may not be very pretty but she is not exactly ___ either.
(a) plain (b) plane

31. Make a ___ turn at the next corner and drive two more blocks.
(a) right (b) rite

32. If you are tired, just think about climbing one __ at a time.
(a) stair (b) stare

33. The doctor worked to save her life but the effort was in ___.
(a) vain (b) vane
(c) vein (d) none of these

34. The television news program reported on all of the ___ issues.
(a) currant (b) current

35. Set another ___ at the table because we are expecting a guest.
(a) place (b) plaice

36. I can not think of anything that you can buy for only one ___.
(a) scent (b) sent
(c) cent (d) none of these

37. My mother lost her ___ because of the disease called glaucoma.
    (a) sight (b) site
    (c) cite (d) none of these

38 It is not unusual to see a wild ___ in the hills near my house.
    (a) boar (b) bore
    (c) boor (d) none of these

39. He kissed her good ___ at the airport as she left for her trip.
    (a) buy (b) by
    (c) bye (d) none of these

40. To remove the seeds from an apple one needs to cut out the ___.
    (a) core (b) corps

Spelling

21

Spelling is the writing of a word or words with the correct letters Diacritics present in an accepted standard order, "the conventions which determine how the graphemes of a writing system are used to write a language." It is one of the elements of orthography and a prescriptive element of language.

Rules of Spelling

☞ **Words ending in -ise and –ize:** Many English words can be spelt with either –ise and –ize. In American English, the spelling with –ize is preferred. In British English, both forms are usually acceptable.

Example:

British Spelling	American Spelling
Baptise/baptize	Baptize
Realize/realise	Realize
Computerize/ computerise	Computerize

Some words have: 'ise' in both British and American English.

Example: *Surprise, revise, advise, comprise, despise.*

☞ **Adverb formation:** We normally change an adjective into an adverb by adding –ly.

Example: Real – Really

Definite – Definitely

Right – Rightly

There are some exceptions to this rule: True – Truly (NOT Truely)Due – Duly

☞ **Changing Y into i:** y usually changes to i.

Example: Happy – Happily

Easy – easily

Exceptions are: Shy – Shyly, Sly – Slyly

☞ **Changing the adjectival words that ends with letters '*le*' to '*ly*':** *le* changes to *ly* after a consonant.

Example: Idle – Idly

☞ **Changing adjectival words that ends with letters '*ic*' into '*ically*':** If an adjective ends in '*ic*', the adverb ends in – *ically.*

Example: Tragic – Tragically

Phonetic – Phonetically

Note: That public is an exception to this rule. Public – Publicly

When the word ends in a consonant: If the accent falls on the last syllable, the consonant is doubled to form the past tense.

Example: Occur → occurred, Transfer → transferred.

☞ When the word ends in a short vowel + consonant, the final consonant is not usually doubled to form the past tense.

Example: Offer → offered (NOT Offerred).

Short monosyllabic words always double their final consonant.

Example: Let → letting, Bat → batting.

☞ ***'ie'* and *'ei'*:** The general rule is that 'i' is used before 'e' except after 'c'.

Example: Believe, friends.

But *receive, deceive, ceiling* (after 'c', we use 'e' before 'i'*)*.

Exceptions:

Example: *Reign, seize.* As you can see, in all of these words, the letter '*e*' goes before the letter '*i*'.

☞ ***Dis* and *mis*:** Never double the 's' of these prefixes. In some words, you may notice a second 's', but remember that it is the first letter of the next syllable.

Example: *Dismiss (NOT* Dissmiss*),* Misspell, Misunderstand, Dispel.

☞ ***Se* and *Ce*:** *Se and sy* are usually verb endings and *ce* and *cy* are usually noun endings.

So, the following words are verbs: license, practise, advise, prophesy.

And the following words are nouns: licence, practice, prophecy, advice.

Exception: The word *promise* is an exception to this rule. Although it ends in *se*, it is a noun. Note that this rule does not hold good when verb and noun are not spelt alike.

☞ ***Us*** and ***ous***: Nouns end in 'us'. Adjectives end in 'ous'. So we have:

Nouns: phosphorus, genius

Adjectives: jealous, tremendous

☞ **If a word ends in *f* or *fe*, sometimes add *s* to make it plural:** roof, roofs

OR

Sometimes change *f* or *fe* to *ves*: half-halves, wife-wives

OR

Sometimes add either: scarf scarfs, scarves

☞ For a single syllabic word, ending in a single consonant preceded by a single vowel – double the consonant letter:

Example: Swim-swimmer, swimming

☞ For a single syllable word, ending in a single consonant preceded by two vowels – do not double the consonant:

Example: Meet-meeting

☞ The following prefixes give negative meaning to the original word:

Example: Unhappy; invisible; illegal; impolite; irregular

☞ The sound of "*shun*" has several different spellings:

Example: Solution, occasion, mission, musician, Dalmatian, crucifixion

☞ Keep the final 'e' if a suffix begins with a consonant:

Example: Care + full = careful, complete + ly = completely, excite + ment = excitement

☞ To make past tense of a verb, add 'ed' in the end of the word unless it is an irregular verb.

Example: Talk - Talked

Ask - Asked

I'm feeling *homesick.*

Practice Exercise

I. Choose the correct spelling.

1. (a) buy (b) buye (c) boy (d) none of these
2. (a) money (b) mony (a) maney (d) none of these
3. (a) schoul (b) school (c) schaul (d) none of these
4. (a) about (b) abowt (c) aboat (d) none of these
5. (a) rane (b) rain (c) rene (d) none of these
6. (a) right (b) righte (c) reght (d) none of these
7. (a) houer (b) hour (c) hoar (d) none of these
8. (a) doctor (b) docter (c) doctar (d) none of these
9. (a) deep (b) diep (c) daep (d) none of these
10. (a) nonne (b) none (c) noene (d) none of these
11. (a) dependant (b) dependent (c) depandent (d) none of these
12. (a) biased (b) biassed (c) biesed (d) none of these
13. (a) cafateria (b) cafeteria (c) cefatria (d) none of these
14. (a) autumn (b) autunm (c) autamn (d) none of these
15. (a) embarrass (b) embarass (c) embaress (d) none of these
16. (a) enviroment (b) environment (c) envirament (d) none of these
17. (a) censor (b) censer (c) cansor (d) none of these
18. (a) labratory (b) laboratory (c) lebratory (d) none of these
19. (a) skying (b) skiing (c) skyeng (d) none of these
20. (a) controlled (b) controled (c) contalled (d) none of these

II. Find the correctly spelt word from the given options.

1. (a) Treachrous (b) Trecherous (c) Trechearous (d) Treacherous
2. (a) Forcast (b) Forecaste (c) Forcaust (d) Forecast
3. (a) Rigerous (b) Rigourous (c) Regerous (d) Rigorous
4. (a) Palete (b) Palet (c) Palate (d) Pelate
5. (a) Bouquete (b) Bouquette (c) Bouquet (d) Boqquet
6. (a) Itinarery (b) Itinerary (c) Itenary (d) Itinarary
7. (a) Survaillance (b) Surveillance (c) Survellance (d) Surveilance
8. (a) Sepulchral (b) Sepilchrle (c) Sepalchrul (d) Sepalchrl
9. (a) Acommodation (b) Accomodaton (c) Accommodation (d) Acomodation
10. (a) Faithfuly (b) Sincerely (c) Truely (d) Affectionatly
11. (a) Friming (b) Burnning (c) Running (d) Fryng
12. (a) Dammage (b) Damaige (c) Dammege (d) Damage
13. (a) Accomplish (b) Acomplush (c) Ackmplesh (d) Accompalish
14. (a) Puerrile (b) Puerrille (c) Purrile (d) Puerile
15. (a) Satelite (b) Sattelite (c) Satellite (d) Sattellite
16. (a) Exaggerate (b) Exeggrate (c) Exagerate (d) Exadgerate
17. (a) Asspersion (b) Voluptuous (c) Voguei (d) Equestrain
18. (a) Hindrance (b) Hinderrance (c) Hindrence (d) Hinderence

19. (a) Parallelled (b) Parralleled
    (c) Paralleled (d) Paraleled

20. (a) Lckadaisicle (b) Lackdaisical
    (c) Lackadisical (d) Lackadaisical

21. (a) Eflorescence (b) Efllorescence
    (c) Efflorescence (d) Efflorascence

22. (a) Exterminatte (b) Inexpliccable
    (c) Offspring (d) Reffere

23. (a) Occasion (b) Occassion
    (c) Ocasion (d) Ocassion

24. (a) Entrepreneur (b) Entrapreneur
    (c) Entrepraneur (d) Enterprenuer

Analogy

22

An analogy is used for drawing comparison in order to show a similarity in some respect between the two chosen subjects/things. When you compare two things for the purpose of explanation, you draw an analogy between them.

Example: Happy–Joyful

Strong–Frail

Types of Analogy Relationship

Synonyms

Synonyms are the words that have the same or nearly the same meaning as another word. In this type of analogy, the candidate is required to find out words that are parallel in meaning.

Example: Love – Affection

Antonyms

Some analogies are based on antonyms the words that have opposite meanings. In this type of analogy, one word in each pair means the opposite of another.

Example: Love – Hate

Part to Whole

This type of analogy expresses a part to whole or part of relationship. The first word will be a part of the second word or vice versa.

Example: Galaxy : Universe.

In this pair, galaxy is a part of the whole universe.

Category/Type

In this type of analogy relationship, one word is the element/member of a group that the other word describes.

Example: Student – Class

Object to Function

This type of analogy tests whether a candidate can determine the function of a specific thing or tool. The first word will be a part of the second word or vice versa.

Example: Shovel – Dig (the function of a shovel is to dig.)

Note: Make sure the function word (certainly a verb) is the primary function of the object (noun) that makes up the other word of the pair.

Performer to Related Action

This kind of analogy usually links a person or object with the action they commonly perform. For example, doctor: diagnose. Here, the doctor's job/profession is to diagnose a patient and give treatment.

Cause and Effect

In this type of analogy, one word in the pair describes a condition or action while the other word describes an outcome or effect to that action or condition.

Example: Light – Illuminate

Degree of Intensity

In this type of analogy relationship, the words in each pair have similar meanings, but one word is stronger, more intense, than the other.

Example: Fanatic – Enthusiastic (being fanatic is an extreme range of being enthusiastic. Though both words are similar in meaning, one word is more intense than the other one.)

The relationship between these two words depends on the degree of intensity of their meaning.

Symbol and Representation

This type of relationship represents or symbolizes the other word.

Example: Lion – Bravery

Analogy Table

The following table shows various types of analogy and their relationship between two objects.

S. No.	Type of Analogy	Relationship	Example
1	Synonym	is similar in meaning to	lucky : fortunate
2	Antonym	is opposite in meaning to	lament : rejoice
3	Part to Whole	is a part of	stanza : poem
4	Category/Type	is a type/kind of	college : art
5	Object to Function	is used to	ruler : measure
6	Performer to Related Action	does/performs	chef : cook
7	Cause and Effect	is a cause or indication of	tornado : destruction
8	Degree of Intensity	is a small or large	irritate : enrage
9	Symbol and Representation	is a symbol of	dove : peace

Practice Exercise

I. Choose the correct option to draw analogy.

1. Paw : Cat :: Hoof : ?
   (a) Lamb (b) Elephant
   (c) Horse (d) None of these
2. Peacock : India :: Bear : ?
   (a) Australia (b) America
   (c) Russia (d) None of these
3. Flow : River :: Stagnant : ?
   (a) Rain (b) Stream
   (c) Pool (d) None of these
4. NATION : ANTINO :: HUNGRY : ?
   (a) HNUGRY
   (b) UHNGYR
   (c) YRNGUH
   (d) None of these
5. Architect : Building :: Sculptor : ?
   (a) Museum
   (b) Stone
   (c) Statue
   (d) None of these
6. Microphone : Loud :: Microscope : ?
   (a) Elongate
   (b) Investigate
   (c) Examine
   (d) None of these
7. Country : President :: State : ?
   (a) Governor (b) M.P
   (c) Legislator (d) None of these
8. Tree : Forest :: Grass : ?
   (a) Road (b) pool
   (c) Park (d) None of these
9. Peace : Chaos :: Creation : ?
   (a) Build
   (b) Construction
   (c) Destruction
   (d) None of these
10. Race : Fatigue :: Fast : ?
    (a) Food (b) Laziness
    (c) Hunger (d) None of these

II. Find out the correct option to establish the relationship as shown in the given expression.

1. 'Dress' is related to 'Body' in the same way as 'Bangles' is related to:
   (a) Glass (b) Lady
   (c) Wrist (d) Beauty
2. Flower' is related to 'Bud' in the same way as 'Fruit' is related to:
   (a) Seed (b) Tree
   (c) Flower (d) Stem
3. 'Jackal' is related to 'Howl' in the same way as 'Cow' is related to:
   (a) Caws (b) Hoot
   (c) Coo (d) Moo
4. 'Smoke' is related to 'Pollution' in the same way as 'War' is related to:
   (a) Victory (b) Treaty
   (c) Defeat (d) Destruction
5. 'Rabbit' is related to 'Burrow' in the same way as 'Lunatic' is related to:
   (a) Prison (b). Cell
   (c) Barrack (d) Asylum

III. See the given analogy and state whether it is True or False.

1. Effect/cause
   Sharp : Blunt :: Sweet : Sour
   (True, False)
2. Antonyms
   Sharp : Blunt :: Sweet : Sour
   (True, False)
3. Action/subject performing action
   Kick : Ball :: Texting : Cell phone
   (True, False)
4. Whole / part
   Fire : Heat :: Study : Good grades
   (True, False)
5. Synonyms
   Strong : Sturdy :: Dry : Wet
   (True, False)

◆◆◆

One Word

23

This chapter deals with the words (One Word) that can be used in place of several words or words which have a more compact meaning than the ones used normally.

Example: The word *'flora'* means all kinds of plants of a particular area or a particular era. Even simple everyday words like *school, court* are examples of such words. The word 'school' reduces the need to say what a school does and is convenient instead of having to say – an institution where children get their education, people can just say school. People's roles at such a place are also easily understood by such words.

Example: The word *teacher* and *student* clearly describes the roles each play at a school. This is what one word substitution means. It could be used to speak of a type of job, a place, a person, any number of things.

A good way to learn such words is to read lots of books. Another way is to use a dictionary and pick a new word a day to learn. Both methods are effective in increasing one's vocabulary.

Practice Exercise

Choose the correct option for the given group of words/phrases:

1. A person who has prejudiced views.
   (a) Bigot (b) Bold
   (c) Brave (d) None of these
2. Something which leads or ends with death.
   (a) Fatal (b) fated
   (c) Fat (d) None of these
3. Only eats plants- normally used for animals
   (a) Omnivorous (b) Carnivorous
   (c) Herbivorous (d) None of these
4. Anything to do with the moon
   (a) Lunatic (b) Lunar
   (c) Moon (d) None of these
5. A person of a different nationality settling down in a new country.
   (a) Immigrant (b) Imminent
   (c) Eminent (d) None of these
6. All kinds of animals living in a particular place
   (a) Plants (b) Fauna
   (c) Flora (d) None of these
7. A follower of a leader–political or religious
   (a) Discipline
   (b) Disciple
   (c) Follower
   (d) None of these
8. A person who is qualified for a post or college or scholarship
   (a) Eligible (b) Illegal
   (c) Able (d) None of these
9. A school for little children or a room in the house for a newborn.
   (a) Primary (b) Secondary
   (c) Nursery (d) None of these
10. Almost see through
    (a) Transparent (b) Opaque
    (c) Clear (d) None of these
11. A house where parentless children are brought up.
    (a) Orphan (b) Orphanage
    (c) School (d) None of these
12. A professional rider in horse races
    (a) Jockey (b) Horse Rider
    (c) Jacky (d) None of these
13. A group of judges
    (a) Jerry (b) Jury
    (c) Judicial (d) None of these
14. A person who can use both right and left hand
    (a) Ambidextrous (b) Amber
    (c) Amorous (d) None of these
15. Dry weather with no rainfall
    (a) Dry (b) Heat
    (c) Drought (d) None of these
16. A person who finds criminals
    (a) Judge (b) Detective/police
    (c) Advocate (d) None of these
17. A brief or short stay in a place
    (a) Sojourn (b) Rest
    (c) Remaining (d) None of these
18. A man whose wife is dead.
    (a) Widower (b) Follower
    (c) Singletan (d) None of these
19. A place where all sorts of animals are kept
    (a) Zoo (b) Farm
    (c) Filed (d) None of these
20. An experienced person
    (a) Veteran (b) old
    (c) grand (d) None of these

Idioms

24

An idiom is a phrase in common use that has a figurative meaning, and sometimes a literal meaning.

An idiom's figurative meaning is separate from the literal meaning.

Example: Flesh and Blood

Meaning: The living material of which people are made of, or it refers to someone's family.

Example: Actions speak louder than words.

Meaning: It's better to actually do something than just talk about it.

Sometimes, the figurative meaning is set in a culture. And the meaning is derived in context of that particular culture. While similar idioms may exist in other languages and culture, the particular cultural references will change and may not be recognizable to everyone.

Example: Enough to cobble dogs with.

Explanation: This incredible phrase is used to refer to a surplus of anything. The humor in the image contained in the phrase becomes apparent when you consider that a cobbler repairs shoes. If a cobbler has enough leather to cobble an animal that has four feet, then that cobbler definitely has a surplus.

Example: We've got enough beer in this party to cobble dogs with.

Idioms with Their Meaning

1. Acid Test

   Meaning: Acid test proves the effectiveness of something.
2. Cut the ground from under feet

   Meaning: When you cut the ground from under someone's feet, you do something which weakens their position.
3. Chase your tail

   Meaning: Spending a lot of time and energy doing a lot of things but actually achieving too little.
4. Whole bag of tricks

   Meaning: Means trying all the clever means to achieve something.
5. Deliver the goods

   Meaning: Do what is expected or promised.
6. Fine-tooth comb

   Meaning: Examining something carefully to not miss out any details.
7. Explore all avenues

   Meaning: Trying out every possibility to get a result.
8. Fast track something

   Meaning: Rating something higher on your priority list to achieve the desired result.
9. Get ducks in a row

   Meaning: Getting your things well organized.
10. Get the show on the road

    Meaning: Putting up a plan or idea into action.
11. Keep your fingers on the pulse

    Meaning: Being constantly aware of the most recent developments.
12. Mean business

    Meaning: Being serious about what you announce.
13. Think on your feet

    Meaning: Adjusting quickly to changes and making fast decisions.
14. Sail through something

    Meaning: Being successful in doing something without difficulty.
15. Tricks of the trade

    Meaning: Clever or expert way of doing something.
16. Not let grass grow under feet

    Meaning: Don't delay in getting something done.

17. Work like a charm

    Meaning: Works very well or has the desired effect.

18. Back-room boys

    Meaning: People who perform important work but have no contact with the public.

19. Dead wood

    Meaning: People or things which are no longer useful or necessary.

20. Get the axe

    Meaning: lose the job.

21. Plum job

    Meaning: Desirable position which is well-paid and considered relatively easy .

22. Shape up or ship out

    Meaning: This expression is used to warn someone that if they do not improvetheir ways, they will have to leave their job.

23. Golden handshake

    Meaning: Big sum of money given to a person when they leave a company or retire.

24. Separate sheep from goats

    Meaning: Examining a group of people and deciding their suitability.

25. Waiting in the wings

    Meaning: Waiting for an opportunity to take action, mostly to replace someone else in their job.

26. Eat, sleep and breathe something:

    Meaning: Being so enthusiastic and passionate about somehting that you think about it all the time.

27. With bells on

    Meaning: When you are delighted and eager to go somewhere, you are said to go with bells on.

28. Fever pitch

    Meaning: When a feeling is very intense and exciting, it is said to be at a fever pitch.

29. Blood, sweat and tears

    Meaning: Something that requires a lot of effort and hard work.

30. Have on the brain

    Meaning: Thinking or talking about it all day long.

31. Fling yourself into

    Meaning: Doing something with a lot of energy and enthusiasm.

32. Raring to go

    Meaning: Being very eager and enthusiastic about the idea of doing something.

33. Xerox subsidy

    Meaning: Using the office photocopier for personal use.

34. Get a grip on yourself

    Meaning: Controlling your feelings to deal with a situation.

35. Hang on by fingernails

    Meaning: Continuing to do something in a very difficult situation.

36. Pull out all the stops

    Meaning: Doing everything you can to make something successful.

37. Buckle down

    Meaning: Doing some hard work with determination and full attention.

38. First out of the gate

    Meaning: Being the first one to make a start at something.

39. Going places

    Meaning: Exhibiting talent and ability that will lead to a successful future.

40. Have one's heart set on

    Meaning: Possessing a determination to obtain something.

41. Make headway

    Meaning: Progress in what you are trying to achieve.

42. Punch above one's weight

    Meaning: Performing beyond your ability.

43. Sink your teeth into

    Meaning: doing something with a lot of energy and enthusiasm.

44. Stand one's ground

    Meaning: Maintaining your position.

45. Close to home

    Meaning: A comment which is true and makes you uncomfortable is close to home.

46. Carry the torch for

    Meaning: Having strong feelings for someone who can not be yours.

47. Cork up something

    Meaning: Failing to express your emotions.

48. Cut to the quick

    Meaning: Hurting someone deeply or offending them.

49. Fish out of water

    Meaning: Feeling uncomfortable in unfamiliar surroundings.

50. Bee in one's bonnet

    Meaning: Carrying an idea which constantly occupies your thoughts.

51. Deep down

    Meaning: Describing what a person really feels deep inside or what is he like.

52. Have your heart in the right place

    Meaning: Refers to a person with good intentions; even though the results are not that impressive.

53. Groan inwardly

    Meaning: Refers to a feeling where you want to express despair, disapproval or distress, but you keep quite.

54. Beard the lion in his den

    Meaning: Challenge someone in his own area.

55. Keep a stiff upper lip

    Meaning: Refers to a person who doesn't show off his emotions.

56. Go bananas

    Meaning: Refers to someone who behaves in a crazy way out of emotions.

57. Lump in your throat

    Meaning: Refers to a tight feeling in your throat because of an emotion like sadness or gratitude.

58. Hard as nails

    Meaning: Refers to a person without sentiments and sympathy for anyone.

59. Lick one's wounds

    Meaning: Trying to regain their confidence or boost up the spirits after a defeat.

60. Proud as a peacock

    Meaning: Refers to an extremely proud person.

61. Tongue-tied

    Meaning: Difficulty in expressing yourself because of nervousness or embarrassment.

62. Look on the bright side

    Meaning: View an unpleasant situation in a positive light.

63. Swallow one's pride

    Meaning: Accepting something humiliating or embarrassing.

64. Makes your flesh crawl

    Meaning: Something that makes you feel disgusting or nervous.

65. Speak volumes

    Meaning: Expresses a reaction without words.

66. Not turn a hair

    Meaning: Refers to not exhibiting any emotion where it is expected.

67. Reduce to tears

    Meaning: Getting into tears because of some one's behavior.

68. In the bag

    Meaning: Refers to a situation when you are sure that success is sure.

69. Blow up in face

    Meaning: Refers to a situation when a plan or project suddenly fails.

70. Bottom fell out

    Meaning: Refers to a situation when a plan or project fails.

71. Cake not worth the candle

    Meaning: Refers to something in which result vs efforts are too less.

72. Chance one's arm

    Meaning: Deciding to do something even though the chances of sucess are very little.

73. Come up roses

    Meaning: Successful end results even though there may be some initial hiccups.

74. Cook someone's goose

Meaning: Spoil other person's chances of success.

75. Cut one's own throat

Meaning: Doing something that will cause your own failure.

76. Foot in the door:

Meaning: Small but good start with a possibility for a bright future.

77. Go great guns

Meaning: Being successful.

78. Dead in the water

Meaning: Plan or project that has ceased to function and is not expected to be re-activated in future.

79. Flying start

Meaning: Something that is immediately successful.

80. Make a go of

Meaning: Succeeding in your enterprise.

81. Go to the dogs

Meaning: Getting comparably less successful than before.

81. Go up in smoke

Meaning: Something that ends before getting a result.

82. Live on the breadline

Meaning: Having very little income.

83. Make or break

Meaning: Circumstances causing total success or total ruin.

84. Landslide victory

Meaning: Overwhelming victory received by a candidate of political party at an election.

85. Let slip through fingers

Meaning: Failing to obtain or keep up a good opportunity.

86. Rags to riches

Meaning: Becoming very rich while starting very poor.

87. On the pig's back

Meaning: Refers to a person in successful and well situation.

88. Miss the boat

Meaning: Failing to take advantage of an opportunity because of slow actions.

89. Smash hit

Meaning: Refers to music, films which are very successful.

90. Murphy's law

Meaning: Means that if anything can go wrong, it will.

91. Place in the sun

Meaning: Finding a place in the sun refers to a position which provides you all the success and happiness you want in your life.

92. Sink or swim

Meaning: fail or succeed.

93. Champagne on a beer budget

Meaning: Wanting expensive things that you can not afford.

94. Top dog

Meaning: Very successful group, company, person, country etc.

95. Keep up appearances

Meaning: Maintaining an outward show of prosperity or well-being while hiding your difficulties

96. Wooden spoon

Meaning: Imaginary prize for the last person in a race.

97. Have the world by its tail

Meaning: Very successful person who can shoose from a lot of opportunities.

98. Live beyond means

Meaning: Spending more money than you can afford.

99. Live in an ivory tower

Meaning: Living a lifestyle that saves you from the real world problems.

100. Hit the road running

Meaning: Start performing immediately.

Practice Exercise

I. Choose the correct option for each of the given idioms.

1. At one's wit's end
   (a) Perplexed (b) Clear up
   (c) Explain (d) Enlighten
2. At one's fingertips
   (a) To take revenge
   (b) Matter of shame
   (c) Complete knowledge
   (d) None of above
3. At the spur of the moment
   (a) Difficult Moment (b) Without Delay
   (c) Great Moment (d) Very Slow
4. All in all
   (a) Every person
   (b) Particular thing same in all
   (c) Call all at once
   (d) Most important
5. At close quarters
   (a) close examinations
   (b) live near to each other
   (c) live far to each other
   (d) in love
6. Apple pie order
   (a) In random order
   (b) Related to fruits packing
   (c) Related to dry fruit packing
   (d) In perfect order
7. Above board
   (a) boasting person
   (b) honest and straightforward
   (c) a man with arrogance
   (d) a dishonest person
8. As fit as a fiddle
   (a) Very weak
   (b) Recovering from illness
   (c) Looks fit but not fit actaully
   (d) None of above
9. At logger heads
   (a) In difficulty (b) to be at strife
   (c) very happy together (d) None of above
10. An apple of discord
    (a) cause of wealth (b) cause of illness
    (c) cause of happiness (d) cause of quarrel
11. At a loss
    (a) at a business loss
    (b) at a relation loss
    (c) to be unable to decide
    (d) none of above
12. At dagger's drawn
    (a) to have bitter enmity
    (b) to be very friendly
    (c) to be unknown
    (d) to be very familiar
13. At large
    (a) very famous (b) not famous
    (c) abscond (d) very far
14. At sea
    (a) baffled (b) very happy
    (c) very excited (d) very sad
15. A bigger bang for your buck
    (a) More for your money
    (b) Not for money
    (c) More for your nature
    (d) More for your smile
16. At sixes and sevens
    (a) in perfect order (b) very happy
    (c) in disorder (d) very sad
17. Argus eyed
    (a) Doubtful (b) Very confident
    (c) Very calm (d) Careful
18. A load of cobblers
    (a) Good news
    (b) Very famous
    (c) Rubbish
    (d) None of above
19. A pig in a poke
    (a) accept deal in a pressure
    (b) accept deal without knowing
    (c) accept deal after detail analysis
    (d) accept deal due to threat

20. At one fell swoop
    (a) After lots of thinking
    (b) In a single action
    (c) By mistake
    (d) Joint action
21. Away with the fairies
    (a) Not facing reality
    (b) On the basis of reality
    (c) Shocking stage
    (d) Very sad
22. Back of beyond
    (a) An ideal place for holidays
    (b) A place with certain memories
    (c) A religious place
    (d) A lonely forsaken place
23. By hook or by crook
    (a) by permission
    (b) by any means
    (c) by noble means
    (d) by request
24. Bandy words
    (a) to argue (b) to request
    (c) to give respect (d) to be polite
25. Break the ice
    (a) To do something with courage
    (b) To win a prize
    (c) To speak first after long silence
    (d) To win some one heart
26. Bad blood
    (a) Wounded in scuffle (b) Bitter relations
    (c) Dishonest (d) Arrogant
27. Black and blue
    (a) To put things in order
    (b) To put things in disorder
    (c) To trust someone
    (d) To beat very badly
28. Brow beat
    (a) to bully (b) to respect
    (c) to praise (d) to rebuke
29. Bid defiance
    (a) to obey (b) to ignore
    (c) to follow (d) none of above
30. Blow one's trumpet
    (a) To praise other
    (b) To praise leader
    (c) To praise ownself
    (d) To praise community
31. Bury the hatchet
    (a) to break peace
    (b) joint operation of killing
    (c) to make peace
    (d) none of above
32. Bring to book
    (a) To punish
    (b) To serve
    (c) To praise
    (d) To write a story
33. Blaze the trail
    (a) To stop a movement
    (b) To join a movement
    (c) To protect a movement
    (d) To start a movement
34. Broken reed
    (a) Continue support
    (b) Support that failed
    (c) Support endlessly
    (d) None of above
35. By dint of
    (a) By force of
    (b) By permission of
    (c) By fear of
    (d) By blessing of
36. Charley horse
    (a) Very rapid (b) Very weak
    (c) Stiffness (d) Boldness
37. Cart before the horse
    (a) To be ready to go
    (b) To be very active
    (c) To do things in reverse order
    (d) To do things in right order
38. Chalk and cheese
    (a) Different from each other
    (b) Having same properties
    (c) Having fun together
    (d) Making plans

39. Cry for the moon
   (a) To wish for something impossible
   (b) To wish for something accessible
   (c) To try to have something by bad means
   (d) None of above

40. Carry the day
   (a) To have great fun
   (b) To do something wrong
   (c) To win a victory
   (d) To loose something

41. Cloven hoof
   (a) the evil intension
   (b) the nice intension
   (c) to do something religious
   (d) to help someone silently

42. Cry over spilt milk
   (a) Approve (b) Be happy
   (c) Praise (d) Repent

43. Call names
   (a) To praise (b) To abuse
   (c) To respect (d) To order

44. Call a spade a spade
   (a) to disrespect
   (b) to say in angre
   (c) to speak plainly
   (d) to manipulate

45. Cut both ends
   (a) very big loss
   (b) very hard worker
   (c) in favour of both sides
   (d) against both sides

46. Cock sure
   (a) In doubt (b) Very uncertain
   (c) Very sure (d) None of above

47. Close shave
   (a) Very touching moment
   (b) A narrow escape
   (c) Nice service
   (d) Bad service

48. Crocodile tears
   (a) True tears (b) Insincere tears
   (c) Very angry (d) Very Sad

49. Carrot and stick policy
   (a) reward and punishment
   (b) dishonest
   (c) arrogant
   (d) selfish policy

50. All and sundry
   (a) Everybody without distinction
   (b) only rich person
   (c) together
   (d) selected people

51. At arm's length
   (a) Length of arm (b) At a distance
   (c) Insult (d) Very near

52. At daggers drawn
   (a) real cause (b) to be puzzled
   (c) at enmity (d) at friendship

53. Bag and baggage
   (a) All the clothing
   (b) Without any belonging
   (c) Leave
   (d) With all one's belongings

54. Bed of roses ?
   (a) very soft bed (b) dull life
   (c) belong to (d) full of joys

55. By leaps and bounds ?
   (a) very fast (b) very slow
   (c) in details (d) aimlessly

II. Fill in the blanks with the correct word to make the idiom complete. (See the given clue)

1. Come ________ water.
   Clue: Any difficult situation or obstacle.

2. _______ killed the cat.
   Clue: Being inquisitive can lead you into a dangerous situation.

3. ____ and no bite.
   Clue: When someone is threatening and/ or aggressive but not willing to engage in a fight.

4. A taste ____________ medicine.
   Clue: When you are mistreated the same way you mistreat others.

5. From ______ riches.

   Clue: To go from being very poor to being very wealthy.

6. _____ trick.

   Clue: When one player scores three goals in one game. This idiom can also mean three scores consecutively.

7. Hold your _____.

   Clue: Be patient

8. Loose _____.

   Clue: Someone who is unpredictable and can cause damage if not kept in check.

9. It's _____ world.

   Clue: You frequently see the same people in different places.

10. Mumbo ______.

    Clue: Nonsense or meaningless speech.

SECTION 2
READING COMPREHENSION

Comprehension of Written Content

Comprehension is the act of understanding or comprehending the matter that you see. Comprehension means understanding the meaning of the matter you are reading. It's the ability to read the text, understand and analyse it, critically and otherwise. This enhances our knowledge basically and our understanding the circumstances we are provided with.

Tips to comprehend the given

1. Read the text thoroughly, carefully and slowly.
2. Read the matter twice, if time permits.
3. Keep a dictionary at hand, and look up difficult words.
4. Follow the storyline and connect the dots while reading.
5. Read books, fiction or non-fiction to improve your reading skills.

Kinds of Written Mediums

In this section, our focus is on gaining understanding through various written mediums like classifieds, dictionaries, articles, etc.

Article

Article is a written work published in a print or electronic medium. It may be for the purpose of propagating the news, research results, academic analysis or debate. One normally sees them in newspapers or magazines and nowadays even on online reporting sites.

Flyer

Flyer is a small handbill which advertises an event or product. Some synonyms are handouts, leaflets, pamphlets, bulletin, etc.

Example:

This picture is an example of a flyer which is letting everyone in an office to know that they are getting flu vaccinations. The flyer tells them the date, location, time and all the other required details.

Dictionary

A dictionary is a book or an electronic resource that arranges the words as per lexicographical rules (in alphabetical order) and gives their meaning, or the equivalent words in a different language, often providing information about pronunciation, origin, and usage.

Example:

uxorious

Meaning: doting upon, foolishly fond of, or affectionately submissive towards one's wife.

Quotes

Keith is genial, straightforward, considerate, clear-eyed. He is also charmingly uxorious, constantly deferring to Kim, who, for her part, is fully abreast of Keith's darting hopes and fears.

-- Martin Amis, "Darts: Gutted for Keith," Visiting Mrs. Nabokov and Other Excursions, 1993

Origin

Uxorious finds its roots in the Latin word ūxor meaning "wife."

The above is from a dictionary. Some dictionaries only give the meaning and nothing much while others provide more information. This example is based on detailed information. It gives you the meaning of the word, how to pronounce it, what it means in the English language, an example of its usage and where it originated and derived from.

Manual Booklet

A manual booklet that instructs or teaches its users on the usage how to handle, use or make things.

Example:

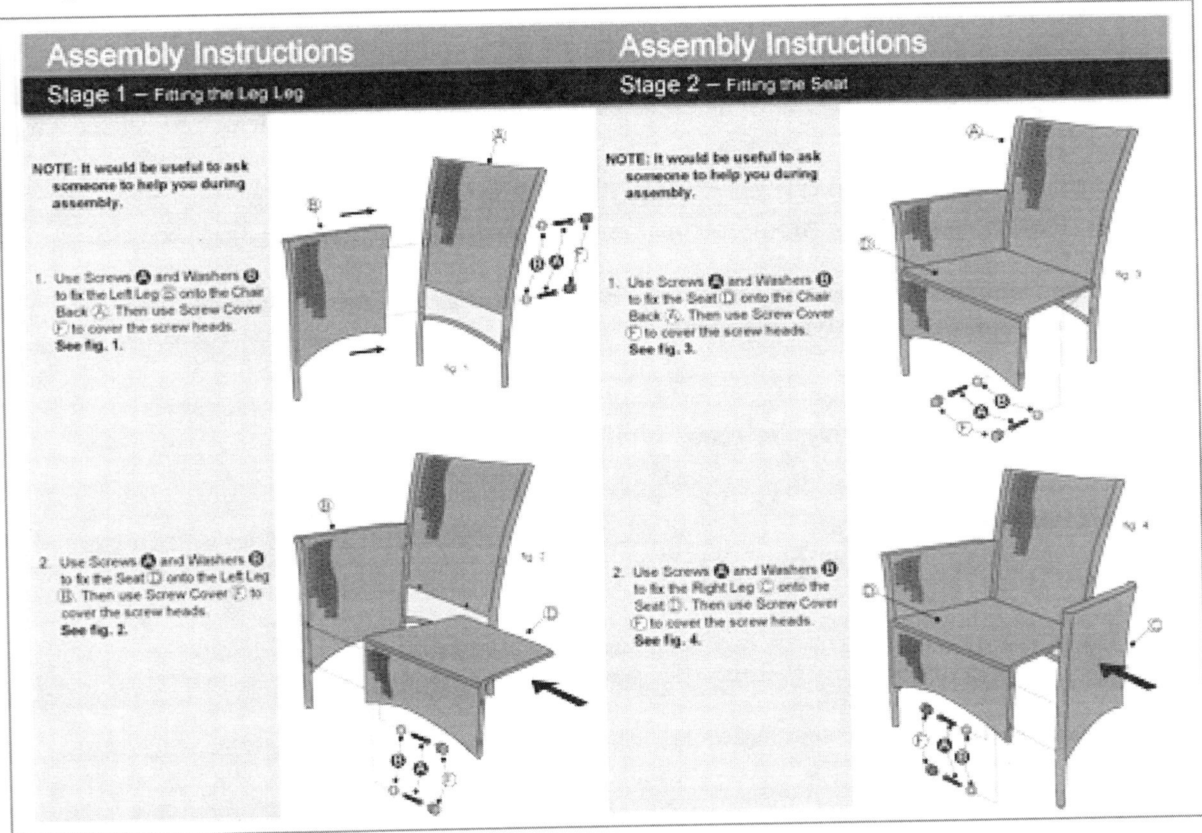

The above diagram is a manual for assembling a *chair.* It gives step by step instructions on how to do it.

Essay

An essay is a piece of literature that is comparatively longer than other literature. It deals with any and all sorts of subject matter.

Practice Exercise

I. CLASSIFIED

FOR SALE

Vasant Marg B-56, 3 BHk, second floor. Good location, metro/ transport 3 mins, with terrace and lift.
47,000/- non negotiable,
No brokers. Call
098XX-XXX-XXX

1. What is for sale?
   (a) A house (b) pool
   (c) flat (d) car
2. How far is Vasant Marg from the metro station?
   (a) three minutes (b) three seconds
   (c) five minutes (d) five seconds
3. Who are the brokers?
   (a) Estate officers
   (b) Their job is to find homes for people and vice versa
   (c) They are the middlemen for such deals
   (d) They tend to break into houses.
4. What is non-negotiable?
   (a) The space (b) The price
   (c) The terrace (d) The rent
5. What are the added benefits?
   (a) Terrace & garden
   (b) Garden and lift
   (c) Lift and terrace
   (d) Lift and pool

II. DICTIONARY

halo

[hay-loh]

noun

plural – halos, haloes

1. Also called nimbus a geometric shape, usually in the form of a disk, circle, ring, or rayed structure, traditionally representing a radiant light around or above the head of a divine or sacred personage, an ancient or medieval monarch, etc.
2. An atmosphere or quality of glory, majesty, sanctity, or the like:
   The halo around Shakespeare's works; She put a halo around her son.
3. Meteorology: Any of a variety of bright circles or arcs centered on the sun or moon, caused by the refraction or reflection of light by ice crystals suspended in the earth's atmosphere and exhibiting prismatic colouration ranging from red inside to blue outside (distinguished from corona).
4. Astronomy: A spherical cloud of gas clusters and stars that form part of a spiral galaxy.

1. Where is this sort of text taken from?
2. What does the [*hay-loh*] portion of the text mean?
3. What sorts of differences are there between the definitions?
4. What is another name for halo?
5. Use the given word in a sentence.

III. DIAGRAM

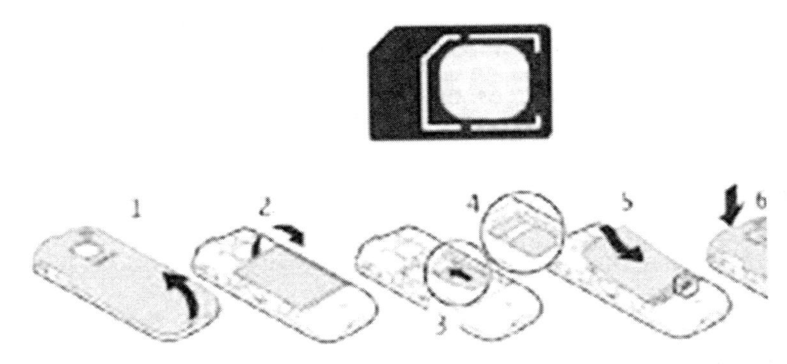

1. What is the above diagram commonly known as?
2. What is another name for such manuals?
3. What does this manual deal with?
4. What do the numbers signify in the diagram?
5. Choose one word to describe the diagram?

IV. ESSAY

KING ARTHUR

King Arthur is the legendary British leader of the late 5th and early 6th centuries, who, according to medieval histories and romances, led the defense of Britain against Saxon invaders in the early 6th century. The details of Arthur's story are mainly composed of folklore, myth and literary invention, and about his historical existence, the historious opinions differ from one another. The sparse historical background of Arthur has been gleaned from various sources like the *Annales Cambriae*, the *Historia Brittonum,* and the writings of Gildas. Arthur's name also occurs in early poetic sources such as Y *Gododdin.*

Arthur is a central figure in the legends making up the 'Matter of Britain'. The legendary Arthur developed as a figure of international interest largely through the popularity of Geoffrey of Monmouth's fanciful and imaginative 12th-century *Historia Regum Britanniae* (*History of the Kings of Britain*). In some Welsh and Breton tales and poems that date from before this work, Arthur appears either as a great warrior defending Britain from human and supernatural enemies or as a magical figure of folklore, sometimes associated with the Welsh Other world, Annwn. How much of Geoffrey's *Historia* (completed in 1138) was adapted from such earlier sources, rather than invented by Geoffrey himself, is unknown.

Although the themes, events and characters of the Arthurian legend varied widely from text to text, and there is no one canonical version, Geoffrey's version of events often served as the starting point for later stories. Geoffrey depicted Arthur as a king of Britain who defeated the Saxons and established an empire over Britain, Ireland, Iceland, Norway and Gaul. Many elements and incidents that are now an integral part of the Arthurian story appear in Geoffrey's *Historia*, including Arthur's father Uther Pendragon, the wizard Merlin, Arthur's wife Guinevere, the sword Excalibur, Arthur's conception at Tintagel, his final battle against Mordred at Camlann, and final rest in Avalon. The 12th-century French writer Chrétien de Troyes, who added Lancelot and the Holy Grail to the story, began the genre of Arthurian romance that became a significant strand of medieval literature. In these French stories, the narrative focus often shifts from King Arthur himself to other characters, such as various Knights of the Round Table. Arthurian literature thrived during the Middle Ages but waned in the centuries that followed until it experienced a major resurgence in the 19th century. In the 21st century, the legend lives on, not only in literature but also in adaptations for theatre, film, television, comics and other media.

1. Is King Arthur a historical figure?
2. What does literary invention imply?
3. Name some of the historical sources that name Arthur.
4. What does the phrase 'Matter of Britain' imply?
5. What initiated the interest in King Arthur?
6. How was Arthur portrayed pertaining to his works?
7. How did such work make Arthur as a historical figure doubtful?
8. What does canonical mean?
9. Was Arthur a conqueror?

   True or False:
10. Are all Arthurian tales focused on Arthur?

    True or False:

V. FINDING NEVERLAND

The story focuses on Scottish writer J. M. Barrie, his platonic relationship with Sylvia Llewelyn Davies, and his close friendship with her sons named George, Jack, Peter, and Michael, who inspired the classic play *Peter Pan, or The Boy Who Never Grew Up.*

Following the dismal reception of his latest play, *Little Mary*, Barrie meets the widowed Sylvia and her four young sons in Kensington Gardens, and a strong friendship develops between them. He proves to be a great playmate and surrogate father-figure for the boys, and their imaginative and boyish antics give him ideas which he incorporates into a play about boys who do not want to grow up, especially one named after young troubled Peter Llewelyn Davies. Although Barrie sees this family as wonderful and inspirational, people question his relationship with the Llewelyn Davies family. Sylvia is a widow: her husband died from cancer and left her with four boys to look after them.

Mary, Barrie's wife, is an unhappy woman suffocated by her husband's lack of success and their subsequent lack of fund and social standing; since Mary seems to enjoy the role of a socialite she is unable to support her husband and unable to keep up their married life further. Mary, who eventually divorces him, and Sylvia's mother Emma du Maurier, object to the amount of time Barrie spends with the Llewelyn Davies family. Emma also seeks to control her daughter and grandsons, especially as Sylvia becomes increasingly weak from an unidentified illness. Along the way, Barrie goes on these adventures with Sylvia and her boys. He, too, is a boy at heart and spending time with the family is special. Barrie and his wife did not have any children of their own. Barrie takes those adventures he has with the boys and sees within them and makes it into a play, Peter Pan.

Producer Charles Frohman skeptically agrees to mount Peter Pan, despite his belief that it holds no appeal for upper-class theatre-goers. Barrie peppers the opening night audience with children from a nearby orphanage, and the adults present react to their infectious delight with an appreciation of their own. The play proves to be a huge success. Barrie is all set for his play, but when Peter arrives alone to the play, Barrie goes to Sylvia's house to check up on her, and misses the show. Peter attends the play and realizes the play is about his brothers and Barrie.

Sylvia is too ill to attend the production, so Barrie arranges to have an abridged production of it performed in her home. He gets the actors, props, and musicians together in the Llewelyn Davies house. At the end of the play, Peter Pan points to the back doors and implies that Sylvia should go off to Neverland. She takes the hands of her boys and slowly walks out into Neverland. The living room and backyard transform into Neverland and Sylvia continues to walk on her own.

In the next scene everyone is at Sylvia's funeral. Barrie discovers that her will says that he and her mother should look after the boys, an arrangement agreeable to both. The film ends with J. M. Barrie finding Peter on the bench in the park where they first met after Peter ran off from the graveyard. Peter is holding his book where he wrote the plays that he ripped apart and that his mother glued back together for him. Barrie sits down and puts his arm around Peter to comfort him. They both fade, and all that is left is the bench.

1. What would you say about Peter Pan after reading the above passage?
2. Explain the family situation of the Llewwelyn Davies?
3. Why did Barrie invite the children from the orphanage on the opening night of Peter Pan?
4. What new meaning does 'Neverland' take on at the end of the fifth paragraph?
5. What does the last scene signify?

SECTION 3
SPOKEN AND WRITTEN EXPRESSIONS

Tips for Speech and Expressions

The mode of communication is divided fundamentally into speech and writing. Different communications systems are used to convey different forms of a single language. While the spoken mode is coded in sounds, the written mode is coded in symbols and the two different codings each bring with them significant features. However, many people imagine spoken and written English are closely related notions. Close examination reveals that there are as many differences as there are connections.

The written mode uses its own versions of speech features, which can be shown in the following table. The written form's most important characteristic is that, unlike the immediacy of speech, there is the opportunity to revise and correct.

Writing is long lasting while speech is ephemeral. Each mode may range from spontaneous, (a casual conversation or a scribbled written note) to planned (a prepared talk or a formal) essay.

Speech	Writing
Pauses	Punctuation (.,;:-)
Hesitation	Punctuation (- ...)
Fillers	usually omitted but can be expressed in written speech as "er"
Non fluency features	usually omitted but can be expressed in written speech as "er" or punctuation (- ...)
Expression of emotions	conventional forms - "aagh!" "grr!" including use of exclamation mark, italics and bold
Grammatical errors	Fewer
Irregular suprasegmentals	None
Incomplete syntax	Rare, expressed as "..."
Overlaps	Expressed as "..." or authorial voice eg *Bill interrupted.*
Instant feedback	Long delays in conventional print, faster in newspapers, faster again in online discussion groups and nearly instant in chat rooms
Phonology	layout, typography
Pronunciation	Spelling
Accent	Spelling
Dialect	Vocabulary
Discourse features	Rare except as vocabulary
Redundancy	Rare

Divergency from topic	Rare
Serial coordinators	Sentences and more logical coordinators
Ill defined sentence structure	Less common. Sentences generally well defined with punctuation defining clauses.
Inexplicit, great use of pronouns	More explicit. Nouns preferred to pronouns.
Paralinguistics - gesture and body language	Limited to typography
Seamless topic change	Topic change by sentence or paragraph

Differences between Writing and Speech

Written and spoken language differ in many ways. However some forms of writing are closer to speech than others, and vice versa. Below are some of the ways in which these two forms of language differ:

- Writing is usually permanent and written texts cannot usually be changed once they have been printed/written out.
- Speech is usually transient, unless recorded, and speakers can correct themselves and change their utterances as they go along.
- A written text can communicate across time and space for as long as the particular language and writing system is still understood.
- Speech is usually used for immediate interactions.
- Written language tends to be more complex and intricate than speech with longer sentences and many subordinate clauses. The punctuation and layout of written texts also have no spoken equivalent. However some forms of written language, such as instant messages and email, are closer to spoken language.
- Spoken language tends to be full of repetitions, incomplete sentences, corrections and interruptions, with the exception of formal speeches and other scripted forms of speech, such as news reports and scripts for plays and films.
- Writers receive no immediate feedback from their readers, except in computer-based communication. Therefore they cannot rely on context to clarify things. So there is more need to explain things clearly and unambiguously than in speech, except in written correspondence between people who know one another well.
- Speech is usually a dynamic interaction between two or more people. Context and shared knowledge play a major role, so it is possible to leave much unsaid or indirectly implied.
- Writers can make use of punctuation, headings, layout, colours and other graphical effects in their written texts. Such things are not available in speech
- Speech can use timing, tone, volume, and timbre to add emotional context.
- Written material can be read repeatedly and closely analysed, and notes can be made on the writing surface. Only recorded speech can be used in this way.
- Some grammatical constructions are only used in writing, as are some kinds of vocabulary, such as some complex chemical and legal terms.
- Some types of vocabulary are used only or mainly in speech. These include slang expressions, and tags like y'know, like, etc.

10 Tips to Improve your Spoken English

Tip 1: Learn Phrases, not Just Individual Words

If you study individual English words in isolation, this is what happens:

When you need to speak, you have to think a lot in order to combine the individual words in the right order, using the right grammar, and in a way that makes sense.

If you focus on learning phrases instead, then you will have ready answers and responses for any situation – no need to over-think. Focusing on phrases will help you speak English in complete sentences more naturally.

Tip 2: Listen More

Most English learners read too much and listen too little. But when babies and children learn English, they listen first – then speak – and later learn to read and write.

Half of a conversation is hearing the other person – and if you don't understand what they're saying, how can you respond correctly? So if you want to improve your English speaking, spend more time listening!

Bonus: Listening more will also help you naturally improve your pronunciation and reduce your accent.

Tip 3: Practice Speaking by Yourself

(both reading aloud and speaking spontaneously)

When you speak English, there are two main difficulties:

- The mental difficulty of thinking of the English words to say
- The physical difficulty of pronouncing the English words correctly

Reading English texts out loud will help you with the second part without having to worry about the first part. It will train your mouth and lips to pronounce English words more easily.

Speaking English spontaneously by yourself is also extremely helpful in developing your ability to put your ideas into words… *without* the pressure of a real conversation.

It might feel a little silly, but remember – this is great training for your spoken English, and there's nobody to hear your mistakes!

Tip 4: Practice Thinking in English

Do not think in your native language and then translate it into English in your head before speaking? It often results in sentences that don't sound natural in English, because the sentence structure is often different in English and your native language. Also, it takes way too much time to think and translate when you're in a conversation. One of the biggest secrets to speaking English fast and fluently is to learn to think directly in English. The great news is that this is a skill you can develop with practice, and you can practice anytime – while taking the bus, while waiting in line, while sitting at home.

Try thinking in English for a few minutes today, to start building this habit!

Tip 5: Get an Online Conversation Partner

You can find a speaking partner on "conversation exchange" websites There are "conversation exchange" websites where you can find a partner who speaks English, but wants to learn your native language.

You can then schedule a conversation session and speak half in English, half in your native language so that both of you can practice.

It's also good to have someone help correct any errors in a relaxed, low-pressure situation.

Tip 6: Remember that Communication is more Important than Grammar

Don't worry too much about grammar when speaking. Do you get nervous when speaking because you're afraid of making a mistake?

Remember that the 1 goal of speaking English is to communicate. Although grammar is important, it is less important than communication when speaking English.

Here's a simple example – if you say:

"Yesterday I go to party on beach."

The sentence isn't grammatically correct, but it DOES successfully communicate your message, and an English speaker will understand you. It's better to say something "wrong" and still communicate successfully than to say nothing!

Also, the grammar of spoken English is more flexible than the grammar of written English – so don't worry too much about grammar when speaking.

Tip 7: Speak Slowly

Slow down when speaking English – don't try to speak too fast

Trying to speak English too fast won't make you sound like a native speaker. Instead, it can actually make it more difficult for the other person to understand you.

Speaking English slowly has two advantages:

- It gives you more time to think of what to say.
- It makes your speech clearer so the other person can understand

Over time and with practice, your spoken English will get faster naturally.

Tip 8: If you Forget a Word, use other Words

It's very common for English learners to stop a sentence in the middle because they've forgotten the word they want to use – but try to be creative. The other person can help you if you describe the word you want by using other English words.

Be creative – use other words when you can't remember the word you want

Tip 9: Relax and have a Positive, Confident Attitude

If you make a mistake or forget a word when you are speaking English – it's OK! Don't be nervous or afraid.

The person who you're talking to will understand and be patient with you. If you are insecure when speaking English, it will be even more difficult to speak.

Relax and think positive! So don't say "My English is terrible" or "Sorry for my bad English." These are negative comments and they're not helpful. Instead, think "I can speak English!" before every conversation in order to give yourself more confidence and help you speak better!

Tip 10: Learn real English Phrases for Everyday Life

Today, you have the opportunity to take an English course in your town or city that focuses on useful English in the context of conversations.

A good *English Speaking Course* teaches you phrases from conversations

The *English Speaking Course* is a simple, fun, and effective way to learn new phrases and expressions– and improve your speaking ability. Each lesson based on conversations, and reading and listening to the dialogues will help you improve your understanding.

It explains and expands upon the vocabulary you heard in the conversations, teaching you new expressions and showing you how to use them.

There are lots of practice phrases which you can listen to and repeat to improve your English speaking.

10 Tips to Improve Your Writing Skills

If you want to develop decent writing skills to succeed at your job but do not have time to work on those skills, mastering a few basic rules can still make a big difference.

Tip 1: Don't Repeat Words or Phrases

Vary the language to avoid annoying or distracting readers with repeated words. Even better, get rid of some of the repeated verbiage, which usually turns out to be overkill anyway.

Tip 2: Don't use Inconsistent Structure for Lists or Heading

Example: Backing up the registry

Searching the registry

Clean the registry

Good practice: Reword where necessary to make the items parallel.

Tip 3: Focus on Subject-Verb Agreement

Sometimes we lose track of what the subject is, and our verb doesn't match.

Example: Neither of the editors are very smart.

One-third of the employees are colour blind.

Good practice: Scrutinize the subject to determine whether it's singular or plural. It's not always obvious.

Tip 4: Use "it" for Companies, Organizations

A company or any collective noun that's being referred to as a single entity should not be treated as plural.

Example: Microsoft said it will look at the problem.

Good practice: Unless there's some compelling exception, use "it."

Tip 5: Don't Hyphenate "ly" Adverbs

Good "ly" adverbs never take a hyphen, but they pop up a lot.

Example: We like to avoid commonly-used expressions.

Good practice: Don't hyphenate ly adverbs. The "ly" says "I modify the word that comes next," so there's no need to tie them together with a hyphen.

Tip 6: Don't use "which" Instead of "that"

We sometimes use "which" to set off an essential clause (instead of "that").

Example: The meeting which was scheduled for 1:00 p.m. has been cancelled. (Incorrect)

The meeting that was scheduled for 1:00 p.m. has been cancelled. (Correct)

Good practice: The commonly accepted convention is to set off a nonessential clause with the word "which" and a comma. If the clause is essential, use "that."

Tip 7: Don't use Deadwood Phrases

Nothing is worse for a reader than having to slog through a sea of unnecessary verbiage.

Example:		**replace with**
a) Has the ability to	⟶	can
b) At this point in time	⟶	now
c) In the event that	⟶	if

Tip 8: Do not use "that" Instead of "who"

Some writers use "that" to refer to people.

Example: The end user that called this morning said he received the parcel. (Incorrect)

The end user who called this morning said he received the parcel. (Correct)

Good practice: When you're referring to people, use "who."

Tip 9: Inconsistent use of the final serial comma

One convention says to use a comma to set off the final item in a series of three or more items; another (equally popular) convention says to leave it out. But some writers bounce between the two rules.

Example: Word, Excel, and Outlook are all installed. (OR: Word, Excel and Outlook are all installed.)

Open the dialog box, click on the Options tab, and select the Enable option. (OR: Open the dialog box, click on the Options tab and select the Enable option.)

Good practice: Decide on one convention and stick to it. Those who read what you've written will have an easier time following your sentence structure if you're consistent.

Tip 10: Using a Comma to Join two Dependent Clauses

Commas are a great source of controversy and often the victim of misguided personal discretion. But there is this rule: Two dependent clauses don't need commas.

Example: I hid the ice cream, and then told my sister where to find it. (Incorrect)

The user said he saved the file, but somehow deleted it. (Incorrect)

Good practice: If the second clause is dependent, do not apply commas.

Practice Exercise

I. Choose the best reply/option to the given statement:

Example: Rita: Good morning! How are you feeling today?

Akhil:______________________

(a) Cool, thanks
(b) I'm doing okay so far. You?
(c) Fine, thank you! What about you?

The correct choice is, choice c, as it is polite and expresses thought for the person being spoken to.

1. Tourist: Excuse me, I'm a bit lost. Could you point me in the right direction?
   Annie:_________________
   (a) Yes, of course. Where would you like to go?
   (b) No, I'm busy.
   (c) Ya, sure.
2. Ankita: The weather is so pleasant today!
   Bhavya:_________________
   (a) So?
   (b) It is, isn't it?
   (c) I don't really care.
3. Aman: My phone isn't working properly.
   Store Attendant: _______________
   (a) I'm on a break.
   (b) Good afternoon! How may I help?
   (c) Wait for a while. I'm a bit busy now.
4. Carol: Thank you for passing the newspaper.
   Christine: ______________
   (a) Whatever
   (b) Sure
   (c) It's ok
5. Anita: Why are you so late?
   Nima: ________________
   (a) Stop getting so angry over such a small issue.
   (b) I'm sorry, I got caught in heavy traffic.
   (c) I woke up late
6. Shubham: I'm in so much trouble at home.
   Palak:________________
   (a) Serves you right
   (b) Doesn't matter. All of us are
   (c) Don't worry, it'll be fine
7. Sweta: Could you please help me move the boxes somewhere?
   Shruti: ______________
   (a) Yes, of course!
   (b) No, it's too heavy for me, let me find someone who can.
   (c) I don't feel like it. Sorry.
8. Aakash: I've cut my hand.
   Raj:_________
   (a) That's because you're so careless.
   (b) Wait, let me find a band aid.
   (c) Don't worry. It's barely a nick.
9. Rhea: I forgot my pen. May I borrow yours?
   Sanchit: ___________
   (a) Yes, here, I have an extra.
   (b) NO
   (c) Sorry, I'm using it.
10. Aditya: That concert was so much funny!
    Anshul:___________
    (a) I didn't want to come.
    (b) I don't care
    (c) Surely it was funny?

II. Choose the correct option to answer each of the following questions.
How would you:

1. Talk to someone who's come to your country for the first time and isn't fluent with the language?
   (a) Slowly and politely, being empathetic
   (b) Talking fast and forcing your opinion on the individual
   (c) Saying that you don't have the time
   (d) None of these
2. Give help a lost stranger?
   (a) Pretend you can't hear her
   (b) Give incorrect directions because you aren't sure yourself
   (c) Help in any way possible
   (d) None of these

3. Address a complaint.
   (a) Ignore it
   (b) Make excuses
   (c) Apologise and promise to correct the mistake
   (d) None of these
4. Give suggestions to a friend about clothes and colours that suit her/him.
   (a) Tell them that they are colour blind and have no taste
   (b) Suggest new styles and colours which suit them better
   (c) Tell them that look okay
5. Decline an invitation to a party.
   (a) Say that you don't feel like coming
   (b) Lie about being ill and go somewhere else
   (c) Thank the host for invitation, and politely decline
   (d) None of these
6. Propose a plan of action at a meeting.
   (a) Wait for your turn and then put forward your plan
   (b) Interrupt everyone else saying that your plan is better
   (c) Belittle everyone else's plan
   (d) None of these
7. Reject a resume.
   (a) Throw the rejected ones into the bin
   (b) Don't reply to the rejected candidates
   (c) Thank them for the applications, say that the position has been filled and wish them good luck for future endeavours
   (d) None of these
8. Congratulate a colleague regarding a promotion.
   (a) Be genuine
   (b) Pass snide remarks
   (c) Pretend like you can't see him
   (d) None of these
9. Invite a professional to join your organisation.
   (a) Write a letter inviting the person to apply for the job
   (b) Make false promises
   (c) Discredit the present employer and say that your organisation is better
   (d) None of these
10. Make a reservation at a restaurant.
   (a) Say that you want a table by hook or by crook
   (b) Turn up at the restaurant without a reservation and create a scene when you don't get a table
   (c) Call up in advance and get a confirmed reservation
   (d) None of these
11. File a complaint against a rude salesman
   (a) Write a letter to the manager telling her about the incident and convey your grievances against the salesman politely
   (b) Write a scathing letter saying that the employee needs to be fired
   (c) Punch him instead of complaining
   (d) None of these
12. Call the maintenance company for fixing the lighting fixtures
   (a) Say that their products are defective and demand a refund
   (b) Describe the problem and ask them to send someone as soon as possible
   (c) Call up and shout at them
   (d) None of these
13. Give suggestions for improving a FMCG.
   (a) Complain instead giving suggestions
   (b) Say that the product should stop being manufactured.
   (c) Describe the problem you encountered, and suggest how they can prevent it from happening again
   (d) None of these
14. Enquire after a friend who was in an accident
   (a) Call and ask how he is, and wish him a speedy recovery
   (b) Call up and make a joke about the accident
   (c) Call up and talk about your problems
   (d) None of these

15. Invite your friend for dinner
    (a) Force them to come
    (b) Call up and ask nicely
    (c) Create a scene if they decline
    (d) None of these

III. Fill in the blanks with the most suitable form of expression.

1. ______ pass the pepper mill.
2. I had_______ a form a while ago and it isn't here yet.
3. _____ remember to pass the fliers around.
4. ________, could you please repeat whatever you just said.
5. I am so _________ for inconveniencing you like this.
6. __________ drop your suggestions in the suggestion box.
7. Shilpa has my sincere _______ for all her assistance.
8. You're ________.
9. _______ don't hesitate before calling and asking for help.
10. I'm afraid that we must decline your _____ for an extension on the due date.
11. You have my _______ apologies for the mix up.
12. ____ Akansha come by later for the documents.
13. With all due _______, I don't believe whatever you're saying .
14. ______ ! Mark would gladly drop you off to the airport.
15. She must ______ for her behaviour at today's meeting.

◆◆◆

SECTION 4
ACHIEVERS' SECTION

Higher Order Thinking Skills (HOTS)

Section–I

A. Choose the correct option for the given idiom.

1. To make ends meet
   (a) A short story
   (b) To earn enough to live
   (c) To skip classes
   (d) None of these
2. Bolt from the blue
   (a) Sudden shock
   (b) To lose a tight game
   (c) To ask for help
   (d) None of these
3. To burn the candle at both ends
   (a) To argue endlessly
   (b) Long power cut
   (c) To work long hours
   (d) None of these
4. To bury the hatchet
   (a) To end enmity
   (b) To hide stolen treasure
   (c) To overexert
   (d) None of these
5. To spill the beans
   (a) To reveal a secret
   (b) To eat clumsily
   (c) To get exhausted
   (d) None of these

B. Choose the correct form of verb to fill in the blanks.

1. She __________ to live in the country.
   (a) enjoys (b) used
   (c) is used (d) None of these
2. Naina ____________ to look for a job in New York.
   (a) has decided (b) is thinking
   (c) had better (d) None of these
3. The children ____________ tidying their bedrooms.
   (a) were made (b) expect you
   (c) are trying (d) None of these
4. The owner of the shop ____________ him to leave.
   (a) stopped (b) wanted
   (c) hoped (d) None of these
5. Her husband ____________ to come home early.
   (a) succeeded
   (b) is looking forward
   (c) reminded her

C. Fill in the blanks with the correct form of verb using simple present or present continuous tense.

1. Look! Sarah (go) ______to the movies.
2. On her right hand, Sarah (carry) ________ her handbag.
3. The handbag (be) ___very beautiful.
4. Sarah usually (put) _____on black shoes but now she (wear) ________white trainers.
5. She (take) _______an umbrella because it (rain) _______.

D. Fill in the blanks with the correct pronoun.

1. It took ____________ twenty minutes to get dressed.
   (a) I (b) me
   (c) us (d) none of these
2. She told _________ an interesting story.
   (a) I (b) me
   (c) us (d) none of these
3. I don't think we should wait for _______
   (a) he
   (b) him
   (c) us
   (d) none of these

4. You pay for your drinks and I will pay for ___________

(a) mine (b) my
(c) us (d) none of these

5. I am angry with both of ___________

(a) they (b) them
(c) me (d) none of these

E. Choose the correct option which has the same analogy as given in the question.

1. Silence: Noise
   (a) Quiet: Peace (b) Baldness: Hair
   (c) Talk: Whisper (d) Sing: Dance
2. Glove : Hand
   (a) Neck : Collar (b) Tie : Shirt
   (c) Socks : Feet (d) Coat : Pocket
3. Scales : Fish
   (a) Bear : Fur (b) Woman : Dress
   (c) Skin : Man (d) Tree : Leaves
4. Candle : Wick
   (a) Hammer : Nail
   (b) Light : Bulb
   (c) Oven : Fire
   (d) Bicycle : Wheel
5. Chalk : Blackboard
   (a) Type : Point (b) Table : Chair
   (c) Door : Handle (d) Ink : Paper

F. Find out the sentences that are written incorrectly in the passive voice.

1. I was eaten an ice cream.
2. The song was sung by a singer.
3. I was deceived by the TV program.
4. The concert was finished at 12 p.m.
5. He was written a novel.

G. Write the correct question for each answer.

1. Ans: My brother loves ice-cream for dessert.
   Q:
2. Ans: On Tuesday, Prateek is going for a movie.
   Q:
3. Ans: Yesterday, Anil and Anu left for Dehradun.
   Q:

Section–II

Answer the questions on the basis of the flyer given below.

1. What does this flyer focus on?
2. Does it specify a certain characteristic in dogs that they are looking for? If so, what is it?
3. What would you call this sort of company?
4. What sort of people would be working here? Give two adjectives.
5. What is the name of the business?

Section–III

Choose the correct option/response in each of the given situations:

1. The tailor doesn't have your suit ready by the due date. He says that he was ill and all his work is backlogged. He asks for two extra days.
   (a) You get angry and shout at him in front of all the other customers, creating a scene and embarrassing him.
   (b) You express your disappointment but say that you understand, agreeing to give him the extra time.
   (c) Make a snarky comment and cancel the order.
   (d) None of these

2. The order you placed at the restaurant is taking long to come, and the restaurant isn't even that busy.
   (a) You call the waiter and ask him about the delay, and ask him to bring the food sooner than later.
   (b) Shout at the waiter for the delay.
   (c) Refuse to pay the bill because of the poor service.
   (d) None of these
3. There is a rush at the station and you accidently bump into someone else, causing him to drop the files in his hands. He expresses his annoyance.
   (a) You walk away and turn a deaf ear to whatever he was saying.
   (b) Become defensive and start arguing with him.
   (c) Apologize and help him to pick up whatever he has dropped.
   (d) None of these
4. You come home a few hours after your curfew from a party. Your parents are waiting for you because they are worried. Once you reach, though they are relieved, they are extremely upset.
   (a) You listen to them and start shouting back.
   (b) You don't listen to a word they say. You arrive and go directly to your room, slamming the door.
   (c) You listen to whatever they're saying and sincerely apologize.
   (d) None of these
5. A top you borrowed from a friend got scorched while you were ironing it.
   (a) You go and buy the exact same top to replace her one, and you never tell her.
   (b) You tell her about the mishap and offer to buy another one.
   (c) You don't tell her at all, and hope that she forgets that she lent it to you in the first place.
   (d) None of these

Short Answer Questions

I. Find out the noun in the following and mention their types

1. Always speak the truth.
2. We all love honesty.
3. I have two children.
4. The lion is the king of the beasts.
5. Solomon was the wisest of all kings.
6. Cleanliness is next to godliness.
7. Birds of a feather flock together.
8. Who teaches you grammar?
9. The Nile is the longest of all rivers.
10. The boy was rewarded for his honesty.
11. He gave me an apple.
12. I recognized his voice at once.
13. You should never tell a lie.
14. Wisdom is better than riches.
15. He is on the jury.
16. Silver and gold are precious metals.
17. Still waters run deep.
18. Old habits die hard.
19. The early bird catches the worm.
20. It was Edison who invented the phonograph.

II. Fill in the blanks with the correct option.

> **Note:** Sometimes you need to use two or more adjectives to describe something or someone.

1. He was wearing a ________ shirt.
   (a) dirty old flannel
   (b) flannel old dirty
   (c) old dirty flannel
   (d) None of these
2. Pass me the ________ cups.
   (a) plastic big blue (b) big blue plastic
   (c) big plastic blue (d) None of these
3. All the girls fell in love with the ________ teacher.
   (a) handsome new American
   (b) American new handsome
   (c) new handsome American
   (d) None of these
4. I used to drive ________ car.
   (a) a blue old German
   (b) an old German blue
   (c) an old blue German
   (d) None of these
5. He recently married a ________ woman.
   (a) young beautiful Greek
   (b) beautiful young Greek
   (c) beautiful Greek young
   (d) None of these
6. This is a ________ movie.
   (a) new Italian wonderful
   (b) wonderful Italian new
   (c) wonderful new Italian
   (d) None of these
7. She is a ________ supermodel.
   (a) beautiful slim Brazilian
   (b) Brazilian beautiful slim
   (c) slim Brazilian beautiful
   (d) None of these
8. It's in the ________ container.
   (a) large blue metal
   (b) blue large metal
   (c) blue metal large
   (d) None of these
9. He sat behind a ________ desk.
   (a) big wooden brown
   (b) big brown wooden
   (c) wooden big brown
   (d) None of these

10. She gave him a ________ vase.
   (a) small Egyptian black
   (b) black Egyptian small
   (c) small black Egyptian
   (d) None of these

III. Read the passage and fill in the blanks with the most suitable word.

Sardar Singh is a salesman. He ___1___ from door to door selling vacuum cleaners. On his first day of work, he decided to sell his goods by ___2___ on the doors of a private housing area.

"My first customer," he thought as he ___3___ the doorbell of the first house. A middle aged woman ___4___ curlers in her hair opened the door.

John began to ___5___ who he was and the product he was selling. The next minute, the door was slammed ___6___.

"Not interested !" Sardar Singh heard her shout ___7___ the closed door. She refused to open the door ___8___ John's persistent knocking.

Sardar Singh was given a similar ___9___ of treatment from the next few houses. ___10___ rather discouraged, he knocked at the door of the ninth household. This ___11___ , the occupants of the house ___12___ him in. They also ___13___ interest in his product. Encouraged by ___14___ , Sardar Singh began to explain the merits of his vacuum cleaner. When the family ___15___ him for a demonstration, he vacuumed the place for them. ___16___ the demonstration, the family, however, did not ___17___ his product. Instead, they politely but firmly told him that they would ___18___ him a call if they want to buy a vacuum cleaner later.

The family never called him ___19___, Sardar Singh suspected that they had not been really interested in his product. ___20___ they had wanted was the 'free service' given by John, who had vacuumed their entire living room.

IV. Put in punctuation marks, italics, and parentheses where required in the following sentences.

1. The men in question John, Mohan, and Sohan deserve awards.
2. Several countries participated in the airlift Italy, Belgium, France, and Luxembourg.
3. Only one course was open to us surrender, said the ex-major, and we did.
4. Judge Carswell later to be nominated for the Supreme Court had ruled against civil rights.
5. In last week's New Yorker, one of my favorite magazines, I enjoyed reading Leland's article How Not to Go Camping.
6. Yes, Jim said, I'll be home by ten.
7. There was only one thing to do study till dawn.
8. Montaigne wrote the following A wise man never loses anything, if he has himself.
9. The following are the primary colors red, blue, and yellow.
10. Arriving on the 8 10 plane were Liz Brooks, my old roommate her husband and Tim, their son.
11. When the teacher commented that her spelling was poor, Lynn replied All the members of my family are poor spellers. Why not me?
12. He used the phrase you know so often that I finally said No, I don't know.
13. The automobile dealer handled three makes of cars Volkswagens, Porsches, and Mercedes Benz.
14. Though Phil said he would arrive on the 9 19 flight, he came instead on the 10 36 flight.
15. Whoever thought said Helen that Jack would be elected class president?
16. In baseball, a show boat is a man who shows off.
17. The minister quoted Isaiah 5 21 in last Sunday's sermon.
18. There was a very interesting article entitled The New Rage for Folk Singing in last Sunday's New York Times newspaper.

19. Whoever is elected secretary of the club Ashley, or Chandra, or Aisha must be prepared to do a great deal of work, said Jumita, the previous secretary.
20. Darwin's On the Origin of Species 1859 caused a great controversy when it appeared.

V. Complete the passages using suitable prepositions.

The rain had just stopped. I went out___1___ the garden. Then I heard a soft mewing. I saw a little white kitten. It was so thin that its bones were showing. It was wet and shivering.

I brought it ___2___ the house and dried it. My brother came ___3___. "Do you know who this kitten belongs ___4___ ?" I asked him.

My brother said he had seen some kittens ___5___ the long grass ___6___ our house. The mother cat was just a stray. He told me to give the kitten some fish.

There was no more fish, so I took some rice and gave it to the kitten. But it would not eat the rice.

"I wonder if it's old enough to eat rice. It may still be feeding ___7___ its mother's milk," said my brother.

I warmed ___8___ some milk and gave it to the kitten but it would not drink the milk. " I wonder if I should give it back to its mother," I said.

"Yes, you'd better do that," said my brother.

My brother and I carried the kitten ___9___ of the house. we heard loud mewing. I was the mother cat. I put ___10___ the kitten. It mewed loudly but stayed still. The mother cat ran quickly to the little kitten. It started licking the kitten all ___11___. The kitten kept mewing loudly.

"Do you think it's telling its mother ___12___ me ?" I asked my brother.

VI. Rearrange the each group of words to form a meaningful sentence:

1. parents watch ? the in evening television Do your
2. Jeremy takes bus mornings. on the o'clock eight Monday always
3. you room, bring to could the Ben, bread ? please the dining
4. Rogers with to likes is friends her when she in London. Mrs go shopping
5. have all them ? are the at books many read There library, you interesting
6. studying at now. is the university He
7. so he could He hardly was think. excited
8. light so had that we was our to cover eyes. The bright
9. that he already She said eaten. had
10. to house. sometimes comes our Brian
11. He as French is English. studying well as
12. was cold that had to our wear It coats. so we
13. my lunch to take always work. I
14. If your buy eye are some drops. sore tomorrow, eyes

VII. Arrange each group of words into a meaningful sentence.

1. Maria / my name / is
2. a comic / Susan / reads
3. play / in the garden / they
4. sings / he / a song
5. have / I / got / a dog
6. sit / on / we / the bench
7. do / my / I / homework
8. her / she / friend / phones
9. computer / games / likes / he
10. her / the / mother / girl / is / helping
11. his / belief / Gandhiji's / greatest / was / in / strength / God
12. dress / on / this / beautiful / looks / you
13. assistants / shop / required / salesmen / and / are
14. had / wish / left / home / I / never / I
15. money / you / me / lend / can / some?
16. Chinese / served / Italian / are / here / meals / and

17. are / cinnamon / benefits / what / the / of?
18. freedom / fought / he / the / India / of / for
19. hit / he / the ball / so hard / lost / it / was/ that
20. repair /all types / works / undertaken / of / are
21. are / the / description / of / beyond / beauties / nature
22. tomato / and / cut / cucumber / slices / some
23. was / clever / Birbal / extremely / witty / and
24. my / bag / lost / in / I / train / the
25. shall / misconduct / be / you / for / your / punished

VIII. Transform each of the following sentences into reported speech.

1. John said, "I love this town."
2. "Are you sure?" He asked me.
3. "I can't drive a lorry," he said.
4. "Be nice to your brother," he said.
5. "Don't be nasty," he said.
6. "Don't waste your money" she said.
7. "What have you decided to do?" she asked him.
8. "I always wake up early," he said.
9. "You should revise your lessons," he said.
10. "Where have you been?" he asked me.

IX Fill in the blanks with the passive form of verb as shown in the bracket.

1. The words _______ by the teacher today. (to explain - Simple Present)
2. We _______ a letter the day before yesterday. (to send - Simple Past)
3. This car _______. It's too old. (not/to steal - will-future)
4. This street _______ because of snow. (already/to close - Present Perfect)
5. A new restaurant _______ next week. (to open - will-future)
6. He _______ to the party yesterday. (to invite - Simple Past)
7. The blue box _______ . (can/not/to see - Simple Present)
8. I _______ the book by my friend last Sunday. (to give - Simple Past)
9. The dishes _______ by my little brother. (not/ to wash - Present Perfect)
10. I _______ by Rakesh. (not/to ask - will-future)

Model Test Paper

Direction (1–2) : Fill in the blanks with suitable word/phrase for each sentence.

1. I am happy you are helping me with the assignment. This kind of work is not really my _________.
   (a) cup and sauce
   (b) cup of tea
   (c) cup of coffee
   (d) tea cup
2. The discussion was by no means_________.It went on for more than four hours!
   (a) cut and dried
   (b) chopped and dried
   (c) cut and shredded
   (d) dried and cut
3. Choose the correct spelling of the word.
   (a) Believe (b) Beleive
   (c) Believ (d) Beleev
4. Choose the correct phrase.
   (a) Down and up (b) Down and out
   (c) Down and town (d) Out and down

Direction (5–6) : Fill in the blanks with the correct word.

5. A class full of very good students means ___________ failures for the teachers to worry about.
   (a) lesser (b) less
   (c) fewer (d) less than
6. He seems to know a lot about you! How long have you ____________him?
   (a) known (b) knew
   (c) been knowing (d) know
7. Spot the error in the sentence.
   Becoming a monitor (a) / often means (b) / to loose friends. (c) No error (d)
8. Complete the conversation with the correct word.
   Ravi: I think it's really exciting to go to new places.
   Teacher: What ____________ keep in mind if you are going to a new place?
   (a) do you have to
   (b) should you
   (c) have you to
   (d) must you have to
9. Change the given direct sentence to indirect.
   "Drive carefully!" Ram said to me.
   (a) Ram said to me drive carefully.
   (b) Ram ordered me drive carefully.
   (c) Ram told me to drive carefully.
   (d) None of the above.

Direction (10–11) : Read the passage and answer the following questions. The fly was finally hers. It had taken Mini hours to trap it, but now, exhausted, it buzzed and crashed hopelessly around inside a pickle jar. Kneeling on a chair, she took a chapatti and spread it with a thick layer of butter, wiping the knife clean against the edge of the dish, the way her mother used to and savored her victory. She was again in control.

10. The event of trapping the fly is compared with ___________________________.
    (a) the taste of chapati and butter
    (b) a war followed by celebrations
    (c) a celebration by the victor
    (d) the defeat of the oppressed
11. Which of the following expressions would you use to describe Mini's emotions after trapping the fly?
    (a) On cloud ten
    (b) Under a cloud
    (c) On cloud nine
    (d) Every dark cloud has a silver lining

Direction (12–13) : Choose one sentence to complete the dialogue.

12. Teacher to student : I thought you had been doing your homework regularly. Why are you still so irregular with your work?
    (a) I will let your parents know that you have failed this year.
    (b) I'm afraid, at this rate, I'll have to give you a 'D' grade.
    (c) I'm expecting you to earn a 'D' grade.
    (d) I think you will do well this year.

13. Mohan : Sohan, it's the Maths class now! I forgot my book.
    (a) Could you share your book with me today?
    (b) Look here! Give me that book of yours!
    (c) Can I buy a Maths book?
    (c) Could I borrow your Maths notebook, please?

Direction (14–15) : Choose the best word.

14. Disaster management ____________ that the areas are mapped beforehand.
    (a) is requires
    (b) requires
    (c) required
    (d) is required

15. "I am happy to inspire so many people, ____________ women and mothers," said Mary Kom.
    (a) and
    (b) special
    (c) especially
    (d) also

Hints and Solutions

SECTION 1: WORD AND STRUCTURE KNOWLEDGE

1. NOUN

Answer Key

I

1. (c)	2. (a)	3. (d)	4. (b)	5. (d)	6. (c)	7. (a)	8. (b)	9. (a)	10. (c)

II

11. (c)	12. (a)	13. (d)	14. (d)	15. (c)	16. (b)	17. (c)	18. (c)	19. (a)	20. (b)

III

21. (a)	22. (a)	23. (c)	24. (c)	25. (b)	26. (b)	27. (c)	28. (d)	29. (a)	30. (b)

IV

1. Herd	2. Nile	3. Habits	4. Orange	5. Voice
6. Hive	7. Wise	8. Cloud	9. Class	10. Hatred

V

1. Proper noun	2. Uncountable	3. Abstract	4. Collective	5. Collective
6. Concrete	7. Material	8. Countable	9. Material/ uncountable	10. Collective

VI

1. Masculine	2. Feminine	3. Masculine	4. Masculine	5. Feminine

2. PRONOUN

Answer Key

I

1. (b)	2. (c)	3. (b)	4. (a)	5. (a)	6. (a)	7. (c)	8. (a)	9. (c)	10. (b)
11. (b)	12. (a)	13. (a)	14. (c)	15. (a)	16. (a)	17. (a)	18. (b)	19. (c)	20. (a)

II

1. Her	2. They	3. Your	4. Her	5. Our
6. Her	7. She	8. Him	9. You	10. My
11. Me	12. She	13. We	14. Her	

III

1. This	2. This	3. Those	4. These	5. That
6. Those	7. These	8. Those	9. This, that	10. Those

IV

1. (b)	2. (c)	3. (a)	4. (d)	5. (d)	6. (b)	7. (a)	8. (c)		

3. ADJECTIVE

Answer Key

1. (b)	2. (a)	3. (a)	4. (c)	5. (c)	6. (a)	7. (a)	8. (a)	9. (b)	10. (a)
11. (b)	12. (a)	13. (a)	14. (d)	15. (b)	16. (a)	17. (c)	18. (b)	19. (d)	20. (c)
21. (a)	22. (d)	23. (d)	24. (d)	25. (a)					

4. ARTICLES

Answer Key

I

1. (b)	2. (b)	3. (a)	4. (a)	5. (b)	6. (a)	7. (a)	8. (b)	9. (a)	

II

1. a, an	2. a, the	3. an	4. an, a, the	5. an
6. a, an	7. an	8. a, an, the	9. a	10. a, the

III

1. x, a, a, an	2. an, a,x	3. a, an	4. a, a	5. an, a, a, x, a
6. a, an	7. an, an	8. a, an	9. a, an	10. an, the
11. a, an, x	12. a, the, an, an	13. an, the, an, a, the	14. a, a, a	15. x, a, a, the
16. an, a, a, an	17. a, an, the	18. an, a, a, a, an	19. a, an, the	20. a, a, an, an

IV

1. an	2. the	3. the	4. the	5. a
6. the	7. the	8. the	9. the	10. the
11. the	12. the	13. the	14. the	

5. VERB

Answer Key

I

1. Was, ran	2. Felt	3. Directed	4. Living	5. Chained
6. Assassinated	7. Feeling	8. Delayed	9. Stopped	10. Played

II

1. Studied	2. Retired	3. Reads	4. Goes	5. Rained
6. Lead	7. Revolves	8. Took	9. Is	10. Has
11. Rises	12. Wins	13. Wait	14. Voted	15. Wanted

III

1. Were	2. Were	3. Had	4. Could have given it	5. Realise
6. Returned	7. Knew	8. Is	9. Were	10. Stop
11. Could	12. Saw	13. Give	14. Belonged	15. Were

IV

1. (b)	2. (d)	3. (c)	4. (a)	5. (a)	6. (b)	7. (b)	8. (a)	9. (c)	10. (d)
11. (d)	12. (c)	13. (d)	14. (d)	15. (b)	16. (d)	17. (d)	18. (d)	19. (d)	20. (d)
21. (b)	22. (d)	23. (a)	24. (d)	25. (b)	26. (a)	27. (c)	28. (a)	29. (b)	30. (b)
31. (d)	32. (b)	33. (a)	34. (a)	35. (c)	36. (c)	37. (c)	38. (c)	39. (c)	40. (d)
41. (d)	42. (d)	43. (c)	44. (c)	45. (b)	46. (c)	47. (c)	48. (d)	49. (c)	50. (b)
51. (a)	52. (c)	53. (a)	54. (b)	55. (b)					

6. ADVERBS

Answer Key

I

1. (a)	2. (a)	3. (c)	4. (b)	5. (c)	6. (a)	7. (a)	8. (c)	9. (c)	10. (a)

II

1. (a)	2. (b)	3. (c)	4. (a)	5. (c)	6. (a)	7. (b)	8. (a)	9. (c)	10. (a)
11. (a)	12. (c)	13. (b)	14. (a)	15. (c)	16. (c)	17. (a)	18. (a)	19. (e)	20. (b)
21. (d)	22. (d)	23. (a)	24. (c)	25. (c)	26. (a)	27. (c)	28. (a)	29. (c)	30. (b)
31. (c)	32. (a)	33. (c)	34. (a)	35. (a)	36. (c)	37. (a)	38. (a)	39. (d)	

7. PREPOSITION

Answer Key

I

1. with	2. for	3. to	4. of	5. with
6. from	7. in	8. with	9. for	10. towards

II

1. (b)	2. (b)	3. (a)	4. (c)	5. (b)	6. (a)	7. (c)	8. (b)	9. (a)	10. (b)

III

1. at	2. at	3. at	4. X	5. at	6. on	7. in	8. on	9. in	10. X
11. X	12. in	13. in	14. X	15. on	16. in	17. on	18. in	19. on	20. on
21. at	22. in	23. on	24. at	25. on	26. on	27. at	28. on	29. on	30. in
31. in	32. at	33. at	34. in	35. in	36. at	37. on	38. in		

IV

1. on	2. for	3. to	4. from	5. for
6. on	7. at	8. to	9. to	10. about
11. to	12. for	13. to	14. about	15. from
16. on	17. on	18. for	19. at	20. to

8. CONJUNCTION

Answer Key

I

1. (b)	2. (c)	3. (a)	4. (c)	5. (c)	6. (d)	7. (a)	8. (c)	9. (a)	10. (c)
11. (d)	12. (b)	13. (a)	14. (b)	15. (c)	16. (a)	17. (a)	18. (d)	19. (d)	20. (a)

II

1. (b)	2. (b)	3. (c)	4. (b)	5. (a)	6. (c)	7. (b)	8. (d)	9. (d)	10. (a)

III

1. (b)	2. (b)	3. (b)	4. (b)	5. (b)	6. (b)	7. (b)	8. (b)	9. (b)	10. (b)
11. (b)	12. (a)	13. (a)	14. (b)	15. (a)	16. (a)	17. (b)	18. (b)	19. (a)	20. (a)
21. (a)	22. (a)	23. (b)	24. (a)	25. (c)	26. (d)	27. (d)	28. (a)	29. (c)	30. (b)
31. (c)	32. (a)	33. (b)	34. (d)						

9. PHRASAL VERBS

Answer Key

I

1. (b)	2. (a)	3. (d)	4. (c)	5. (b)	6. (d)	7. (b)	8. (c)	9. (d)	10. (b)
11. (d)	12. (a)	13. (b)	14. (d)	15. (c)	16. (a)	17. (a)	18. (c)	19. (c)	20. (d)
21. (b)	22. (a)	23. (b)	24. (a)	25. (d)	26. (c)	27. (a)	28. (c)		

II

1. look up	2. get on	3. turn on	4. give up	5. take off
6. stand up	7. put out	8. look after	9. put on	10. get off

III

1. account for	2. carry on	3. clean up	4. died out	5. fallen behind
6. gave away	7. handed in	8. feel up	9. hand round	10. called on
11. asked for	12. hold on	13. looked after	14. run into	15. saw, off
16. took on	17. wear away	18. run out	19. talked over	20. waited for

IV

1. wind up	2. called out	3. getting on	4. laid out	5. make out
6. move in	7. see about	8. sold out	9. works at	10. be back

10. PUNCTUATION

Answer Key

I

1. (a)	2. (c)	3. (d)	4. (a)	5. (d)	6. (a)	7. (a)	8. (b)	9. (d)	10. (c)
11. (d)	12. (c)	13. (c)	14. (a)	15. (a)	16. (d)	17. (d)	18. (c)	19. (d)	20. (d)

II

1. Why are you not resting?	2. I just came back from the theatre.
3. Don't be such an idiot.	4. Where are the apples kept?
5. How could you do that to a good friend?	6. Rani went and bought the ice-cream.
7. I hope you succeed in life.	8. Robert Browning is a famous poet.
9. Why is it taking so long?	10. When will we be reaching Dehradun?

III

Kunal is one of the most laid-back people I know. He is tall and slim with black hair, and he always wears a T-shirt and black jeans. His jeans have holes in them, and his converse boots are scruffy too. He usually sits at the back of the class, and he often seems to be sleepy. However, when the result of exam given out he always gets an "A" grade. I don't think he's as lazy as he appears to be.

IV

1. We had a great time in France – the kids really enjoyed it.	2. Some people work best in the mornings; others do better in the evenings.
3. What are you doing next weekend?	4. Mother had to go into hospital; she had heart problem.
5. Did you know why I was upset?	6. It is a fine idea; let us hope that it is going to work.
7. We will be arriving at least on Monday morning, I think so.	8. A textbook can be a 'wall' between teacher and class.
9. The girl's father sat in a corner.	10. In the words of Murphy's Law: Anything that can go wrong will go wrong.
11. A grandparent's job is easier than a parent's.	12. It looks as if the sun goes around the earth, but in reality the earth goes round the sun.
13. He neither smiled, spoke, nor looked at me.	14. Long ago, in a distant country, there lived a beautiful princess.
15. It was my aunt who took Shiv yesterday, not my father.	16. Deepika was invited to the party, but she was ill, so Lara went instead of her.
17. Sorry to disturb you, could I speak to you for a moment?	18. Is it any use expecting them to be on time?
19. Jai is going to sleep during the wedding was rather embarrassing.	20. Having lost all my money, I went home.

11. TENSES

Answer Key

I									
1. (d)	2. (a)	3. (d)	4. (c)	5. (b)	6. (c)	7. (d)	8. (b)	9. (a)	10. (b)
11. (d)	12. (b)	13. (c)	14. (b)	15. (a)	16. (b)	17. (d)	18. (d)	19. (d)	20. (c)
21. (c)	22. (a)	23. (a)	24. (b)	25. (c)	26. (d)	27. (a)	28. (d)	29. (a)	30. (c)

12. CONDITIONALS

Answer Key

1. go	2. didn't rain	3. had worn	4. would have watched	5. had not signed
6. would live	7. switch off	8. would have understood	9. explained	10. might have arrived
11. won't play	12. grew	13. would see	14. didn't have to do	15. hadn't stayed up
16. wait	17. would miss	18. would have helped	19. had used	20. would be
21. can stay	22. had seen	23. would be	24. expands	25. should have received
26. hadn't torn off	27. tidies	28. would you do	29. were	30. wait

13. VOICE

Answer Key

I

1. (b)	2. (b)	3. (b)	4. (b)	5. (a)	6. (b)	7. (c)	8. (b)	9. (a)	10. (a)
11. (c)	12. (c)								

II

1. (d)	2. (c)	3. (b)	4. (b)	5. (a)	6. (a)	7. (a)	8. (d)	9. (a)	10. (c)
11. (b)	12. (b)	13. (a)	14. (d)	15. (d)	16. (d)	17. (d)	18. (b)	19. (d)	

III

1. The fire damaged the building.	2. Who taught you French?
3. The manager will give you a ticket.	4. Spectators thronged the streets.
5. Everyone will blame us.	6. The wind blew down the trees.
7. The police caught the thieves.	8. Alice posted the letter.
9. The hostess received us.	10. Someone killed the snake with a stick.

IV

1. The door is opened by him.	2. The table is set by us.
3. A lot of money is paid by her.	4. A picture is drawn by me.
5. Blue shoes are worn by them.	6. You are not helped by them.
7. The book is not opened by him.	8. The letter is not written by you.
9. Are you picked up by your mum?	10. Was the thief caught by the police officer?

14. REPORTED SPEECH

Answer Key

I

1. (c)	2. (a)	3. (a)	4. (c)	5. (c)	6. (d)	7. (b)	8. (a)	9. (c)	10. (a)
11. (c)	12. (b)								

II

1. (c)	2. (b)	3. (b)	4. (a)	5. (b)	6. (b)	7. (b)	8. (b)	9. (c)	10. (a)
11. (b)	12. (b)	13. (b)	14. (c)	15. (b)					

III

1. that he loved that town.	2. if / whether I liked soccer.
3. that he couldn't drive a lorry.	4. to be nice to my brother.
5. not to be nasty.	6. not to waste their money.
7. what he had decided to do.	8. that he always woke up early.
9. to revise their lessons.	10. where I had been.

IV

1. She asked where her jacket was.	2. Naina asked us how we were.
3. He asked if he had to do it.	4. The mother asked her daughter where she had been.
5. She asked her girlfriend which dress she liked best.	6. She wanted to know what they were doing.
7. He wanted to know if I was going to the cinema.	8. The teacher wanted to know who spoke English.
9. She asked me how I knew that.	10. My friend asked me if Priyanka had talked to Kunal.

V

1. He said, "I like this song."	2. "Where is your sister?" she asked me.
3. "I don't speak Assamese," she said.	4. "Say hello to Satya," they said.
5. "The film began at seven o'clock," he said.	6. "Don't play on the grass, boys," she said.
7. "Where have you spent your money?" she asked him.	8. "I never make mistakes," he said.
9. "Does she know Dr. Roy?" he wanted to know.	10. "Don't try this at home," the stuntman told the audience.

15. CONCORD

Answer Key									
I									
1. (c)	2. (b)	3. (d)	4. (c)	5. (b)	6. (c)	7. (a)	8. a)	9. (b)	10. (c)
11. (d)	12. (d)	13. (b)	14. (c)	15. (c)	16. (a)	17. (b)	18. (d)	19. (c)	20. (a)
21. (b)	22. (a)								

16. QUESTION FORMS

Answer Key	
I	
1. What would you have done?	2. What are we going to do tomorrow?
3. What were her last words?	4. What shall we do?
5. What better could they have done?	6. What would we have eaten?
7. When will they have scored three points?	8. When should we start?
9. When must we go to bed tomorrow night?	10. When would you have started to get ready?
11. When will the report be ready?	12. When had you seen him last?
13. Where shall we dine tonight?	14. Where will he have been 65 by age?
15. Where would you have got your car washed?	16. Where would you go if you had 100 dollars?
17. Where have all the cookies gone?	18. Where are they going to play baseball tonight?
19. Why would you do that?	20. Why should we help them?
21. Why were you all playing in the street?	22. Why would he have got a new car?
23. Why do we have to mow the grass?	24. Why have the criminal shouldn't committed the crime?
25. Who will be coming to reunion the family?	26. Who will be the first to walk on Mars?
27. Who has been a major soccer to a league?	28. Whose glasses were you wearing?
29. Who could have done a better job?	30. Who shall we appoint as the next president?

II	
1. Yes/no	2. Choice
3. Yes/no	4. Question/word
5. Question/word	6. Question/word
7. Choice	8. Question/word
9. Question/word	10. Opinion
III	
1. What is she opening?	2. Where are the boys hiding?
3. Who prefers porridge for breakfast?	4. What does Prasad have on Thursday?
5. When did Anil and Anu go to the swimming pool?	6. Where is the plane landing?
7. What is ringing?	8. Why does Chitra have to stop?
9. What does Ashima's new bike cost?	10. Who is walking along the beach of the river?

17. COLLOCATIONS

Answer Key

I									
1. (b)	2. (a)	3. (a)	4. (b)	5. (a)	6. (c)	7. (b)	8. (b)	9. (a)	10. (c)
II									
1. (d)	2. (e)	3. (d)	4. (e)	5. (a)	6. (c)	7. (b)	8. (c)	9. (a)	10. (d)
11. (e)	12. (a)	13. (b)	14. (b)	15. (b)	16. (c)	17. (a)	18. (e)	19. (d)	20. (e)
21. (b)	22. (c)	23. (c)	24. (d)	25. (e)	26. (a)	27. (b)	28. (a)	29. (c)	30. (d)
31. (b)	32. (d)	33. (e)	34. (a)	35. (b)	36. (e)	37. (c)	38. (a)	39. (d)	40. (e)
41. (a)	42. (b)	43. (c)	44. (d)	45. (e)	46. (a)	47. (b)	48. (c)	49. (d)	50. (e)

18. JUMBLED WORDS

Answer Key				
1. Scramble	2. Balance	3. Universe	4. Professor	5. Atlantis
6. Paradise	7. Statement	8. Experience	9. Offspring	10. Overcoat
11. Glorious	12. Child	13. Justify	14. Equal	15. Specific
16. Enrich	17. Adventure	18. Debate	19. Famous	20. Natural
21. Cell	22. Life	23. Bacteria	24. Evolution	25. Microscope
26. Virus	27. Organism	28. Cloning	29. Gene	30. Ecology
31. Energy	32. Chromosome	33. Plant	34. Fungi	35. Biologist
36. Animal	37. Growth	38. Fossil	39. Protein	40. Nucleus
41. Lake	42. Gold	43. Volcano	44. Earthquake	45. Mountain
46. River	47. Desert	48. Ocean	49. Rock	50. Water
51. Tree	52. Lava	53. Continent	54. Magma	55. Forest
56. Iceberg	57. Grass	58. Soil	59. Rain	60. World

19. SYNONYMS AND ANTONYMS

Answer Key

I

1. (b)	2. (a)	3. (c)	4. (c)	5. (a)	6. (b)	7. (b)	8. (c)	9. (a)	10. (c)

II

1. (d)	2. (c)	3. (a)	4. (d)	5. (a)	6. (c)	7. (d)	8. (d)	9. (b)	10. (c)
11. (d)	12. (b)	13. (a)	14. (d)	15. (d)	16. (b)	17. (d)	18. (d)	19. (c)	20. (c)
21. (d)	22. (d)	23. (a)	24. (a)	25. (d)	26. (d)	27. (d)	28. (b)	29. (b)	30. (c)
31. (b)	32. (b)	33. (d)	34. (c)	35. (a)	36. (c)	37. (c)	38. (a)	39. (d)	40. (d)
41. (a)	42. (a)	43. (a)	44. (a)	45. (c)	46. (c)	47. (a)	48. (d)	49. (d)	50. (b)
51. (a)	52. (b)	53. (b)	54. (d)	55. (b)	56. (c)	57. (b)	58. (d)	59. (d)	60. (c)
61. (a)	62. (b)	63. (d)	64. (d)	65. (b)	66. (d)	67. (a)	68. (d)	69. (a)	70. (c)
71. (a)	72. (c)	73. (a)	74. (b)	75. (d)	76. (a)	77. (d)	78. (c)	79. (c)	80. (b)
81. (d)	82. (b)	83. (c)	84. (d)	85. (c)	86. (a)	87. (c)	88. (d)	89. (a)	90. (a)
91. (d)	92. (b)	93. (c)	94. (c)	95. (c)	96. (d)	97. (b)	98. (b)	99. (a)	100. (b)
101. (b)	102. (d)	103. (b)	104. (c)	105. (c)	106. (d)	107. (b)	108. (d)	109. (c)	110. (a)
111. (d)	112. (c)	113. (c)	114. (c)	115. (a)	116. (a)	117. (c)	118. (b)	119. (c)	120. (b)
121. (d)	122. (b)	123. (d)	124. (a)	125. (b)	126. (d)	127. (a)	128. (a)	129. (b)	130. (b)
131. (a)	132. (c)	133. (c)	134. (b)	135. (a)	136. (c)	137. (c)	138. (a)	139. (d)	140. (b)
141. (d)	142. (a)	143. (d)	144. (d)	145. (b)	146. (b)	147. (d)	148. (d)	149. (d)	150. (c)
151. (b)	152. (b)	153. (d)	154. (d)	155. (a)	156. (d)	157. (c)	158. (d)	159. (c)	160. (c)
161. (b)	162. (c)	163. (c)	164. (b)	165. (a)	166. (b)	167. (a)	168. (c)	169. (d)	170. (a)
171. (c)	172. (d)	173. (d)	174. (a)	175. (d)	176. (b)	177. (a)	178. (c)	179. (a)	180. (b)
181. (b)	182. (d)	183. (b)	184. (d)	185. (a)	186. (c)	187. (d)	188. (b)	189. (a)	190. (b)
191. (c)	192. (a)	193. (b)	194. (d)	195. (a)	196. (c)	197. (c)	198. (a)		

III									
1. (a)	2. (b)	3. (d)	4. (a)	5. (d)	6. (c)	7. (b)	8. (b)	9. (c)	10. (b)
11. (d)	12. (b)	13. (a)	14. (a)	15. (b)	16. (c)	17. (c)	18. (a)	19. (b)	20. (a)
21. (c)	22. (a)	23. (b)	24. (d)	25. (b)	26. (d)	27. (a)	28. (d)	29. (a)	30. (a)
31. (a)	32. (b)	33. (a)	34. (d)	35. (a)	36. (a)	37. (b)	38. (b)	39. (a)	40. (c)
41. (a)	42. (d)	43. (a)	44. (a)	45. (b)	46. (b)	47. (c)	48. (d)	49. (d)	50. (c)
51. (d)	52. (a)	53. (d)	54. (d)	55. (a)	56. (b)	57. (c)	58. (c)	59. (b)	60. (a)
61. (a)	62. (d)	63. (c)	64. (c)	65. (c)	66. (d)	67. (a)	68. (a)	69. (d)	70. (d)
71. (a)	72. (d)	73. (c)	74. (c)	75. (b)	76. (d)	77. (d)	78. (c)	79. (d)	80. (c)
81. (d)	82. (a)	83. (a)	84. (a)	85. (d)	86. (c)	87. (b)	88. (b)	89. (a)	90. (d)
91. (b)	92. (c)	93. (c)	94. (a)	95. (b)	96. (d)	97. (d)	98. (d)	99. (a)	100. (b)
101. (c)	102. (d)	103. (d)	104. (a)	105. (c)	106. (c)	107. (b)	108. (b)	109. (a)	110. (d)
111. (a)	112. (b)	113. (c)	114. (c)	115. (a)	116. (b)	117. (c)	118. (c)	119. (d)	120. (b)
121. (c)	122. (d)	123. (a)	124. (c)	125. (b)	126. (d)	127. (d)	128. (c)	129. (c)	130. (c)
131. (c)	132. (a)	133. (d)	134. (a)	135. (b)	136. (b)	137. (a)	138. (b)	139. (b)	140. (a)
141. (d)	142. (c)	143. (b)	144. (c)	145. (b)	146. (b)	147. (d)	148. (c)	149. (d)	150. (a)
151. (c)	152. (c)	153. (b)	154. (b)	155. (b)	156. (d)	157. (b)	158. (a)	159. (d)	160. (b)
161. (b)	162. (a)	163. (c)	164. (c)	165. (d)	166. (d)	167. (b)	168. (c)	169. (d)	170. (d)
171. (c)	172. (c)	173. (b)	174. (c)	175. (b)	176. (d)	177. (d)	178. (d)	179. (b)	180. (a)
181. (a)	182. (c)	183. (d)	184. (b)	185. (b)	186. (c)	187. (b)	188. (c)	189. (a)	190. (b)
191. (c)	192. (d)	193. (a)	194. (b)	195. (c)	196. (c)	197. (b)	198. (c)	199. (b)	200. (b)

20. HOMOPHONES AND HOMONYMS

Answer Key									
I									
1. (a)	2. (b)	3. (b)	4. (b)	5. (a)	6. (a)	7. (a)	8. (a)	9. (a)	10. (b)
II									
1. (a)	2. (b)	3. (b)	4. (b)	5. (c)	6. (b)	7. (b)	8. (a)	9. (b)	10. (a)
11. (b)	12. (b)	13. (a)	14. (b)	15. (a)	16. (b)	17. (b)	18. (b)	19. (a)	20. (b)
21. (b)	22. (b)	23. (a)	24. (b)	25. (b)	26. (a)	27. (b)	28. (b)	29. (a)	30. (a)
31. (b)	32. (b)	33. (b)	34. (b)	35. (b)	36. (c)	37. (b)	38. (a)	39. (b)	40. (b)
III									
1. (c)	2. (a)	3. (b)	4. (c)	5. (b)	6. (c)	7. (a)	8. (b)	9. (b)	10. (a)
11. (a)	12. (a)	13. (b)	14. (b)	15. (b)	16. (a)	17. (a)	18. (a)	19. (b)	20. (a)
21. (a)	22. (a)	23. (a)	24. (b)	25. (c)	26. (b)	27. (b)	28. (a)	29. (a)	30. (a)
31. (a)	32. (a)	33. (a)	34. (b)	35. (a)	36. (c)	37. (a)	38. (a)	39. (c)	40. (a)

21. SPELLING

Answer Key									
I									
1. (a)	2. (a)	3. (b)	4. (a)	5. (b)	6. (a)	7. (b)	8. (a)	9. (a)	10. (b)
11. (b)	12. (a)	13. (b)	14. (a)	15. (a)	16. (b)	17. (a)	18. (b)	19. (b)	20. (a)
II									
1. (d)	2. (d)	3. (d)	4. (c)	5. (c)	6. (b)	7. (b)	8. (a)	9. (c)	10. (b)
11. (c)	12. (d)	13. (a)	14. (d)	15. (c)	16. (a)	17. (b)	18. (a)	19. (c)	20. (d)
21. (c)	22. (c)	23. (a)	24. (d)						

22. ANALOGY

Answer Key

I									
1. (c)	2. (c)	3. (c)	4. (b)	5. (c)	6. (c)	7. (a)	8. (c)	9. (c)	10. (b)
II									
1. (c)	2. (a)	3. (d)	4. (d)	5. (d)					
III									
1. (F)	2. (T)	3. (T)	4. (T)	5. (F)					

23. ONE WORD

Answer Key

1. (a)	2. (a)	3. (c)	4. (b)	5. (a)	6. (b)	7. (b)	8. (a)	9. (c)	10. (b)
11. (b)	12. (a)	13. (b)	14. (a)	15. (c)	16. (b)	17. (a)	18. (a)	19. (a)	20. (a)

24. IDIOMS

Answer Key

I									
1. (a)	2. (c)	3. (b)	4. (d)	5. (a)	6. (d)	7. (b)	8. (d)	9. (b)	10. (d)
11. (c)	12. (a)	13. (c)	14. (a)	15. (a)	16. (c)	17. (d)	18. (c)	19. (b)	20. (b)
21. (a)	22. (d)	23. (b)	24. (a)	25. (c)	26. (b)	27. (d)	28. (a)	29. (b)	30. (c)
31. (c)	32. (a)	33. (d)	34. (b)	35. (a)	36. (c)	37. (c)	38. (a)	39. (a)	40. (c)
41. (a)	42. (d)	43. (b)	44. (c)	45. (c)	46. (c)	47. (b)	48. (b)	49. (a)	50. (a)
51. (b)	52. (c)	53. (d)	54. (d)	55. (a)					

II				
1. hell or high	2. curiosity	3. all bark	4. of your own	5. rags to
6. hat	7. horses	8. cannon	9. a small	10. jumbo

SECTION 2: READING COMPREHENSION

1. COMPREHENSION OF WRITTEN MEDIUMS

Answer Key					
I	1. (c)	2. (a)	3. (c)	4. (d)	5. (c)
II	9. True	10. False			

SECTION 3: SPOKEN AND WRITTEN EXPRESSIONS

1. TIPS FOR SPOKEN AND EXPRESSIONS

Answer Key									
I									
1. (a)	2. (b)	3. (b)	4. (c)	5. (b)	6. (c)	7. (a)	8. (b)	9. (c)	10. (c)
II									
1. (a)	2. (c)	3. (c)	4. (b)	5. (c)	6. (a)	7. (c)	8. (a)	9. (a)	10. (c)
11. (a)	12. (b)	13. (c)	14. (a)	15. (b)					

III				
1. please	2. requested	3. kindly	4. excuse me	5. sorry
6. kindly	7. thanks	8. welcome	9. please	10. request
11. sincerest	12. may	13. respect	14. of course	15. apologise

SECTION 4: ACHIEVERS' SECTION

HIGHER ORDER THINKING SKILLS (HOTS)

Answer Key

	I				
A	1. (b)	2. (a)	3. (c)	4. (a)	5. (a)
B	1. (b)	2. (a)	3. (c)	4. (b)	5. (c)
C	1 is going	2. is carrying	3. is	4. puts, is wearing	5. is taking, is raining
D	1. (b)	2. (b)	3. (b)	4. (a)	5. (b)
E	1. (b)	2. (c)	3. (c)	4. (d)	5. (d)
F	1. I was eaten an ice cream		5. He was written a novel.		
G	1. What does your brother like/love for dessert? 2. When is Prateek going for a movie? 3. Where did Anil and Anu leave for yesterday?				
	II				
	1. Dog walking 2. Outgoing, adventurous, likes exploring 3. A dog walking company 4. Athletic, animal-lovers, nature loving, energetic, strong, patient 5. My Pet Biz				
	III				
	1. (b)	2. (a)	3. (c)	4. (c)	5. (b)

SHORT ANSWER QUESTIONS

Answer Key

I

1. truth	2. honesty	3. children	4. beasts	5. Solomon, kings
6. Cleanliness	7. Birds	8. grammar	9. Nile, rivers	10. boy, honesty
11. apple	12. voice	13. lie	14. Wisdom	15. jury
16. silver, metals	17. waters	18. habits	19. bird, worm	20. Edison, phonograph

II

1. (a)	2. (b)	3. (a)	4. (c)	5. (b)	6. (c)	7. (a)	8. (a)	9. (b)	10. (c)

III

1. goes	2. knocking	3. pressed	4. with	5. explain
6. shut	7. behind	8. despite	9. kind	10. Feeling
11. time	12. let	13. showed	14. this	15. asked
16. After	17. buy	18. give	19. up	20. What

IV

1. The men in question (John, Mohan, and Sohan deserve awards.	2. Several countries participated in the airlift: Italy, Belgium, France, and Luxembourg.
3. "Only one course was open to us: surrender," said the ex-major, "and we did."	4. Judge Carswell—later to be nominated for the Supreme Court—had ruled against civil rights.
5. In last week's New Yorker, one of my favorite magazines, I enjoyed reading Leland's article "How Not to Go Camping."	6. "Yes," Jim said, "I'll be home by ten."
7. There was only one thing to do—study till dawn.	8. Montaigne wrote the following: "A wise man never loses anything, if he has himself."
9. The following are the primary colors: red, blue, and yellow.	10. Arriving on the 8:10 plane were Liz Brooks, my old roommate; her husband; and Tim, their son.
11. When the teacher commented that her spelling was poor, Lynn replied, "All the members of my family are poor spellers. Why not me?"	12. He used the phrase "you know" so often that I finally said, "No, I don't know."
13. The automobile dealer handled three makes of cars: Volkswagens, Porsches, and Mercedes Benz.	14. Though Phil said he would arrive on the 9:19 flight, he came instead on the 10:36 flight.

15. "Whoever thought," said Helen, "that Jack would be elected class president?"	16. In baseball, a "show boat" is a man who shows off.
17. The minister quoted Isaiah 5:21 in last Sunday's sermon.	18. There was a very interesting article entitled "The New Rage for Folk Singing" in last Sunday's New York Times newspaper.
19. "Whoever is elected secretary of the club—Ashley, or Chandra, or Aisha—must be prepared to do a great deal of work," said Jumita, the previous secretary.	20. Darwin's On the Origin of Species (1859) caused a great controversy when it appeared.

V

1. into	2. into	3. in	4. to	5. in
6. near	7. on	8. up	9. out	10. down
11. over	12. about			

VI

1. Do your parents watch television in the evening?	2. Jeremy always takes the eight o'clock bus on Monday mornings.
3. Ben, could you bring the bread to the dining room, please?	4. Mrs Rogers likes to go shopping with her friends when she is in London.
5. There are many interesting books at the library, have you read them all?	6. Now he is studying at the university.
7. He could hardly think he was so excited.	8. The light was so bright that we had to cover our eyes.
9. She said that he had already eaten.	10. Sometimes Brian comes to our house.
11. He is studying English as well as French.	12. It was so cold that we had to wear our coats.
13. I always take my lunch to work.	14. If your eyes are sore, buy some eye drops tomorrow.

VII

1. My name is Maria.	2. Susan reads a comic.
3. They play in the garden.	4. He sings a song.
5. I have got a dog.	6. We sit on the bench.
7. I do my homework.	8. She phones her friend.
9. He likes computer games.	10. The girl is helping her mother.
11. Gandhiji's greatest strength was his belief in God.	12. This dress looks beautiful on you.

13. Salesmen and assistants are required at shop.	14. I wish I had never left the home.
15. Can you lend me some money?	16. Here Chinese and Italian meals are served.
17. What are the benefits of cinnamon?	18. He fought for the freedom of India.
19. He hit the ball so hard that it was lost	20. All types of repair works are undertaken.
21. The beauties of nature are beyond the description.	22. Cut some slices of tomato and cucumber.
23. Birbal was extremely clever and witty.	24. I lost my bag in the train.
25. You shall be punished for your misconduct.	
VIII	
1. John said that he loved that town.	2. He asked me if / whether I liked soccer.
3. He said that he couldn't drive a lorry.	4. He asked me to be nice to my brother.
5. He urged me not to be nasty.	6. She told the boys not to waste their money.
7. She asked him what he had decided to do.	8. He said that he always woke up early.
9. He advised the students to revise their lessons.	10. He wanted to know where I had been.
IX	
1. The words are explained by the teacher today.	2. We were sent a letter the day before yesterday.
3. This car will not be stolen. It's too old.	4. This street has already been closed because of snow.
5. A new restaurant will be opened next week.	6. He was invited to the party yesterday.
7. The blue box cannot be seen.	8. I was given the book by my friend last Sunday.
9. The dishes have not been washed by my little brother.	10. I will not be asked by Rakesh.

MODEL TEST PAPER

Answer Key									
1. (b)	2. (a)	3. (a)	4. (b)	5. (c)	6. (c)	7. (c)	8. (a)	9. (c)	10. (c)
11. (c)	12. (b)	13. (a)	14. (b)	15. (c)					

OMR ANSWER SHEET

1. NAME (IN ENGLISH CAPITAL LETTERS ONLY)

2. FATHER'S NAME (IN ENGLISH CAPITAL LETTERS ONLY)

Students must write and darken the respective circles completely for School Code, Class and Roll No. columns, othewise their Answer Sheets will not be evaluated.

3. SCHOOL CODE

A–Z	A–Z	0–9	0–9	0–9	0–9

4. % of Marks / Grade

In Last Class

Percentage OR Grade

Percentage			Grade
0–9	0–9	0–9	A–J

5. CLASS

0, 1, 2	0, 1, 2, 4, 5, 6, 7, 8, 9, M, B

6. ROLL NO.

0–9	0–9	0–9

7. GENDER

MALE ○

FEMALE ○

8. STREAM (Only for Class XI and XII Students)

MATHEMATICS ○

BIOLOGY ○

OTHERS ○

9. MARK YOUR ANSWERS WITH HB PENCIL/BALL POINT PEN (BLUE/BLACK)

Q.					Q.				
1.	A	B	C	D	26.	A	B	C	D
2.	A	B	C	D	27.	A	B	C	D
3.	A	B	C	D	28.	A	B	C	D
4.	A	B	C	D	29.	A	B	C	D
5.	A	B	C	D	30.	A	B	C	D
6.	A	B	C	D	31.	A	B	C	D
7.	A	B	C	D	32.	A	B	C	D
8.	A	B	C	D	33.	A	B	C	D
9.	A	B	C	D	34.	A	B	C	D
10.	A	B	C	D	35.	A	B	C	D
11.	A	B	C	D	36.	A	B	C	D
12.	A	B	C	D	37.	A	B	C	D
13.	A	B	C	D	38.	A	B	C	D
14.	A	B	C	D	39.	A	B	C	D
15.	A	B	C	D	40.	A	B	C	D
16.	A	B	C	D	41.	A	B	C	D
17.	A	B	C	D	42.	A	B	C	D
18.	A	B	C	D	43.	A	B	C	D
19.	A	B	C	D	44.	A	B	C	D
20.	A	B	C	D	45.	A	B	C	D
21.	A	B	C	D	46.	A	B	C	D
22.	A	B	C	D	47.	A	B	C	D
23.	A	B	C	D	48.	A	B	C	D
24.	A	B	C	D	49.	A	B	C	D
25.	A	B	C	D	50.	A	B	C	D

V&S Publisher, Head Office: F-2/16 Ansari Road, Daryaganj, New Delhi-110002, Ph: 011-23240026-27, *Email:info@vspublishers.com*
Regional Office: 5-1-707/1, Brij Bhawan (Beside Central Bank of India Lane) Bank Street, Koti, Hyderabad-500 095, Ph: 040-24737290, *Email: vspublishershyd@gmail.com*
Branch: Jaywant Industrial Estate, 1st Floor–108, Tardeo Road Opposite Sobo Central Mall, Mumbai - 400 034, Ph: 022-23510736, *Email: vspublishersmum@gmail.com*

OMR ANSWER SHEET

1. NAME (IN ENGLISH CAPITAL LETTERS ONLY)

2. FATHER'S NAME (IN ENGLISH CAPITAL LETTERS ONLY)

Students must write and darken the respective circles completely for School Code, Class and Roll No. columns, othewise their Answer Sheets will not be evaluated.

3. SCHOOL CODE

A–Z	A–Z	0–9	0–9	0–9	0–9

4. % of Marks | Grade

In Last Class

Percentage OR Grade

Percentage			Grade
0–9	0–9	0–9	A–J

5. CLASS

0, 1, 2	0, 1, 2, 4, 5, 6, 7, 8, 9, M, B

6. ROLL NO.

0–9	0–9	0–9

7. GENDER

MALE ○

FEMALE ○

8. STREAM (Only for Class XI and XII Students)

MATHEMATICS ○

BIOLOGY ○

OTHERS ○

9. MARK YOUR ANSWERS WITH HB PENCIL/BALL POINT PEN (BLUE/BLACK)

Q.					Q.				
1.	A	B	C	D	26.	A	B	C	D
2.	A	B	C	D	27.	A	B	C	D
3.	A	B	C	D	28.	A	B	C	D
4.	A	B	C	D	29.	A	B	C	D
5.	A	B	C	D	30.	A	B	C	D
6.	A	B	C	D	31.	A	B	C	D
7.	A	B	C	D	32.	A	B	C	D
8.	A	B	C	D	33.	A	B	C	D
9.	A	B	C	D	34.	A	B	C	D
10.	A	B	C	D	35.	A	B	C	D
11.	A	B	C	D	36.	A	B	C	D
12.	A	B	C	D	37.	A	B	C	D
13.	A	B	C	D	38.	A	B	C	D
14.	A	B	C	D	39.	A	B	C	D
15.	A	B	C	D	40.	A	B	C	D
16.	A	B	C	D	41.	A	B	C	D
17.	A	B	C	D	42.	A	B	C	D
18.	A	B	C	D	43.	A	B	C	D
19.	A	B	C	D	44.	A	B	C	D
20.	A	B	C	D	45.	A	B	C	D
21.	A	B	C	D	46.	A	B	C	D
22.	A	B	C	D	47.	A	B	C	D
23.	A	B	C	D	48.	A	B	C	D
24.	A	B	C	D	49.	A	B	C	D
25.	A	B	C	D	50.	A	B	C	D

V&S Publisher, Head Office: F-2/16 Ansari Road, Daryaganj, New Delhi-110002, Ph: 011-23240026-27, Email:info@vspublishers.com
Regional Office: 5-1-707/1, Brij Bhawan (Beside Central Bank of India Lane) Bank Street, Koti, Hyderabad-500 095, Ph: 040-24737290, Email: vspublishershyd@gmail.com
Branch: Jaywant Industrial Estate, 1st Floor–108, Tardeo Road Opposite Sobo Central Mall, Mumbai - 400 034, Ph: 022-23510736, Email: vspublishersmum@gmail.com

OMR ANSWER SHEET

1. NAME (IN ENGLISH CAPITAL LETTERS ONLY)

2. FATHER'S NAME (IN ENGLISH CAPITAL LETTERS ONLY)

Students must write and darken the respective circles completely for School Code, Class and Roll No. columns, othewise their Answer Sheets will not be evaluated.

3. SCHOOL CODE

Columns 1–2: A B C D E F G H I J K L M N O P Q R S T U V W X Y Z

Columns 3–6: 0 1 2 3 4 5 6 7 8 9

4. % of Marks | Grade

In Last Class

Percentage OR Grade

Percentage (3 columns): 0 1 2 3 4 5 6 7 8 9

Grade: A B C D E F G H I J

5. CLASS

Column 1: 0 1 2

Column 2: 0 1 2 4 5 6 7 8 9 M B

6. ROLL NO.

Columns 1–3: 0 1 2 3 4 5 6 7 8 9

7. GENDER

MALE ○

FEMALE ○

8. STREAM (Only for Class XI and XII Students)

MATHEMATICS ○

BIOLOGY ○

OTHERS ○

9. MARK YOUR ANSWERS WITH HB PENCIL/BALL POINT PEN (BLUE/BLACK)

1.	A	B	C	D	26.	A	B	C	D
2.	A	B	C	D	27.	A	B	C	D
3.	A	B	C	D	28.	A	B	C	D
4.	A	B	C	D	29.	A	B	C	D
5.	A	B	C	D	30.	A	B	C	D
6.	A	B	C	D	31.	A	B	C	D
7.	A	B	C	D	32.	A	B	C	D
8.	A	B	C	D	33.	A	B	C	D
9.	A	B	C	D	34.	A	B	C	D
10.	A	B	C	D	35.	A	B	C	D
11.	A	B	C	D	36.	A	B	C	D
12.	A	B	C	D	37.	A	B	C	D
13.	A	B	C	D	38.	A	B	C	D
14.	A	B	C	D	39.	A	B	C	D
15.	A	B	C	D	40.	A	B	C	D
16.	A	B	C	D	41.	A	B	C	D
17.	A	B	C	D	42.	A	B	C	D
18.	A	B	C	D	43.	A	B	C	D
19.	A	B	C	D	44.	A	B	C	D
20.	A	B	C	D	45.	A	B	C	D
21.	A	B	C	D	46.	A	B	C	D
22.	A	B	C	D	47.	A	B	C	D
23.	A	B	C	D	48.	A	B	C	D
24.	A	B	C	D	49.	A	B	C	D
25.	A	B	C	D	50.	A	B	C	D

V&S Publisher, Head Office: F-2/16 Ansari Road, Daryaganj, New Delhi-110002, Ph: 011-23240026-27, Email:info@vspublishers.com
Regional Office: 5-1-707/1, Brij Bhawan (Beside Central Bank of India Lane) Bank Street, Koti, Hyderabad-500 095, Ph: 040-24737290, Email: vspublishershyd@gmail.com
Branch: Jaywant Industrial Estate, 1st Floor–108, Tardeo Road Opposite Sobo Central Mall, Mumbai - 400 034, Ph: 022-23510736, Email: vspublishersmum@gmail.com

OMR ANSWER SHEET

1. NAME (IN ENGLISH CAPITAL LETTERS ONLY)

2. FATHER'S NAME (IN ENGLISH CAPITAL LETTERS ONLY)

Students must write and darken the respective circles completely for School Code, Class and Roll No. columns, othewise their Answer Sheets will not be evaluated.

3. SCHOOL CODE

A–Z	A–Z	0–9	0–9	0–9	0–9

4. % of Marks | Grade

In Last Class

Percentage OR Grade

0–9	0–9	0–9	A–J

5. CLASS

0, 1, 2	0, 1, 2, 4, 5, 6, 7, 8, 9, M, B

6. ROLL NO.

0–9	0–9	0–9

7. GENDER

MALE ◯

FEMALE ◯

8. STREAM (Only for Class XI and XII Students)

MATHEMATICS ◯

BIOLOGY ◯

OTHERS ◯

9. MARK YOUR ANSWERS WITH HB PENCIL/BALL POINT PEN (BLUE/BLACK)

1.	A	B	C	D	26.	A	B	C	D
2.	A	B	C	D	27.	A	B	C	D
3.	A	B	C	D	28.	A	B	C	D
4.	A	B	C	D	29.	A	B	C	D
5.	A	B	C	D	30.	A	B	C	D
6.	A	B	C	D	31.	A	B	C	D
7.	A	B	C	D	32.	A	B	C	D
8.	A	B	C	D	33.	A	B	C	D
9.	A	B	C	D	34.	A	B	C	D
10.	A	B	C	D	35.	A	B	C	D
11.	A	B	C	D	36.	A	B	C	D
12.	A	B	C	D	37.	A	B	C	D
13.	A	B	C	D	38.	A	B	C	D
14.	A	B	C	D	39.	A	B	C	D
15.	A	B	C	D	40.	A	B	C	D
16.	A	B	C	D	41.	A	B	C	D
17.	A	B	C	D	42.	A	B	C	D
18.	A	B	C	D	43.	A	B	C	D
19.	A	B	C	D	44.	A	B	C	D
20.	A	B	C	D	45.	A	B	C	D
21.	A	B	C	D	46.	A	B	C	D
22.	A	B	C	D	47.	A	B	C	D
23.	A	B	C	D	48.	A	B	C	D
24.	A	B	C	D	49.	A	B	C	D
25.	A	B	C	D	50.	A	B	C	D

V&S Publisher, Head Office: F-2/16 Ansari Road, Daryaganj, New Delhi-110002, Ph: 011-23240026-27, Email:info@vspublishers.com
Regional Office: 5-1-707/1, Brij Bhawan (Beside Central Bank of India Lane) Bank Street, Koti, Hyderabad-500 095, Ph: 040-24737290, Email: vspublishershyd@gmail.com
Branch: Jaywant Industrial Estate, 1st Floor–108, Tardeo Road Opposite Sobo Central Mall, Mumbai - 400 034, Ph: 022-23510736, Email: vspublishersmum@gmail.com

OMR ANSWER SHEET

1. NAME (IN ENGLISH CAPITAL LETTERS ONLY)

2. FATHER'S NAME (IN ENGLISH CAPITAL LETTERS ONLY)

Students must write and darken the respective circles completely for School Code, Class and Roll No. columns, othewise their Answer Sheets will not be evaluated.

3. SCHOOL CODE

A–Z	A–Z	0–9	0–9	0–9	0–9

4. % of Marks / Grade

In Last Class

Percentage OR Grade

0–9	0–9	0–9	A–J

5. CLASS

0, 1, 2	0, 1, 2, 4, 5, 6, 7, 8, 9, M, B

6. ROLL NO.

0–9	0–9	0–9

7. GENDER

MALE ○

FEMALE ○

8. STREAM
(Only for Class XI and XII Students)

MATHEMATICS ○

BIOLOGY ○

OTHERS ○

9. MARK YOUR ANSWERS WITH HB PENCIL/BALL POINT PEN (BLUE/BLACK)

No.					No.				
1.	Ⓐ	Ⓑ	Ⓒ	Ⓓ	26.	Ⓐ	Ⓑ	Ⓒ	Ⓓ
2.	Ⓐ	Ⓑ	Ⓒ	Ⓓ	27.	Ⓐ	Ⓑ	Ⓒ	Ⓓ
3.	Ⓐ	Ⓑ	Ⓒ	Ⓓ	28.	Ⓐ	Ⓑ	Ⓒ	Ⓓ
4.	Ⓐ	Ⓑ	Ⓒ	Ⓓ	29.	Ⓐ	Ⓑ	Ⓒ	Ⓓ
5.	Ⓐ	Ⓑ	Ⓒ	Ⓓ	30.	Ⓐ	Ⓑ	Ⓒ	Ⓓ
6.	Ⓐ	Ⓑ	Ⓒ	Ⓓ	31.	Ⓐ	Ⓑ	Ⓒ	Ⓓ
7.	Ⓐ	Ⓑ	Ⓒ	Ⓓ	32.	Ⓐ	Ⓑ	Ⓒ	Ⓓ
8.	Ⓐ	Ⓑ	Ⓒ	Ⓓ	33.	Ⓐ	Ⓑ	Ⓒ	Ⓓ
9.	Ⓐ	Ⓑ	Ⓒ	Ⓓ	34.	Ⓐ	Ⓑ	Ⓒ	Ⓓ
10.	Ⓐ	Ⓑ	Ⓒ	Ⓓ	35.	Ⓐ	Ⓑ	Ⓒ	Ⓓ
11.	Ⓐ	Ⓑ	Ⓒ	Ⓓ	36.	Ⓐ	Ⓑ	Ⓒ	Ⓓ
12.	Ⓐ	Ⓑ	Ⓒ	Ⓓ	37.	Ⓐ	Ⓑ	Ⓒ	Ⓓ
13.	Ⓐ	Ⓑ	Ⓒ	Ⓓ	38.	Ⓐ	Ⓑ	Ⓒ	Ⓓ
14.	Ⓐ	Ⓑ	Ⓒ	Ⓓ	39.	Ⓐ	Ⓑ	Ⓒ	Ⓓ
15.	Ⓐ	Ⓑ	Ⓒ	Ⓓ	40.	Ⓐ	Ⓑ	Ⓒ	Ⓓ
16.	Ⓐ	Ⓑ	Ⓒ	Ⓓ	41.	Ⓐ	Ⓑ	Ⓒ	Ⓓ
17.	Ⓐ	Ⓑ	Ⓒ	Ⓓ	42.	Ⓐ	Ⓑ	Ⓒ	Ⓓ
18.	Ⓐ	Ⓑ	Ⓒ	Ⓓ	43.	Ⓐ	Ⓑ	Ⓒ	Ⓓ
19.	Ⓐ	Ⓑ	Ⓒ	Ⓓ	44.	Ⓐ	Ⓑ	Ⓒ	Ⓓ
20.	Ⓐ	Ⓑ	Ⓒ	Ⓓ	45.	Ⓐ	Ⓑ	Ⓒ	Ⓓ
21.	Ⓐ	Ⓑ	Ⓒ	Ⓓ	46.	Ⓐ	Ⓑ	Ⓒ	Ⓓ
22.	Ⓐ	Ⓑ	Ⓒ	Ⓓ	47.	Ⓐ	Ⓑ	Ⓒ	Ⓓ
23.	Ⓐ	Ⓑ	Ⓒ	Ⓓ	48.	Ⓐ	Ⓑ	Ⓒ	Ⓓ
24.	Ⓐ	Ⓑ	Ⓒ	Ⓓ	49.	Ⓐ	Ⓑ	Ⓒ	Ⓓ
25.	Ⓐ	Ⓑ	Ⓒ	Ⓓ	50.	Ⓐ	Ⓑ	Ⓒ	Ⓓ

V&S Publisher, Head Office: F-2/16 Ansari Road, Daryaganj, New Delhi-110002, Ph: 011-23240026-27, *Email:info@vspublishers.com*
Regional Office: 5-1-707/1, Brij Bhawan (Beside Central Bank of India Lane) Bank Street, Koti, Hyderabad-500 095, Ph: 040-24737290, *Email: vspublishershyd@gmail.com*
Branch: Jaywant Industrial Estate, 1st Floor–108, Tardeo Road Opposite Sobo Central Mall, Mumbai - 400 034, Ph: 022-23510736, *Email: vspublishersmum@gmail.com*

OMR ANSWER SHEET

1. NAME (IN ENGLISH CAPITAL LETTERS ONLY)

2. FATHER'S NAME (IN ENGLISH CAPITAL LETTERS ONLY)

Students must write and darken the respective circles completely for School Code, Class and Roll No. columns, othewise their Answer Sheets will not be evaluated.

3. SCHOOL CODE

Ⓐ–Ⓩ	Ⓐ–Ⓩ	⓪–⑨	⓪–⑨	⓪–⑨	⓪–⑨

4. % of Marks | Grade

In Last Class

Percentage OR Grade

Percentage			Grade
⓪–⑨	⓪–⑨	⓪–⑨	Ⓐ–Ⓙ

5. CLASS

⓪ ① ②	⓪ ① ② ④ ⑤ ⑥ ⑦ ⑧ ⑨ Ⓜ Ⓑ

6. ROLL NO.

⓪–⑨	⓪–⑨	⓪–⑨

7. GENDER

MALE ○

FEMALE ○

8. STREAM
(Only for Class XI and XII Students)

MATHEMATICS ○

BIOLOGY ○

OTHERS ○

9. MARK YOUR ANSWERS WITH HB PENCIL/BALL POINT PEN (BLUE/BLACK)

1.	Ⓐ	Ⓑ	Ⓒ	Ⓓ	26.	Ⓐ	Ⓑ	Ⓒ	Ⓓ
2.	Ⓐ	Ⓑ	Ⓒ	Ⓓ	27.	Ⓐ	Ⓑ	Ⓒ	Ⓓ
3.	Ⓐ	Ⓑ	Ⓒ	Ⓓ	28.	Ⓐ	Ⓑ	Ⓒ	Ⓓ
4.	Ⓐ	Ⓑ	Ⓒ	Ⓓ	29.	Ⓐ	Ⓑ	Ⓒ	Ⓓ
5.	Ⓐ	Ⓑ	Ⓒ	Ⓓ	30.	Ⓐ	Ⓑ	Ⓒ	Ⓓ
6.	Ⓐ	Ⓑ	Ⓒ	Ⓓ	31.	Ⓐ	Ⓑ	Ⓒ	Ⓓ
7.	Ⓐ	Ⓑ	Ⓒ	Ⓓ	32.	Ⓐ	Ⓑ	Ⓒ	Ⓓ
8.	Ⓐ	Ⓑ	Ⓒ	Ⓓ	33.	Ⓐ	Ⓑ	Ⓒ	Ⓓ
9.	Ⓐ	Ⓑ	Ⓒ	Ⓓ	34.	Ⓐ	Ⓑ	Ⓒ	Ⓓ
10.	Ⓐ	Ⓑ	Ⓒ	Ⓓ	35.	Ⓐ	Ⓑ	Ⓒ	Ⓓ
11.	Ⓐ	Ⓑ	Ⓒ	Ⓓ	36.	Ⓐ	Ⓑ	Ⓒ	Ⓓ
12.	Ⓐ	Ⓑ	Ⓒ	Ⓓ	37.	Ⓐ	Ⓑ	Ⓒ	Ⓓ
13.	Ⓐ	Ⓑ	Ⓒ	Ⓓ	38.	Ⓐ	Ⓑ	Ⓒ	Ⓓ
14.	Ⓐ	Ⓑ	Ⓒ	Ⓓ	39.	Ⓐ	Ⓑ	Ⓒ	Ⓓ
15.	Ⓐ	Ⓑ	Ⓒ	Ⓓ	40.	Ⓐ	Ⓑ	Ⓒ	Ⓓ
16.	Ⓐ	Ⓑ	Ⓒ	Ⓓ	41.	Ⓐ	Ⓑ	Ⓒ	Ⓓ
17.	Ⓐ	Ⓑ	Ⓒ	Ⓓ	42.	Ⓐ	Ⓑ	Ⓒ	Ⓓ
18.	Ⓐ	Ⓑ	Ⓒ	Ⓓ	43.	Ⓐ	Ⓑ	Ⓒ	Ⓓ
19.	Ⓐ	Ⓑ	Ⓒ	Ⓓ	44.	Ⓐ	Ⓑ	Ⓒ	Ⓓ
20.	Ⓐ	Ⓑ	Ⓒ	Ⓓ	45.	Ⓐ	Ⓑ	Ⓒ	Ⓓ
21.	Ⓐ	Ⓑ	Ⓒ	Ⓓ	46.	Ⓐ	Ⓑ	Ⓒ	Ⓓ
22.	Ⓐ	Ⓑ	Ⓒ	Ⓓ	47.	Ⓐ	Ⓑ	Ⓒ	Ⓓ
23.	Ⓐ	Ⓑ	Ⓒ	Ⓓ	48.	Ⓐ	Ⓑ	Ⓒ	Ⓓ
24.	Ⓐ	Ⓑ	Ⓒ	Ⓓ	49.	Ⓐ	Ⓑ	Ⓒ	Ⓓ
25.	Ⓐ	Ⓑ	Ⓒ	Ⓓ	50.	Ⓐ	Ⓑ	Ⓒ	Ⓓ

V&S Publisher, Head Office: F-2/16 Ansari Road, Daryaganj, New Delhi-110002, Ph: 011-23240026-27, *Email:info@vspublishers.com*
Regional Office: 5-1-707/1, Brij Bhawan (Beside Central Bank of India Lane) Bank Street, Koti, Hyderabad-500 095, Ph: 040-24737290, *Email: vspublishershyd@gmail.com*
Branch: Jaywant Industrial Estate, 1st Floor–108, Tardeo Road Opposite Sobo Central Mall, Mumbai - 400 034, Ph: 022-23510736, *Email: vspublishersmum@gmail.com*

OMR ANSWER SHEET

1. NAME (IN ENGLISH CAPITAL LETTERS ONLY)

2. FATHER'S NAME (IN ENGLISH CAPITAL LETTERS ONLY)

Students must write and darken the respective circles completely for School Code, Class and Roll No. columns, othewise their Answer Sheets will not be evaluated.

3. SCHOOL CODE

A B C D E F G H I J K L M N O P Q R S T U V W X Y Z

A B C D E F G H I J K L M N O P Q R S T U V W X Y Z

0 1 2 3 4 5 6 7 8 9

0 1 2 3 4 5 6 7 8 9

0 1 2 3 4 5 6 7 8 9

0 1 2 3 4 5 6 7 8 9

4. % of Marks | Grade

In Last Class

Percentage OR Grade

0 1 2 3 4 5 6 7 8 9

0 1 2 3 4 5 6 7 8 9

0 1 2 3 4 5 6 7 8 9

A B C D E F G H I J

5. CLASS

0 1 2

0 1 2 4 5 6 7 8 9 M B

6. ROLL NO.

0 1 2 3 4 5 6 7 8 9

0 1 2 3 4 5 6 7 8 9

0 1 2 3 4 5 6 7 8 9

7. GENDER

MALE ○

FEMALE ○

8. STREAM (Only for Class XI and XII Students)

MATHEMATICS ○

BIOLOGY ○

OTHERS ○

9. MARK YOUR ANSWERS WITH HB PENCIL/BALL POINT PEN (BLUE/BLACK)

1.	A	B	C	D	26.	A	B	C	D
2.	A	B	C	D	27.	A	B	C	D
3.	A	B	C	D	28.	A	B	C	D
4.	A	B	C	D	29.	A	B	C	D
5.	A	B	C	D	30.	A	B	C	D
6.	A	B	C	D	31.	A	B	C	D
7.	A	B	C	D	32.	A	B	C	D
8.	A	B	C	D	33.	A	B	C	D
9.	A	B	C	D	34.	A	B	C	D
10.	A	B	C	D	35.	A	B	C	D
11.	A	B	C	D	36.	A	B	C	D
12.	A	B	C	D	37.	A	B	C	D
13.	A	B	C	D	38.	A	B	C	D
14.	A	B	C	D	39.	A	B	C	D
15.	A	B	C	D	40.	A	B	C	D
16.	A	B	C	D	41.	A	B	C	D
17.	A	B	C	D	42.	A	B	C	D
18.	A	B	C	D	43.	A	B	C	D
19.	A	B	C	D	44.	A	B	C	D
20.	A	B	C	D	45.	A	B	C	D
21.	A	B	C	D	46.	A	B	C	D
22.	A	B	C	D	47.	A	B	C	D
23.	A	B	C	D	48.	A	B	C	D
24.	A	B	C	D	49.	A	B	C	D
25.	A	B	C	D	50.	A	B	C	D

V&S Publisher, Head Office: F-2/16 Ansari Road, Daryaganj, New Delhi-110002, Ph: 011-23240026-27, Email:info@vspublishers.com
Regional Office: 5-1-707/1, Brij Bhawan (Beside Central Bank of India Lane) Bank Street, Koti, Hyderabad-500 095, Ph: 040-24737290, Email: vspublishershyd@gmail.com
Branch: Jaywant Industrial Estate, 1st Floor–108, Tardeo Road Opposite Sobo Central Mall, Mumbai - 400 034, Ph: 022-23510736, Email: vspublishersmum@gmail.com

OMR ANSWER SHEET

1. NAME (IN ENGLISH CAPITAL LETTERS ONLY)

2. FATHER'S NAME (IN ENGLISH CAPITAL LETTERS ONLY)

Students must write and darken the respective circles completely for School Code, Class and Roll No. columns, othewise their Answer Sheets will not be evaluated.

3. SCHOOL CODE

A–Z	A–Z	0–9	0–9	0–9	0–9

4. % of Marks | Grade

In Last Class

Percentage OR Grade

Percentage			Grade
0–9	0–9	0–9	A–J

5. CLASS

0, 1, 2	0, 1, 2, 4, 5, 6, 7, 8, 9, M, B

6. ROLL NO.

0–9	0–9	0–9

7. GENDER

MALE ○
FEMALE ○

8. STREAM
(Only for Class XI and XII Students)

MATHEMATICS ○
BIOLOGY ○
OTHERS ○

9. MARK YOUR ANSWERS WITH HB PENCIL/BALL POINT PEN (BLUE/BLACK)

Q.					Q.				
1.	A	B	C	D	26.	A	B	C	D
2.	A	B	C	D	27.	A	B	C	D
3.	A	B	C	D	28.	A	B	C	D
4.	A	B	C	D	29.	A	B	C	D
5.	A	B	C	D	30.	A	B	C	D
6.	A	B	C	D	31.	A	B	C	D
7.	A	B	C	D	32.	A	B	C	D
8.	A	B	C	D	33.	A	B	C	D
9.	A	B	C	D	34.	A	B	C	D
10.	A	B	C	D	35.	A	B	C	D
11.	A	B	C	D	36.	A	B	C	D
12.	A	B	C	D	37.	A	B	C	D
13.	A	B	C	D	38.	A	B	C	D
14.	A	B	C	D	39.	A	B	C	D
15.	A	B	C	D	40.	A	B	C	D
16.	A	B	C	D	41.	A	B	C	D
17.	A	B	C	D	42.	A	B	C	D
18.	A	B	C	D	43.	A	B	C	D
19.	A	B	C	D	44.	A	B	C	D
20.	A	B	C	D	45.	A	B	C	D
21.	A	B	C	D	46.	A	B	C	D
22.	A	B	C	D	47.	A	B	C	D
23.	A	B	C	D	48.	A	B	C	D
24.	A	B	C	D	49.	A	B	C	D
25.	A	B	C	D	50.	A	B	C	D

V&S Publisher, Head Office: F-2/16 Ansari Road, Daryaganj, New Delhi-110002, Ph: 011-23240026-27, Email:info@vspublishers.com
Regional Office: 5-1-707/1, Brij Bhawan (Beside Central Bank of India Lane) Bank Street, Koti, Hyderabad-500 095, Ph: 040-24737290, Email: vspublishershyd@gmail.com
Branch: Jaywant Industrial Estate, 1st Floor–108, Tardeo Road Opposite Sobo Central Mall, Mumbai - 400 034, Ph: 022-23510736, Email: vspublishersmum@gmail.com

OMR ANSWER SHEET

1. NAME (IN ENGLISH CAPITAL LETTERS ONLY)

2. FATHER'S NAME (IN ENGLISH CAPITAL LETTERS ONLY)

Students must write and darken the respective circles completely for School Code, Class and Roll No. columns, othewise their Answer Sheets will not be evaluated.

3. SCHOOL CODE

A–Z	A–Z	0–9	0–9	0–9	0–9

4. % of Marks / Grade

In Last Class

Percentage OR Grade

Percentage			Grade
0–9	0–9	0–9	A–J

5. CLASS

0, 1, 2	0, 1, 2, 4, 5, 6, 7, 8, 9, M, B

6. ROLL NO.

0–9	0–9	0–9

7. GENDER

MALE ○

FEMALE ○

8. STREAM
(Only for Class XI and XII Students)

MATHEMATICS ○

BIOLOGY ○

OTHERS ○

9. MARK YOUR ANSWERS WITH HB PENCIL/BALL POINT PEN (BLUE/BLACK)

1.	Ⓐ Ⓑ Ⓒ Ⓓ	26.	Ⓐ Ⓑ Ⓒ Ⓓ
2.	Ⓐ Ⓑ Ⓒ Ⓓ	27.	Ⓐ Ⓑ Ⓒ Ⓓ
3.	Ⓐ Ⓑ Ⓒ Ⓓ	28.	Ⓐ Ⓑ Ⓒ Ⓓ
4.	Ⓐ Ⓑ Ⓒ Ⓓ	29.	Ⓐ Ⓑ Ⓒ Ⓓ
5.	Ⓐ Ⓑ Ⓒ Ⓓ	30.	Ⓐ Ⓑ Ⓒ Ⓓ
6.	Ⓐ Ⓑ Ⓒ Ⓓ	31.	Ⓐ Ⓑ Ⓒ Ⓓ
7.	Ⓐ Ⓑ Ⓒ Ⓓ	32.	Ⓐ Ⓑ Ⓒ Ⓓ
8.	Ⓐ Ⓑ Ⓒ Ⓓ	33.	Ⓐ Ⓑ Ⓒ Ⓓ
9.	Ⓐ Ⓑ Ⓒ Ⓓ	34.	Ⓐ Ⓑ Ⓒ Ⓓ
10.	Ⓐ Ⓑ Ⓒ Ⓓ	35.	Ⓐ Ⓑ Ⓒ Ⓓ
11.	Ⓐ Ⓑ Ⓒ Ⓓ	36.	Ⓐ Ⓑ Ⓒ Ⓓ
12.	Ⓐ Ⓑ Ⓒ Ⓓ	37.	Ⓐ Ⓑ Ⓒ Ⓓ
13.	Ⓐ Ⓑ Ⓒ Ⓓ	38.	Ⓐ Ⓑ Ⓒ Ⓓ
14.	Ⓐ Ⓑ Ⓒ Ⓓ	39.	Ⓐ Ⓑ Ⓒ Ⓓ
15.	Ⓐ Ⓑ Ⓒ Ⓓ	40.	Ⓐ Ⓑ Ⓒ Ⓓ
16.	Ⓐ Ⓑ Ⓒ Ⓓ	41.	Ⓐ Ⓑ Ⓒ Ⓓ
17.	Ⓐ Ⓑ Ⓒ Ⓓ	42.	Ⓐ Ⓑ Ⓒ Ⓓ
18.	Ⓐ Ⓑ Ⓒ Ⓓ	43.	Ⓐ Ⓑ Ⓒ Ⓓ
19.	Ⓐ Ⓑ Ⓒ Ⓓ	44.	Ⓐ Ⓑ Ⓒ Ⓓ
20.	Ⓐ Ⓑ Ⓒ Ⓓ	45.	Ⓐ Ⓑ Ⓒ Ⓓ
21.	Ⓐ Ⓑ Ⓒ Ⓓ	46.	Ⓐ Ⓑ Ⓒ Ⓓ
22.	Ⓐ Ⓑ Ⓒ Ⓓ	47.	Ⓐ Ⓑ Ⓒ Ⓓ
23.	Ⓐ Ⓑ Ⓒ Ⓓ	48.	Ⓐ Ⓑ Ⓒ Ⓓ
24.	Ⓐ Ⓑ Ⓒ Ⓓ	49.	Ⓐ Ⓑ Ⓒ Ⓓ
25.	Ⓐ Ⓑ Ⓒ Ⓓ	50.	Ⓐ Ⓑ Ⓒ Ⓓ

V&S Publisher, Head Office: F-2/16 Ansari Road, Daryaganj, New Delhi-110002, Ph: 011-23240026-27, *Email:info@vspublishers.com*
Regional Office: 5-1-707/1, Brij Bhawan (Beside Central Bank of India Lane) Bank Street, Koti, Hyderabad-500 095, Ph: 040-24737290, *Email: vspublishershyd@gmail.com*
Branch: Jaywant Industrial Estate, 1st Floor–108, Tardeo Road Opposite Sobo Central Mall, Mumbai - 400 034, Ph: 022-23510736, *Email: vspublishersmum@gmail.com*

OMR ANSWER SHEET

1. NAME (IN ENGLISH CAPITAL LETTERS ONLY)

2. FATHER'S NAME (IN ENGLISH CAPITAL LETTERS ONLY)

Students must write and darken the respective circles completely for School Code, Class and Roll No. columns, othewise their Answer Sheets will not be evaluated.

3. SCHOOL CODE

A	A	0	0	0	0
B	B	1	1	1	1
C	C	2	2	2	2
D	D	3	3	3	3
E	E	4	4	4	4
F	F	5	5	5	5
G	G	6	6	6	6
H	H	7	7	7	7
I	I	8	8	8	8
J	J	9	9	9	9
K	K				
L	L				
M	M				
N	N				
O	O				
P	P				
Q	Q				
R	R				
S	S				
T	T				
U	U				
V	V				
W	W				
X	X				
Y	Y				
Z	Z				

4. % of Marks / Grade

In Last Class

Percentage			OR	Grade
0	0	0		A
1	1	1		B
2	2	2		C
3	3	3		D
4	4	4		E
5	5	5		F
6	6	6		G
7	7	7		H
8	8	8		I
9	9	9		J

5. CLASS		6. ROLL NO.		
0	0	0	0	0
1	1	1	1	1
2	2	2	2	2
	4	3	3	3
	5	4	4	4
	6	5	5	5
	7	6	6	6
	8	7	7	7
	9	8	8	8
	M	9	9	9
	B			

7. GENDER

MALE ○

FEMALE ○

8. STREAM (Only for Class XI and XII Students)

MATHEMATICS ○

BIOLOGY ○

OTHERS ○

9. MARK YOUR ANSWERS WITH HB PENCIL/BALL POINT PEN (BLUE/BLACK)

1.	A	B	C	D	26.	A	B	C	D
2.	A	B	C	D	27.	A	B	C	D
3.	A	B	C	D	28.	A	B	C	D
4.	A	B	C	D	29.	A	B	C	D
5.	A	B	C	D	30.	A	B	C	D
6.	A	B	C	D	31.	A	B	C	D
7.	A	B	C	D	32.	A	B	C	D
8.	A	B	C	D	33.	A	B	C	D
9.	A	B	C	D	34.	A	B	C	D
10.	A	B	C	D	35.	A	B	C	D
11.	A	B	C	D	36.	A	B	C	D
12.	A	B	C	D	37.	A	B	C	D
13.	A	B	C	D	38.	A	B	C	D
14.	A	B	C	D	39.	A	B	C	D
15.	A	B	C	D	40.	A	B	C	D
16.	A	B	C	D	41.	A	B	C	D
17.	A	B	C	D	42.	A	B	C	D
18.	A	B	C	D	43.	A	B	C	D
19.	A	B	C	D	44.	A	B	C	D
20.	A	B	C	D	45.	A	B	C	D
21.	A	B	C	D	46.	A	B	C	D
22.	A	B	C	D	47.	A	B	C	D
23.	A	B	C	D	48.	A	B	C	D
24.	A	B	C	D	49.	A	B	C	D
25.	A	B	C	D	50.	A	B	C	D

V&S Publisher, Head Office: F-2/16 Ansari Road, Daryaganj, New Delhi-110002, Ph: 011-23240026-27, *Email:info@vspublishers.com*

Regional Office: 5-1-707/1, Brij Bhawan (Beside Central Bank of India Lane) Bank Street, Koti, Hyderabad-500 095, Ph: 040-24737290, *Email: vspublishershyd@gmail.com*

Branch: Jaywant Industrial Estate, 1st Floor–108, Tardeo Road Opposite Sobo Central Mall, Mumbai - 400 034, Ph: 022-23510736, *Email: vspublishersmum@gmail.com*

OMR ANSWER SHEET

1. NAME (IN ENGLISH CAPITAL LETTERS ONLY)

2. FATHER'S NAME (IN ENGLISH CAPITAL LETTERS ONLY)

Students must write and darken the respective circles completely for School Code, Class and Roll No. columns, othewise their Answer Sheets will not be evaluated.

3. SCHOOL CODE

Ⓐ–Ⓩ | Ⓐ–Ⓩ | 0–9 | 0–9 | 0–9 | 0–9

4. % of Marks | Grade

In Last Class

Percentage OR Grade

0–9 | 0–9 | 0–9 | A B C D E F G H I J

5. CLASS

0 1 2 | 0 1 2 4 5 6 7 8 9 M B

6. ROLL NO.

0–9 | 0–9 | 0–9

7. GENDER

MALE ○

FEMALE ○

8. STREAM
(Only for Class XI and XII Students)

MATHEMATICS ○

BIOLOGY ○

OTHERS ○

9. MARK YOUR ANSWERS WITH HB PENCIL/BALL POINT PEN (BLUE/BLACK)

1.	Ⓐ	Ⓑ	Ⓒ	Ⓓ	26.	Ⓐ	Ⓑ	Ⓒ	Ⓓ
2.	Ⓐ	Ⓑ	Ⓒ	Ⓓ	27.	Ⓐ	Ⓑ	Ⓒ	Ⓓ
3.	Ⓐ	Ⓑ	Ⓒ	Ⓓ	28.	Ⓐ	Ⓑ	Ⓒ	Ⓓ
4.	Ⓐ	Ⓑ	Ⓒ	Ⓓ	29.	Ⓐ	Ⓑ	Ⓒ	Ⓓ
5.	Ⓐ	Ⓑ	Ⓒ	Ⓓ	30.	Ⓐ	Ⓑ	Ⓒ	Ⓓ
6.	Ⓐ	Ⓑ	Ⓒ	Ⓓ	31.	Ⓐ	Ⓑ	Ⓒ	Ⓓ
7.	Ⓐ	Ⓑ	Ⓒ	Ⓓ	32.	Ⓐ	Ⓑ	Ⓒ	Ⓓ
8.	Ⓐ	Ⓑ	Ⓒ	Ⓓ	33.	Ⓐ	Ⓑ	Ⓒ	Ⓓ
9.	Ⓐ	Ⓑ	Ⓒ	Ⓓ	34.	Ⓐ	Ⓑ	Ⓒ	Ⓓ
10.	Ⓐ	Ⓑ	Ⓒ	Ⓓ	35.	Ⓐ	Ⓑ	Ⓒ	Ⓓ
11.	Ⓐ	Ⓑ	Ⓒ	Ⓓ	36.	Ⓐ	Ⓑ	Ⓒ	Ⓓ
12.	Ⓐ	Ⓑ	Ⓒ	Ⓓ	37.	Ⓐ	Ⓑ	Ⓒ	Ⓓ
13.	Ⓐ	Ⓑ	Ⓒ	Ⓓ	38.	Ⓐ	Ⓑ	Ⓒ	Ⓓ
14.	Ⓐ	Ⓑ	Ⓒ	Ⓓ	39.	Ⓐ	Ⓑ	Ⓒ	Ⓓ
15.	Ⓐ	Ⓑ	Ⓒ	Ⓓ	40.	Ⓐ	Ⓑ	Ⓒ	Ⓓ
16.	Ⓐ	Ⓑ	Ⓒ	Ⓓ	41.	Ⓐ	Ⓑ	Ⓒ	Ⓓ
17.	Ⓐ	Ⓑ	Ⓒ	Ⓓ	42.	Ⓐ	Ⓑ	Ⓒ	Ⓓ
18.	Ⓐ	Ⓑ	Ⓒ	Ⓓ	43.	Ⓐ	Ⓑ	Ⓒ	Ⓓ
19.	Ⓐ	Ⓑ	Ⓒ	Ⓓ	44.	Ⓐ	Ⓑ	Ⓒ	Ⓓ
20.	Ⓐ	Ⓑ	Ⓒ	Ⓓ	45.	Ⓐ	Ⓑ	Ⓒ	Ⓓ
21.	Ⓐ	Ⓑ	Ⓒ	Ⓓ	46.	Ⓐ	Ⓑ	Ⓒ	Ⓓ
22.	Ⓐ	Ⓑ	Ⓒ	Ⓓ	47.	Ⓐ	Ⓑ	Ⓒ	Ⓓ
23.	Ⓐ	Ⓑ	Ⓒ	Ⓓ	48.	Ⓐ	Ⓑ	Ⓒ	Ⓓ
24.	Ⓐ	Ⓑ	Ⓒ	Ⓓ	49.	Ⓐ	Ⓑ	Ⓒ	Ⓓ
25.	Ⓐ	Ⓑ	Ⓒ	Ⓓ	50.	Ⓐ	Ⓑ	Ⓒ	Ⓓ

V&S Publisher, Head Office: F-2/16 Ansari Road, Daryaganj, New Delhi-110002, Ph: 011-23240026-27, Email:info@vspublishers.com
Regional Office: 5-1-707/1, Brij Bhawan (Beside Central Bank of India Lane) Bank Street, Koti, Hyderabad-500 095, Ph: 040-24737290, Email: vspublishershyd@gmail.com
Branch: Jaywant Industrial Estate, 1st Floor–108, Tardeo Road Opposite Sobo Central Mall, Mumbai - 400 034, Ph: 022-23510736, Email: vspublishersmum@gmail.com

OMR ANSWER SHEET

1. NAME (IN ENGLISH CAPITAL LETTERS ONLY)

2. FATHER'S NAME (IN ENGLISH CAPITAL LETTERS ONLY)

Students must write and darken the respective circles completely for School Code, Class and Roll No. columns, othewise their Answer Sheets will not be evaluated.

3. SCHOOL CODE

A–Z	A–Z	0–9	0–9	0–9	0–9

4. % of Marks | Grade

In Last Class

Percentage OR Grade

Percentage			Grade
0–9	0–9	0–9	A–J

5. CLASS

0, 1, 2	0, 1, 2, 4, 5, 6, 7, 8, 9, M, B

6. ROLL NO.

0–9	0–9	0–9

7. GENDER

MALE ○

FEMALE ○

8. STREAM
(Only for Class XI and XII Students)

MATHEMATICS ○

BIOLOGY ○

OTHERS ○

9. MARK YOUR ANSWERS WITH HB PENCIL/BALL POINT PEN (BLUE/BLACK)

Q.					Q.				
1.	A	B	C	D	26.	A	B	C	D
2.	A	B	C	D	27.	A	B	C	D
3.	A	B	C	D	28.	A	B	C	D
4.	A	B	C	D	29.	A	B	C	D
5.	A	B	C	D	30.	A	B	C	D
6.	A	B	C	D	31.	A	B	C	D
7.	A	B	C	D	32.	A	B	C	D
8.	A	B	C	D	33.	A	B	C	D
9.	A	B	C	D	34.	A	B	C	D
10.	A	B	C	D	35.	A	B	C	D
11.	A	B	C	D	36.	A	B	C	D
12.	A	B	C	D	37.	A	B	C	D
13.	A	B	C	D	38.	A	B	C	D
14.	A	B	C	D	39.	A	B	C	D
15.	A	B	C	D	40.	A	B	C	D
16.	A	B	C	D	41.	A	B	C	D
17.	A	B	C	D	42.	A	B	C	D
18.	A	B	C	D	43.	A	B	C	D
19.	A	B	C	D	44.	A	B	C	D
20.	A	B	C	D	45.	A	B	C	D
21.	A	B	C	D	46.	A	B	C	D
22.	A	B	C	D	47.	A	B	C	D
23.	A	B	C	D	48.	A	B	C	D
24.	A	B	C	D	49.	A	B	C	D
25.	A	B	C	D	50.	A	B	C	D

V&S Publisher, Head Office: F-2/16 Ansari Road, Daryaganj, New Delhi-110002, Ph: 011-23240026-27, Email:info@vspublishers.com
Regional Office: 5-1-707/1, Brij Bhawan (Beside Central Bank of India Lane) Bank Street, Koti, Hyderabad-500 095, Ph: 040-24737290, Email: vspublishershyd@gmail.com
Branch: Jaywant Industrial Estate, 1st Floor–108, Tardeo Road Opposite Sobo Central Mall, Mumbai - 400 034, Ph: 022-23510736, Email: vspublishersmum@gmail.com

OMR ANSWER SHEET

1. NAME (IN ENGLISH CAPITAL LETTERS ONLY)

2. FATHER'S NAME (IN ENGLISH CAPITAL LETTERS ONLY)

Students must write and darken the respective circles completely for School Code, Class and Roll No. columns, othewise their Answer Sheets will not be evaluated.

3. SCHOOL CODE

Ⓐ–Ⓩ	Ⓐ–Ⓩ	⓪–⑨	⓪–⑨	⓪–⑨	⓪–⑨

4. % of Marks / Grade

In Last Class

Percentage OR Grade

⓪–⑨	⓪–⑨	⓪–⑨	Ⓐ–Ⓙ

5. CLASS

⓪ ① ②	⓪ ① ② ④ ⑤ ⑥ ⑦ ⑧ ⑨ Ⓜ Ⓑ

6. ROLL NO.

⓪–⑨	⓪–⑨	⓪–⑨

7. GENDER

MALE ○

FEMALE ○

8. STREAM
(Only for Class XI and XII Students)

MATHEMATICS ○

BIOLOGY ○

OTHERS ○

9. MARK YOUR ANSWERS WITH HB PENCIL/BALL POINT PEN (BLUE/BLACK)

Q.					Q.				
1.	Ⓐ	Ⓑ	Ⓒ	Ⓓ	26.	Ⓐ	Ⓑ	Ⓒ	Ⓓ
2.	Ⓐ	Ⓑ	Ⓒ	Ⓓ	27.	Ⓐ	Ⓑ	Ⓒ	Ⓓ
3.	Ⓐ	Ⓑ	Ⓒ	Ⓓ	28.	Ⓐ	Ⓑ	Ⓒ	Ⓓ
4.	Ⓐ	Ⓑ	Ⓒ	Ⓓ	29.	Ⓐ	Ⓑ	Ⓒ	Ⓓ
5.	Ⓐ	Ⓑ	Ⓒ	Ⓓ	30.	Ⓐ	Ⓑ	Ⓒ	Ⓓ
6.	Ⓐ	Ⓑ	Ⓒ	Ⓓ	31.	Ⓐ	Ⓑ	Ⓒ	Ⓓ
7.	Ⓐ	Ⓑ	Ⓒ	Ⓓ	32.	Ⓐ	Ⓑ	Ⓒ	Ⓓ
8.	Ⓐ	Ⓑ	Ⓒ	Ⓓ	33.	Ⓐ	Ⓑ	Ⓒ	Ⓓ
9.	Ⓐ	Ⓑ	Ⓒ	Ⓓ	34.	Ⓐ	Ⓑ	Ⓒ	Ⓓ
10.	Ⓐ	Ⓑ	Ⓒ	Ⓓ	35.	Ⓐ	Ⓑ	Ⓒ	Ⓓ
11.	Ⓐ	Ⓑ	Ⓒ	Ⓓ	36.	Ⓐ	Ⓑ	Ⓒ	Ⓓ
12.	Ⓐ	Ⓑ	Ⓒ	Ⓓ	37.	Ⓐ	Ⓑ	Ⓒ	Ⓓ
13.	Ⓐ	Ⓑ	Ⓒ	Ⓓ	38.	Ⓐ	Ⓑ	Ⓒ	Ⓓ
14.	Ⓐ	Ⓑ	Ⓒ	Ⓓ	39.	Ⓐ	Ⓑ	Ⓒ	Ⓓ
15.	Ⓐ	Ⓑ	Ⓒ	Ⓓ	40.	Ⓐ	Ⓑ	Ⓒ	Ⓓ
16.	Ⓐ	Ⓑ	Ⓒ	Ⓓ	41.	Ⓐ	Ⓑ	Ⓒ	Ⓓ
17.	Ⓐ	Ⓑ	Ⓒ	Ⓓ	42.	Ⓐ	Ⓑ	Ⓒ	Ⓓ
18.	Ⓐ	Ⓑ	Ⓒ	Ⓓ	43.	Ⓐ	Ⓑ	Ⓒ	Ⓓ
19.	Ⓐ	Ⓑ	Ⓒ	Ⓓ	44.	Ⓐ	Ⓑ	Ⓒ	Ⓓ
20.	Ⓐ	Ⓑ	Ⓒ	Ⓓ	45.	Ⓐ	Ⓑ	Ⓒ	Ⓓ
21.	Ⓐ	Ⓑ	Ⓒ	Ⓓ	46.	Ⓐ	Ⓑ	Ⓒ	Ⓓ
22.	Ⓐ	Ⓑ	Ⓒ	Ⓓ	47.	Ⓐ	Ⓑ	Ⓒ	Ⓓ
23.	Ⓐ	Ⓑ	Ⓒ	Ⓓ	48.	Ⓐ	Ⓑ	Ⓒ	Ⓓ
24.	Ⓐ	Ⓑ	Ⓒ	Ⓓ	49.	Ⓐ	Ⓑ	Ⓒ	Ⓓ
25.	Ⓐ	Ⓑ	Ⓒ	Ⓓ	50.	Ⓐ	Ⓑ	Ⓒ	Ⓓ

V&S Publisher, Head Office: F-2/16 Ansari Road, Daryaganj, New Delhi-110002, Ph: 011-23240026-27, *Email:info@vspublishers.com*
Regional Office: 5-1-707/1, Brij Bhawan (Beside Central Bank of India Lane) Bank Street, Koti, Hyderabad-500 095, Ph: 040-24737290, *Email: vspublishershyd@gmail.com*
Branch: Jaywant Industrial Estate, 1st Floor–108, Tardeo Road Opposite Sobo Central Mall, Mumbai - 400 034, Ph: 022-23510736, *Email: vspublishersmum@gmail.com*

OMR ANSWER SHEET

1. NAME (IN ENGLISH CAPITAL LETTERS ONLY)

2. FATHER'S NAME (IN ENGLISH CAPITAL LETTERS ONLY)

Students must write and darken the respective circles completely for School Code, Class and Roll No. columns, othewise their Answer Sheets will not be evaluated.

3. SCHOOL CODE

Ⓐ–Ⓩ	Ⓐ–Ⓩ	0–9	0–9	0–9	0–9

4. % of Marks | Grade

In Last Class

Percentage OR Grade

Percentage			Grade
0–9	0–9	0–9	A–J

5. CLASS

0, 1, 2	0, 1, 2, 4, 5, 6, 7, 8, 9, M, B

6. ROLL NO.

0–9	0–9	0–9

7. GENDER

MALE ◯

FEMALE ◯

8. STREAM
(Only for Class XI and XII Students)

MATHEMATICS ◯

BIOLOGY ◯

OTHERS ◯

9. MARK YOUR ANSWERS WITH HB PENCIL/BALL POINT PEN (BLUE/BLACK)

1.	Ⓐ	Ⓑ	Ⓒ	Ⓓ	26.	Ⓐ	Ⓑ	Ⓒ	Ⓓ
2.	Ⓐ	Ⓑ	Ⓒ	Ⓓ	27.	Ⓐ	Ⓑ	Ⓒ	Ⓓ
3.	Ⓐ	Ⓑ	Ⓒ	Ⓓ	28.	Ⓐ	Ⓑ	Ⓒ	Ⓓ
4.	Ⓐ	Ⓑ	Ⓒ	Ⓓ	29.	Ⓐ	Ⓑ	Ⓒ	Ⓓ
5.	Ⓐ	Ⓑ	Ⓒ	Ⓓ	30.	Ⓐ	Ⓑ	Ⓒ	Ⓓ
6.	Ⓐ	Ⓑ	Ⓒ	Ⓓ	31.	Ⓐ	Ⓑ	Ⓒ	Ⓓ
7.	Ⓐ	Ⓑ	Ⓒ	Ⓓ	32.	Ⓐ	Ⓑ	Ⓒ	Ⓓ
8.	Ⓐ	Ⓑ	Ⓒ	Ⓓ	33.	Ⓐ	Ⓑ	Ⓒ	Ⓓ
9.	Ⓐ	Ⓑ	Ⓒ	Ⓓ	34.	Ⓐ	Ⓑ	Ⓒ	Ⓓ
10.	Ⓐ	Ⓑ	Ⓒ	Ⓓ	35.	Ⓐ	Ⓑ	Ⓒ	Ⓓ
11.	Ⓐ	Ⓑ	Ⓒ	Ⓓ	36.	Ⓐ	Ⓑ	Ⓒ	Ⓓ
12.	Ⓐ	Ⓑ	Ⓒ	Ⓓ	37.	Ⓐ	Ⓑ	Ⓒ	Ⓓ
13.	Ⓐ	Ⓑ	Ⓒ	Ⓓ	38.	Ⓐ	Ⓑ	Ⓒ	Ⓓ
14.	Ⓐ	Ⓑ	Ⓒ	Ⓓ	39.	Ⓐ	Ⓑ	Ⓒ	Ⓓ
15.	Ⓐ	Ⓑ	Ⓒ	Ⓓ	40.	Ⓐ	Ⓑ	Ⓒ	Ⓓ
16.	Ⓐ	Ⓑ	Ⓒ	Ⓓ	41.	Ⓐ	Ⓑ	Ⓒ	Ⓓ
17.	Ⓐ	Ⓑ	Ⓒ	Ⓓ	42.	Ⓐ	Ⓑ	Ⓒ	Ⓓ
18.	Ⓐ	Ⓑ	Ⓒ	Ⓓ	43.	Ⓐ	Ⓑ	Ⓒ	Ⓓ
19.	Ⓐ	Ⓑ	Ⓒ	Ⓓ	44.	Ⓐ	Ⓑ	Ⓒ	Ⓓ
20.	Ⓐ	Ⓑ	Ⓒ	Ⓓ	45.	Ⓐ	Ⓑ	Ⓒ	Ⓓ
21.	Ⓐ	Ⓑ	Ⓒ	Ⓓ	46.	Ⓐ	Ⓑ	Ⓒ	Ⓓ
22.	Ⓐ	Ⓑ	Ⓒ	Ⓓ	47.	Ⓐ	Ⓑ	Ⓒ	Ⓓ
23.	Ⓐ	Ⓑ	Ⓒ	Ⓓ	48.	Ⓐ	Ⓑ	Ⓒ	Ⓓ
24.	Ⓐ	Ⓑ	Ⓒ	Ⓓ	49.	Ⓐ	Ⓑ	Ⓒ	Ⓓ
25.	Ⓐ	Ⓑ	Ⓒ	Ⓓ	50.	Ⓐ	Ⓑ	Ⓒ	Ⓓ

V&S Publisher, Head Office: F-2/16 Ansari Road, Daryaganj, New Delhi-110002, Ph: 011-23240026-27, *Email:info@vspublishers.com*
Regional Office: 5-1-707/1, Brij Bhawan (Beside Central Bank of India Lane) Bank Street, Koti, Hyderabad-500 095, Ph: 040-24737290, *Email: vspublishershyd@gmail.com*
Branch: Jaywant Industrial Estate, 1st Floor–108, Tardeo Road Opposite Sobo Central Mall, Mumbai - 400 034, Ph: 022-23510736, *Email: vspublishersmum@gmail.com*

OMR ANSWER SHEET

1. NAME (IN ENGLISH CAPITAL LETTERS ONLY)

2. FATHER'S NAME (IN ENGLISH CAPITAL LETTERS ONLY)

Students must write and darken the respective circles completely for School Code, Class and Roll No. columns, othewise their Answer Sheets will not be evaluated.

3. SCHOOL CODE

A	A	0	0	0	0
B	B	1	1	1	1
C	C	2	2	2	2
D	D	3	3	3	3
E	E	4	4	4	4
F	F	5	5	5	5
G	G	6	6	6	6
H	H	7	7	7	7
I	I	8	8	8	8
J	J	9	9	9	9
K	K				
L	L				
M	M				
N	N				
O	O				
P	P				
Q	Q				
R	R				
S	S				
T	T				
U	U				
V	V				
W	W				
X	X				
Y	Y				
Z	Z				

4. % of Marks | Grade

In Last Class

Percentage			OR	Grade
0	0	0		A
1	1	1		B
2	2	2		C
3	3	3		D
4	4	4		E
5	5	5		F
6	6	6		G
7	7	7		H
8	8	8		I
9	9	9		J

5. CLASS

0	0
1	1
2	2
	4
	5
	6
	7
	8
	9
	M
	B

6. ROLL NO.

0	0	0
1	1	1
2	2	2
3	3	3
4	4	4
5	5	5
6	6	6
7	7	7
8	8	8
9	9	9

7. GENDER

MALE ○

FEMALE ○

8. STREAM
(Only for Class XI and XII Students)

MATHEMATICS ○

BIOLOGY ○

OTHERS ○

9. MARK YOUR ANSWERS WITH HB PENCIL/BALL POINT PEN (BLUE/BLACK)

1.	A	B	C	D	26.	A	B	C	D
2.	A	B	C	D	27.	A	B	C	D
3.	A	B	C	D	28.	A	B	C	D
4.	A	B	C	D	29.	A	B	C	D
5.	A	B	C	D	30.	A	B	C	D
6.	A	B	C	D	31.	A	B	C	D
7.	A	B	C	D	32.	A	B	C	D
8.	A	B	C	D	33.	A	B	C	D
9.	A	B	C	D	34.	A	B	C	D
10.	A	B	C	D	35.	A	B	C	D
11.	A	B	C	D	36.	A	B	C	D
12.	A	B	C	D	37.	A	B	C	D
13.	A	B	C	D	38.	A	B	C	D
14.	A	B	C	D	39.	A	B	C	D
15.	A	B	C	D	40.	A	B	C	D
16.	A	B	C	D	41.	A	B	C	D
17.	A	B	C	D	42.	A	B	C	D
18.	A	B	C	D	43.	A	B	C	D
19.	A	B	C	D	44.	A	B	C	D
20.	A	B	C	D	45.	A	B	C	D
21.	A	B	C	D	46.	A	B	C	D
22.	A	B	C	D	47.	A	B	C	D
23.	A	B	C	D	48.	A	B	C	D
24.	A	B	C	D	49.	A	B	C	D
25.	A	B	C	D	50.	A	B	C	D

V&S Publisher, Head Office: F-2/16 Ansari Road, Daryaganj, New Delhi-110002, Ph: 011-23240026-27, *Email:info@vspublishers.com*
Regional Office: 5-1-707/1, Brij Bhawan (Beside Central Bank of India Lane) Bank Street, Koti, Hyderabad-500 095, Ph: 040-24737290, *Email: vspublishershyd@gmail.com*
Branch: Jaywant Industrial Estate, 1st Floor–108, Tardeo Road Opposite Sobo Central Mall, Mumbai - 400 034, Ph: 022-23510736, *Email: vspublishersmum@gmail.com*

OMR ANSWER SHEET

1. NAME (IN ENGLISH CAPITAL LETTERS ONLY)

2. FATHER'S NAME (IN ENGLISH CAPITAL LETTERS ONLY)

Students must write and darken the respective circles completely for School Code, Class and Roll No. columns, othewise their Answer Sheets will not be evaluated.

3. SCHOOL CODE

Columns 1–2: A B C D E F G H I J K L M N O P Q R S T U V W X Y Z

Columns 3–6: 0 1 2 3 4 5 6 7 8 9

4. % of Marks | Grade

In Last Class

Percentage OR Grade

Percentage: 0 1 2 3 4 5 6 7 8 9 (three columns)

Grade: A B C D E F G H I J

5. CLASS

Column 1: 0 1 2

Column 2: 0 1 2 4 5 6 7 8 9 M B

6. ROLL NO.

0 1 2 3 4 5 6 7 8 9 (three columns)

7. GENDER

MALE ○

FEMALE ○

8. STREAM
(Only for Class XI and XII Students)

MATHEMATICS ○

BIOLOGY ○

OTHERS ○

9. MARK YOUR ANSWERS WITH HB PENCIL/BALL POINT PEN (BLUE/BLACK)

No.					No.				
1.	A	B	C	D	26.	A	B	C	D
2.	A	B	C	D	27.	A	B	C	D
3.	A	B	C	D	28.	A	B	C	D
4.	A	B	C	D	29.	A	B	C	D
5.	A	B	C	D	30.	A	B	C	D
6.	A	B	C	D	31.	A	B	C	D
7.	A	B	C	D	32.	A	B	C	D
8.	A	B	C	D	33.	A	B	C	D
9.	A	B	C	D	34.	A	B	C	D
10.	A	B	C	D	35.	A	B	C	D
11.	A	B	C	D	36.	A	B	C	D
12.	A	B	C	D	37.	A	B	C	D
13.	A	B	C	D	38.	A	B	C	D
14.	A	B	C	D	39.	A	B	C	D
15.	A	B	C	D	40.	A	B	C	D
16.	A	B	C	D	41.	A	B	C	D
17.	A	B	C	D	42.	A	B	C	D
18.	A	B	C	D	43.	A	B	C	D
19.	A	B	C	D	44.	A	B	C	D
20.	A	B	C	D	45.	A	B	C	D
21.	A	B	C	D	46.	A	B	C	D
22.	A	B	C	D	47.	A	B	C	D
23.	A	B	C	D	48.	A	B	C	D
24.	A	B	C	D	49.	A	B	C	D
25.	A	B	C	D	50.	A	B	C	D

V&S Publisher, Head Office: F-2/16 Ansari Road, Daryaganj, New Delhi-110002, Ph: 011-23240026-27, *Email:info@vspublishers.com*
Regional Office: 5-1-707/1, Brij Bhawan (Beside Central Bank of India Lane) Bank Street, Koti, Hyderabad-500 095, Ph: 040-24737290, *Email: vspublishershyd@gmail.com*
Branch: Jaywant Industrial Estate, 1st Floor–108, Tardeo Road Opposite Sobo Central Mall, Mumbai - 400 034, Ph: 022-23510736, *Email: vspublishersmum@gmail.com*

OMR ANSWER SHEET

1. NAME (IN ENGLISH CAPITAL LETTERS ONLY)

2. FATHER'S NAME (IN ENGLISH CAPITAL LETTERS ONLY)

Students must write and darken the respective circles completely for School Code, Class and Roll No. columns, othewise their Answer Sheets will not be evaluated.

3. SCHOOL CODE

A–Z	A–Z	0–9	0–9	0–9	0–9

4. % of Marks / Grade

In Last Class

Percentage OR Grade

0–9	0–9	0–9	A–J

5. CLASS

0, 1, 2	0, 1, 2, 4, 5, 6, 7, 8, 9, M, B

6. ROLL NO.

0–9	0–9	0–9

7. GENDER

MALE ○

FEMALE ○

8. STREAM
(Only for Class XI and XII Students)

MATHEMATICS ○

BIOLOGY ○

OTHERS ○

9. MARK YOUR ANSWERS WITH HB PENCIL/BALL POINT PEN (BLUE/BLACK)

1.	A	B	C	D	26.	A	B	C	D
2.	A	B	C	D	27.	A	B	C	D
3.	A	B	C	D	28.	A	B	C	D
4.	A	B	C	D	29.	A	B	C	D
5.	A	B	C	D	30.	A	B	C	D
6.	A	B	C	D	31.	A	B	C	D
7.	A	B	C	D	32.	A	B	C	D
8.	A	B	C	D	33.	A	B	C	D
9.	A	B	C	D	34.	A	B	C	D
10.	A	B	C	D	35.	A	B	C	D
11.	A	B	C	D	36.	A	B	C	D
12.	A	B	C	D	37.	A	B	C	D
13.	A	B	C	D	38.	A	B	C	D
14.	A	B	C	D	39.	A	B	C	D
15.	A	B	C	D	40.	A	B	C	D
16.	A	B	C	D	41.	A	B	C	D
17.	A	B	C	D	42.	A	B	C	D
18.	A	B	C	D	43.	A	B	C	D
19.	A	B	C	D	44.	A	B	C	D
20.	A	B	C	D	45.	A	B	C	D
21.	A	B	C	D	46.	A	B	C	D
22.	A	B	C	D	47.	A	B	C	D
23.	A	B	C	D	48.	A	B	C	D
24.	A	B	C	D	49.	A	B	C	D
25.	A	B	C	D	50.	A	B	C	D

V&S Publisher, Head Office: F-2/16 Ansari Road, Daryaganj, New Delhi-110002, Ph: 011-23240026-27, Email:info@vspublishers.com
Regional Office: 5-1-707/1, Brij Bhawan (Beside Central Bank of India Lane) Bank Street, Koti, Hyderabad-500 095, Ph: 040-24737290, Email: vspublishershyd@gmail.com
Branch: Jaywant Industrial Estate, 1st Floor–108, Tardeo Road Opposite Sobo Central Mall, Mumbai - 400 034, Ph: 022-23510736, Email: vspublishersmum@gmail.com

OMR ANSWER SHEET

1. NAME (IN ENGLISH CAPITAL LETTERS ONLY)

2. FATHER'S NAME (IN ENGLISH CAPITAL LETTERS ONLY)

Students must write and darken the respective circles completely for School Code, Class and Roll No. columns, othewise their Answer Sheets will not be evaluated.

3. SCHOOL CODE

A–Z	A–Z	0–9	0–9	0–9	0–9

4. % of Marks | Grade

In Last Class

Percentage OR Grade

Percentage			Grade
0–9	0–9	0–9	A–J

5. CLASS

0, 1, 2	0, 1, 2, 4, 5, 6, 7, 8, 9, M, B

6. ROLL NO.

0–9	0–9	0–9

7. GENDER

MALE ○

FEMALE ○

8. STREAM
(Only for Class XI and XII Students)

MATHEMATICS ○

BIOLOGY ○

OTHERS ○

9. MARK YOUR ANSWERS WITH HB PENCIL/BALL POINT PEN (BLUE/BLACK)

1.	A	B	C	D	26.	A	B	C	D
2.	A	B	C	D	27.	A	B	C	D
3.	A	B	C	D	28.	A	B	C	D
4.	A	B	C	D	29.	A	B	C	D
5.	A	B	C	D	30.	A	B	C	D
6.	A	B	C	D	31.	A	B	C	D
7.	A	B	C	D	32.	A	B	C	D
8.	A	B	C	D	33.	A	B	C	D
9.	A	B	C	D	34.	A	B	C	D
10.	A	B	C	D	35.	A	B	C	D
11.	A	B	C	D	36.	A	B	C	D
12.	A	B	C	D	37.	A	B	C	D
13.	A	B	C	D	38.	A	B	C	D
14.	A	B	C	D	39.	A	B	C	D
15.	A	B	C	D	40.	A	B	C	D
16.	A	B	C	D	41.	A	B	C	D
17.	A	B	C	D	42.	A	B	C	D
18.	A	B	C	D	43.	A	B	C	D
19.	A	B	C	D	44.	A	B	C	D
20.	A	B	C	D	45.	A	B	C	D
21.	A	B	C	D	46.	A	B	C	D
22.	A	B	C	D	47.	A	B	C	D
23.	A	B	C	D	48.	A	B	C	D
24.	A	B	C	D	49.	A	B	C	D
25.	A	B	C	D	50.	A	B	C	D

V&S Publisher, Head Office: F-2/16 Ansari Road, Daryaganj, New Delhi-110002, Ph: 011-23240026-27, Email:info@vspublishers.com
Regional Office: 5-1-707/1, Brij Bhawan (Beside Central Bank of India Lane) Bank Street, Koti, Hyderabad-500 095, Ph: 040-24737290, Email: vspublishershyd@gmail.com
Branch: Jaywant Industrial Estate, 1st Floor–108, Tardeo Road Opposite Sobo Central Mall, Mumbai - 400 034, Ph: 022-23510736, Email: vspublishersmum@gmail.com

OMR ANSWER SHEET

1. NAME (IN ENGLISH CAPITAL LETTERS ONLY)

2. FATHER'S NAME (IN ENGLISH CAPITAL LETTERS ONLY)

Students must write and darken the respective circles completely for School Code, Class and Roll No. columns, othewise their Answer Sheets will not be evaluated.

3. SCHOOL CODE

Ⓐ–Ⓩ	Ⓐ–Ⓩ	⓪–⑨	⓪–⑨	⓪–⑨	⓪–⑨

4. % of Marks | Grade

In Last Class

Percentage OR Grade

Percentage (3 columns)	Grade
⓪–⑨ / ⓪–⑨ / ⓪–⑨	Ⓐ Ⓑ Ⓒ Ⓓ Ⓔ Ⓕ Ⓖ Ⓗ Ⓘ Ⓙ

5. CLASS

⓪ ① ②	⓪ ① ② ④ ⑤ ⑥ ⑦ ⑧ ⑨ Ⓜ Ⓑ

6. ROLL NO.

⓪–⑨	⓪–⑨	⓪–⑨

7. GENDER

MALE ○

FEMALE ○

8. STREAM
(Only for Class XI and XII Students)

MATHEMATICS ○

BIOLOGY ○

OTHERS ○

9. MARK YOUR ANSWERS WITH HB PENCIL/BALL POINT PEN (BLUE/BLACK)

1.	Ⓐ Ⓑ Ⓒ Ⓓ	26.	Ⓐ Ⓑ Ⓒ Ⓓ
2.	Ⓐ Ⓑ Ⓒ Ⓓ	27.	Ⓐ Ⓑ Ⓒ Ⓓ
3.	Ⓐ Ⓑ Ⓒ Ⓓ	28.	Ⓐ Ⓑ Ⓒ Ⓓ
4.	Ⓐ Ⓑ Ⓒ Ⓓ	29.	Ⓐ Ⓑ Ⓒ Ⓓ
5.	Ⓐ Ⓑ Ⓒ Ⓓ	30.	Ⓐ Ⓑ Ⓒ Ⓓ
6.	Ⓐ Ⓑ Ⓒ Ⓓ	31.	Ⓐ Ⓑ Ⓒ Ⓓ
7.	Ⓐ Ⓑ Ⓒ Ⓓ	32.	Ⓐ Ⓑ Ⓒ Ⓓ
8.	Ⓐ Ⓑ Ⓒ Ⓓ	33.	Ⓐ Ⓑ Ⓒ Ⓓ
9.	Ⓐ Ⓑ Ⓒ Ⓓ	34.	Ⓐ Ⓑ Ⓒ Ⓓ
10.	Ⓐ Ⓑ Ⓒ Ⓓ	35.	Ⓐ Ⓑ Ⓒ Ⓓ
11.	Ⓐ Ⓑ Ⓒ Ⓓ	36.	Ⓐ Ⓑ Ⓒ Ⓓ
12.	Ⓐ Ⓑ Ⓒ Ⓓ	37.	Ⓐ Ⓑ Ⓒ Ⓓ
13.	Ⓐ Ⓑ Ⓒ Ⓓ	38.	Ⓐ Ⓑ Ⓒ Ⓓ
14.	Ⓐ Ⓑ Ⓒ Ⓓ	39.	Ⓐ Ⓑ Ⓒ Ⓓ
15.	Ⓐ Ⓑ Ⓒ Ⓓ	40.	Ⓐ Ⓑ Ⓒ Ⓓ
16.	Ⓐ Ⓑ Ⓒ Ⓓ	41.	Ⓐ Ⓑ Ⓒ Ⓓ
17.	Ⓐ Ⓑ Ⓒ Ⓓ	42.	Ⓐ Ⓑ Ⓒ Ⓓ
18.	Ⓐ Ⓑ Ⓒ Ⓓ	43.	Ⓐ Ⓑ Ⓒ Ⓓ
19.	Ⓐ Ⓑ Ⓒ Ⓓ	44.	Ⓐ Ⓑ Ⓒ Ⓓ
20.	Ⓐ Ⓑ Ⓒ Ⓓ	45.	Ⓐ Ⓑ Ⓒ Ⓓ
21.	Ⓐ Ⓑ Ⓒ Ⓓ	46.	Ⓐ Ⓑ Ⓒ Ⓓ
22.	Ⓐ Ⓑ Ⓒ Ⓓ	47.	Ⓐ Ⓑ Ⓒ Ⓓ
23.	Ⓐ Ⓑ Ⓒ Ⓓ	48.	Ⓐ Ⓑ Ⓒ Ⓓ
24.	Ⓐ Ⓑ Ⓒ Ⓓ	49.	Ⓐ Ⓑ Ⓒ Ⓓ
25.	Ⓐ Ⓑ Ⓒ Ⓓ	50.	Ⓐ Ⓑ Ⓒ Ⓓ

V&S Publisher, Head Office: F-2/16 Ansari Road, Daryaganj, New Delhi-110002, Ph: 011-23240026-27, *Email:info@vspublishers.com*
Regional Office: 5-1-707/1, Brij Bhawan (Beside Central Bank of India Lane) Bank Street, Koti, Hyderabad-500 095, Ph: 040-24737290, *Email: vspublishershyd@gmail.com*
Branch: Jaywant Industrial Estate, 1st Floor–108, Tardeo Road Opposite Sobo Central Mall, Mumbai - 400 034, Ph: 022-23510736, *Email: vspublishersmum@gmail.com*

OMR ANSWER SHEET

1. NAME (IN ENGLISH CAPITAL LETTERS ONLY)

2. FATHER'S NAME (IN ENGLISH CAPITAL LETTERS ONLY)

Students must write and darken the respective circles completely for School Code, Class and Roll No. columns, othewise their Answer Sheets will not be evaluated.

3. SCHOOL CODE

A–Z	A–Z	0–9	0–9	0–9	0–9

4. % of Marks / Grade In Last Class

Percentage OR Grade

Percentage: 0–9 (three columns); Grade: A–J

5. CLASS

Column 1: 0, 1, 2; Column 2: 0, 1, 2, 4, 5, 6, 7, 8, 9, M, B

6. ROLL NO.

Three columns: 0–9

7. GENDER

MALE ○

FEMALE ○

8. STREAM (Only for Class XI and XII Students)

MATHEMATICS ○

BIOLOGY ○

OTHERS ○

9. MARK YOUR ANSWERS WITH HB PENCIL/BALL POINT PEN (BLUE/BLACK)

1.	Ⓐ Ⓑ Ⓒ Ⓓ	26.	Ⓐ Ⓑ Ⓒ Ⓓ
2.	Ⓐ Ⓑ Ⓒ Ⓓ	27.	Ⓐ Ⓑ Ⓒ Ⓓ
3.	Ⓐ Ⓑ Ⓒ Ⓓ	28.	Ⓐ Ⓑ Ⓒ Ⓓ
4.	Ⓐ Ⓑ Ⓒ Ⓓ	29.	Ⓐ Ⓑ Ⓒ Ⓓ
5.	Ⓐ Ⓑ Ⓒ Ⓓ	30.	Ⓐ Ⓑ Ⓒ Ⓓ
6.	Ⓐ Ⓑ Ⓒ Ⓓ	31.	Ⓐ Ⓑ Ⓒ Ⓓ
7.	Ⓐ Ⓑ Ⓒ Ⓓ	32.	Ⓐ Ⓑ Ⓒ Ⓓ
8.	Ⓐ Ⓑ Ⓒ Ⓓ	33.	Ⓐ Ⓑ Ⓒ Ⓓ
9.	Ⓐ Ⓑ Ⓒ Ⓓ	34.	Ⓐ Ⓑ Ⓒ Ⓓ
10.	Ⓐ Ⓑ Ⓒ Ⓓ	35.	Ⓐ Ⓑ Ⓒ Ⓓ
11.	Ⓐ Ⓑ Ⓒ Ⓓ	36.	Ⓐ Ⓑ Ⓒ Ⓓ
12.	Ⓐ Ⓑ Ⓒ Ⓓ	37.	Ⓐ Ⓑ Ⓒ Ⓓ
13.	Ⓐ Ⓑ Ⓒ Ⓓ	38.	Ⓐ Ⓑ Ⓒ Ⓓ
14.	Ⓐ Ⓑ Ⓒ Ⓓ	39.	Ⓐ Ⓑ Ⓒ Ⓓ
15.	Ⓐ Ⓑ Ⓒ Ⓓ	40.	Ⓐ Ⓑ Ⓒ Ⓓ
16.	Ⓐ Ⓑ Ⓒ Ⓓ	41.	Ⓐ Ⓑ Ⓒ Ⓓ
17.	Ⓐ Ⓑ Ⓒ Ⓓ	42.	Ⓐ Ⓑ Ⓒ Ⓓ
18.	Ⓐ Ⓑ Ⓒ Ⓓ	43.	Ⓐ Ⓑ Ⓒ Ⓓ
19.	Ⓐ Ⓑ Ⓒ Ⓓ	44.	Ⓐ Ⓑ Ⓒ Ⓓ
20.	Ⓐ Ⓑ Ⓒ Ⓓ	45.	Ⓐ Ⓑ Ⓒ Ⓓ
21.	Ⓐ Ⓑ Ⓒ Ⓓ	46.	Ⓐ Ⓑ Ⓒ Ⓓ
22.	Ⓐ Ⓑ Ⓒ Ⓓ	47.	Ⓐ Ⓑ Ⓒ Ⓓ
23.	Ⓐ Ⓑ Ⓒ Ⓓ	48.	Ⓐ Ⓑ Ⓒ Ⓓ
24.	Ⓐ Ⓑ Ⓒ Ⓓ	49.	Ⓐ Ⓑ Ⓒ Ⓓ
25.	Ⓐ Ⓑ Ⓒ Ⓓ	50.	Ⓐ Ⓑ Ⓒ Ⓓ

V&S Publisher, Head Office: F-2/16 Ansari Road, Daryaganj, New Delhi-110002, Ph: 011-23240026-27, *Email:info@vspublishers.com*
Regional Office: 5-1-707/1, Brij Bhawan (Beside Central Bank of India Lane) Bank Street, Koti, Hyderabad-500 095, Ph: 040-24737290, *Email: vspublishershyd@gmail.com*
Branch: Jaywant Industrial Estate, 1st Floor–108, Tardeo Road Opposite Sobo Central Mall, Mumbai - 400 034, Ph: 022-23510736, *Email: vspublishersmum@gmail.com*

OMR ANSWER SHEET

1. NAME (IN ENGLISH CAPITAL LETTERS ONLY)

2. FATHER'S NAME (IN ENGLISH CAPITAL LETTERS ONLY)

Students must write and darken the respective circles completely for School Code, Class and Roll No. columns, othewise their Answer Sheets will not be evaluated.

3. SCHOOL CODE

A B C D E F G H I J K L M N O P Q R S T U V W X Y Z
A B C D E F G H I J K L M N O P Q R S T U V W X Y Z
0 1 2 3 4 5 6 7 8 9
0 1 2 3 4 5 6 7 8 9
0 1 2 3 4 5 6 7 8 9
0 1 2 3 4 5 6 7 8 9

4. % of Marks	Grade
In Last Class	

Percentage OR Grade

0 1 2 3 4 5 6 7 8 9
0 1 2 3 4 5 6 7 8 9
0 1 2 3 4 5 6 7 8 9

A B C D E F G H I J

5. CLASS

0 1 2
0 1 2 4 5 6 7 8 9 M B

6. ROLL NO.

0 1 2 3 4 5 6 7 8 9
0 1 2 3 4 5 6 7 8 9
0 1 2 3 4 5 6 7 8 9

7. GENDER

MALE ○
FEMALE ○

8. STREAM (Only for Class XI and XII Students)

MATHEMATICS ○
BIOLOGY ○
OTHERS ○

9. MARK YOUR ANSWERS WITH HB PENCIL/BALL POINT PEN (BLUE/BLACK)

Q					Q				
1.	A	B	C	D	26.	A	B	C	D
2.	A	B	C	D	27.	A	B	C	D
3.	A	B	C	D	28.	A	B	C	D
4.	A	B	C	D	29.	A	B	C	D
5.	A	B	C	D	30.	A	B	C	D
6.	A	B	C	D	31.	A	B	C	D
7.	A	B	C	D	32.	A	B	C	D
8.	A	B	C	D	33.	A	B	C	D
9.	A	B	C	D	34.	A	B	C	D
10.	A	B	C	D	35.	A	B	C	D
11.	A	B	C	D	36.	A	B	C	D
12.	A	B	C	D	37.	A	B	C	D
13.	A	B	C	D	38.	A	B	C	D
14.	A	B	C	D	39.	A	B	C	D
15.	A	B	C	D	40.	A	B	C	D
16.	A	B	C	D	41.	A	B	C	D
17.	A	B	C	D	42.	A	B	C	D
18.	A	B	C	D	43.	A	B	C	D
19.	A	B	C	D	44.	A	B	C	D
20.	A	B	C	D	45.	A	B	C	D
21.	A	B	C	D	46.	A	B	C	D
22.	A	B	C	D	47.	A	B	C	D
23.	A	B	C	D	48.	A	B	C	D
24.	A	B	C	D	49.	A	B	C	D
25.	A	B	C	D	50.	A	B	C	D

V&S Publisher, Head Office: F-2/16 Ansari Road, Daryaganj, New Delhi-110002, Ph: 011-23240026-27, Email:info@vspublishers.com
Regional Office: 5-1-707/1, Brij Bhawan (Beside Central Bank of India Lane) Bank Street, Koti, Hyderabad-500 095, Ph: 040-24737290, Email: vspublishershyd@gmail.com
Branch: Jaywant Industrial Estate, 1st Floor–108, Tardeo Road Opposite Sobo Central Mall, Mumbai - 400 034, Ph: 022-23510736, Email: vspublishersmum@gmail.com

OMR ANSWER SHEET

1. NAME (IN ENGLISH CAPITAL LETTERS ONLY)

2. FATHER'S NAME (IN ENGLISH CAPITAL LETTERS ONLY)

Students must write and darken the respective circles completely for School Code, Class and Roll No. columns, othewise their Answer Sheets will not be evaluated.

3. SCHOOL CODE

A–Z	A–Z	0–9	0–9	0–9	0–9

4. % of Marks | Grade

In Last Class

Percentage OR Grade

0–9	0–9	0–9	A–J

5. CLASS

0, 1, 2	0, 1, 2, 4, 5, 6, 7, 8, 9, M, B

6. ROLL NO.

0–9	0–9	0–9

7. GENDER

MALE ◯

FEMALE ◯

8. STREAM (Only for Class XI and XII Students)

MATHEMATICS ◯

BIOLOGY ◯

OTHERS ◯

9. MARK YOUR ANSWERS WITH HB PENCIL/BALL POINT PEN (BLUE/BLACK)

1.	Ⓐ	Ⓑ	Ⓒ	Ⓓ	26.	Ⓐ	Ⓑ	Ⓒ	Ⓓ
2.	Ⓐ	Ⓑ	Ⓒ	Ⓓ	27.	Ⓐ	Ⓑ	Ⓒ	Ⓓ
3.	Ⓐ	Ⓑ	Ⓒ	Ⓓ	28.	Ⓐ	Ⓑ	Ⓒ	Ⓓ
4.	Ⓐ	Ⓑ	Ⓒ	Ⓓ	29.	Ⓐ	Ⓑ	Ⓒ	Ⓓ
5.	Ⓐ	Ⓑ	Ⓒ	Ⓓ	30.	Ⓐ	Ⓑ	Ⓒ	Ⓓ
6.	Ⓐ	Ⓑ	Ⓒ	Ⓓ	31.	Ⓐ	Ⓑ	Ⓒ	Ⓓ
7.	Ⓐ	Ⓑ	Ⓒ	Ⓓ	32.	Ⓐ	Ⓑ	Ⓒ	Ⓓ
8.	Ⓐ	Ⓑ	Ⓒ	Ⓓ	33.	Ⓐ	Ⓑ	Ⓒ	Ⓓ
9.	Ⓐ	Ⓑ	Ⓒ	Ⓓ	34.	Ⓐ	Ⓑ	Ⓒ	Ⓓ
10.	Ⓐ	Ⓑ	Ⓒ	Ⓓ	35.	Ⓐ	Ⓑ	Ⓒ	Ⓓ
11.	Ⓐ	Ⓑ	Ⓒ	Ⓓ	36.	Ⓐ	Ⓑ	Ⓒ	Ⓓ
12.	Ⓐ	Ⓑ	Ⓒ	Ⓓ	37.	Ⓐ	Ⓑ	Ⓒ	Ⓓ
13.	Ⓐ	Ⓑ	Ⓒ	Ⓓ	38.	Ⓐ	Ⓑ	Ⓒ	Ⓓ
14.	Ⓐ	Ⓑ	Ⓒ	Ⓓ	39.	Ⓐ	Ⓑ	Ⓒ	Ⓓ
15.	Ⓐ	Ⓑ	Ⓒ	Ⓓ	40.	Ⓐ	Ⓑ	Ⓒ	Ⓓ
16.	Ⓐ	Ⓑ	Ⓒ	Ⓓ	41.	Ⓐ	Ⓑ	Ⓒ	Ⓓ
17.	Ⓐ	Ⓑ	Ⓒ	Ⓓ	42.	Ⓐ	Ⓑ	Ⓒ	Ⓓ
18.	Ⓐ	Ⓑ	Ⓒ	Ⓓ	43.	Ⓐ	Ⓑ	Ⓒ	Ⓓ
19.	Ⓐ	Ⓑ	Ⓒ	Ⓓ	44.	Ⓐ	Ⓑ	Ⓒ	Ⓓ
20.	Ⓐ	Ⓑ	Ⓒ	Ⓓ	45.	Ⓐ	Ⓑ	Ⓒ	Ⓓ
21.	Ⓐ	Ⓑ	Ⓒ	Ⓓ	46.	Ⓐ	Ⓑ	Ⓒ	Ⓓ
22.	Ⓐ	Ⓑ	Ⓒ	Ⓓ	47.	Ⓐ	Ⓑ	Ⓒ	Ⓓ
23.	Ⓐ	Ⓑ	Ⓒ	Ⓓ	48.	Ⓐ	Ⓑ	Ⓒ	Ⓓ
24.	Ⓐ	Ⓑ	Ⓒ	Ⓓ	49.	Ⓐ	Ⓑ	Ⓒ	Ⓓ
25.	Ⓐ	Ⓑ	Ⓒ	Ⓓ	50.	Ⓐ	Ⓑ	Ⓒ	Ⓓ

V&S Publisher, Head Office: F-2/16 Ansari Road, Daryaganj, New Delhi-110002, Ph: 011-23240026-27, Email:info@vspublishers.com
Regional Office: 5-1-707/1, Brij Bhawan (Beside Central Bank of India Lane) Bank Street, Koti, Hyderabad-500 095, Ph: 040-24737290, Email: vspublishershyd@gmail.com
Branch: Jaywant Industrial Estate, 1st Floor–108, Tardeo Road Opposite Sobo Central Mall, Mumbai - 400 034, Ph: 022-23510736, Email: vspublishersmum@gmail.com

OMR ANSWER SHEET

1. NAME (IN ENGLISH CAPITAL LETTERS ONLY)

2. FATHER'S NAME (IN ENGLISH CAPITAL LETTERS ONLY)

Students must write and darken the respective circles completely for School Code, Class and Roll No. columns, othewise their Answer Sheets will not be evaluated.

3. SCHOOL CODE

A–Z	A–Z	0–9	0–9	0–9	0–9

4. % of Marks | Grade

In Last Class

Percentage OR Grade

Percentage	Grade
0–9, 0–9, 0–9	A B C D E F G H I J

5. CLASS

0 1 2	0 1 2 4 5 6 7 8 9 M B

6. ROLL NO.

0–9	0–9	0–9

7. GENDER

MALE ○

FEMALE ○

8. STREAM
(Only for Class XI and XII Students)

MATHEMATICS ○

BIOLOGY ○

OTHERS ○

9. MARK YOUR ANSWERS WITH HB PENCIL/BALL POINT PEN (BLUE/BLACK)

No.					No.				
1.	A	B	C	D	26.	A	B	C	D
2.	A	B	C	D	27.	A	B	C	D
3.	A	B	C	D	28.	A	B	C	D
4.	A	B	C	D	29.	A	B	C	D
5.	A	B	C	D	30.	A	B	C	D
6.	A	B	C	D	31.	A	B	C	D
7.	A	B	C	D	32.	A	B	C	D
8.	A	B	C	D	33.	A	B	C	D
9.	A	B	C	D	34.	A	B	C	D
10.	A	B	C	D	35.	A	B	C	D
11.	A	B	C	D	36.	A	B	C	D
12.	A	B	C	D	37.	A	B	C	D
13.	A	B	C	D	38.	A	B	C	D
14.	A	B	C	D	39.	A	B	C	D
15.	A	B	C	D	40.	A	B	C	D
16.	A	B	C	D	41.	A	B	C	D
17.	A	B	C	D	42.	A	B	C	D
18.	A	B	C	D	43.	A	B	C	D
19.	A	B	C	D	44.	A	B	C	D
20.	A	B	C	D	45.	A	B	C	D
21.	A	B	C	D	46.	A	B	C	D
22.	A	B	C	D	47.	A	B	C	D
23.	A	B	C	D	48.	A	B	C	D
24.	A	B	C	D	49.	A	B	C	D
25.	A	B	C	D	50.	A	B	C	D

V&S Publisher, Head Office: F-2/16 Ansari Road, Daryaganj, New Delhi-110002, Ph: 011-23240026-27, Email:info@vspublishers.com
Regional Office: 5-1-707/1, Brij Bhawan (Beside Central Bank of India Lane) Bank Street, Koti, Hyderabad-500 095, Ph: 040-24737290, Email: vspublishershyd@gmail.com
Branch: Jaywant Industrial Estate, 1st Floor–108, Tardeo Road Opposite Sobo Central Mall, Mumbai - 400 034, Ph: 022-23510736, Email: vspublishersmum@gmail.com

OMR ANSWER SHEET

1. NAME (IN ENGLISH CAPITAL LETTERS ONLY)

2. FATHER'S NAME (IN ENGLISH CAPITAL LETTERS ONLY)

Students must write and darken the respective circles completely for School Code, Class and Roll No. columns, othewise their Answer Sheets will not be evaluated.

3. SCHOOL CODE

Ⓐ–Ⓩ | Ⓐ–Ⓩ | 0–9 | 0–9 | 0–9 | 0–9

4. % of Marks | Grade

In Last Class

Percentage OR Grade

0–9 | 0–9 | 0–9 | Ⓐ–Ⓙ

5. CLASS

0 1 2 | 0 1 2 4 5 6 7 8 9 M B

6. ROLL NO.

0–9 | 0–9 | 0–9

7. GENDER

MALE ○

FEMALE ○

8. STREAM (Only for Class XI and XII Students)

MATHEMATICS ○

BIOLOGY ○

OTHERS ○

9. MARK YOUR ANSWERS WITH HB PENCIL/BALL POINT PEN (BLUE/BLACK)

No.					No.				
1.	Ⓐ	Ⓑ	Ⓒ	Ⓓ	26.	Ⓐ	Ⓑ	Ⓒ	Ⓓ
2.	Ⓐ	Ⓑ	Ⓒ	Ⓓ	27.	Ⓐ	Ⓑ	Ⓒ	Ⓓ
3.	Ⓐ	Ⓑ	Ⓒ	Ⓓ	28.	Ⓐ	Ⓑ	Ⓒ	Ⓓ
4.	Ⓐ	Ⓑ	Ⓒ	Ⓓ	29.	Ⓐ	Ⓑ	Ⓒ	Ⓓ
5.	Ⓐ	Ⓑ	Ⓒ	Ⓓ	30.	Ⓐ	Ⓑ	Ⓒ	Ⓓ
6.	Ⓐ	Ⓑ	Ⓒ	Ⓓ	31.	Ⓐ	Ⓑ	Ⓒ	Ⓓ
7.	Ⓐ	Ⓑ	Ⓒ	Ⓓ	32.	Ⓐ	Ⓑ	Ⓒ	Ⓓ
8.	Ⓐ	Ⓑ	Ⓒ	Ⓓ	33.	Ⓐ	Ⓑ	Ⓒ	Ⓓ
9.	Ⓐ	Ⓑ	Ⓒ	Ⓓ	34.	Ⓐ	Ⓑ	Ⓒ	Ⓓ
10.	Ⓐ	Ⓑ	Ⓒ	Ⓓ	35.	Ⓐ	Ⓑ	Ⓒ	Ⓓ
11.	Ⓐ	Ⓑ	Ⓒ	Ⓓ	36.	Ⓐ	Ⓑ	Ⓒ	Ⓓ
12.	Ⓐ	Ⓑ	Ⓒ	Ⓓ	37.	Ⓐ	Ⓑ	Ⓒ	Ⓓ
13.	Ⓐ	Ⓑ	Ⓒ	Ⓓ	38.	Ⓐ	Ⓑ	Ⓒ	Ⓓ
14.	Ⓐ	Ⓑ	Ⓒ	Ⓓ	39.	Ⓐ	Ⓑ	Ⓒ	Ⓓ
15.	Ⓐ	Ⓑ	Ⓒ	Ⓓ	40.	Ⓐ	Ⓑ	Ⓒ	Ⓓ
16.	Ⓐ	Ⓑ	Ⓒ	Ⓓ	41.	Ⓐ	Ⓑ	Ⓒ	Ⓓ
17.	Ⓐ	Ⓑ	Ⓒ	Ⓓ	42.	Ⓐ	Ⓑ	Ⓒ	Ⓓ
18.	Ⓐ	Ⓑ	Ⓒ	Ⓓ	43.	Ⓐ	Ⓑ	Ⓒ	Ⓓ
19.	Ⓐ	Ⓑ	Ⓒ	Ⓓ	44.	Ⓐ	Ⓑ	Ⓒ	Ⓓ
20.	Ⓐ	Ⓑ	Ⓒ	Ⓓ	45.	Ⓐ	Ⓑ	Ⓒ	Ⓓ
21.	Ⓐ	Ⓑ	Ⓒ	Ⓓ	46.	Ⓐ	Ⓑ	Ⓒ	Ⓓ
22.	Ⓐ	Ⓑ	Ⓒ	Ⓓ	47.	Ⓐ	Ⓑ	Ⓒ	Ⓓ
23.	Ⓐ	Ⓑ	Ⓒ	Ⓓ	48.	Ⓐ	Ⓑ	Ⓒ	Ⓓ
24.	Ⓐ	Ⓑ	Ⓒ	Ⓓ	49.	Ⓐ	Ⓑ	Ⓒ	Ⓓ
25.	Ⓐ	Ⓑ	Ⓒ	Ⓓ	50.	Ⓐ	Ⓑ	Ⓒ	Ⓓ

V&S Publisher, Head Office: F-2/16 Ansari Road, Daryaganj, New Delhi-110002, Ph: 011-23240026-27, Email:info@vspublishers.com
Regional Office: 5-1-707/1, Brij Bhawan (Beside Central Bank of India Lane) Bank Street, Koti, Hyderabad-500 095, Ph: 040-24737290, Email: vspublishershyd@gmail.com
Branch: Jaywant Industrial Estate, 1st Floor–108, Tardeo Road Opposite Sobo Central Mall, Mumbai - 400 034, Ph: 022-23510736, Email: vspublishersmum@gmail.com

40771